Studies in European Economic and Regulation

Volume 6

Series editor
Kai Purnhagen
Law and Governance Group, Faculty of Law
Wageningen University, Erasmus University
Wageningen and Rotterdam, The Netherlands

The series shall focus on studies devoted to the analysis of European Economic Law. It shall firstly embrace all features of EU economic law in general (e.g. EU law such as fundamental freedoms and their relationship to fundamental rights, as well as other economic law such as arbitration and WTO law) and more specifically (antitrust law, unfair competition law, financial market law, consumer law). This series shall cover both classical internal analysis (doctrine) as well as external analysis, where European Economic Law and Regulation is the subject of analysis (Law and Economics, Sociological Analysis, Comparative Law and the like).

The series accepts monographs focusing on a specific topic, as well as edited collections of articles covering a specific theme or collections of articles by a single author. All contributions are accepted exclusively after a rigorous double-blind peer-review process.

More information about this series at http://www.springer.com/series/11710

Hanna Schebesta

Damages in EU Public Procurement Law

 Springer

Hanna Schebesta
Department of Law
European University Institute
Florence, Italy

Law & Governance Group
Wageningen University
Wageningen, The Netherlands

ISSN 2214-2037   ISSN 2214-2045   (electronic)
Studies in European Economic Law and Regulation
ISBN 978-3-319-79509-6   ISBN 978-3-319-23612-4   (eBook)
DOI 10.1007/978-3-319-23612-4

Printed on acid-free paper

Springer International Publishing AG Switzerland is part of Springer Science+Business Media (www.
springer.com)

Meiner Mutter

Preface

The present book is a revised version of my dissertation that was defended at the European University Institute (EUI, Florence, Italy) in September 2013. My dissertation was a project that bridged the highly specific field of procurement damages with that of general EU law, leading 'Towards an EU law of damages'. As a monograph, it would have been overwhelming; I therefore decided to rework and shorten the manuscript with a focus on public procurement for a specialised audience.

The individual chapters were substantially rewritten and updated, taking into account case law up to April 2015. Additionally, I have taken the legislative action in the field of competition law as an opportunity to put forward several recommendations specifically geared at the European legislator for a revision of the public procurement damage regime.

Although in many ways this book has outgrown the dissertation it is based on, some acknowledgements are due to the same people. I am grateful to Prof. Hans-Wolfgang Micklitz for his supervision and advice, which then and now provides useful guidance time and again. I thank Prof. Giorgio Monti (EUI), Prof. Alexandra (Sacha) Prechal (Court of Justice of the European Union) and Prof. Laurence W. Gormley (University of Groningen and College of Europe) for having been members of the examining board of my thesis and particularly for their very instructive reports. I have picked up many of the comments in the revisions. In addition, I want to thank the two anonymous reviewers and Dr Kai Purnhagen, the editor of this series, for their valuable feedback on the book manuscript.

For my research at the EUI, I received a DAAD grant. I am grateful to the German government for funding PhD positions at this institution, which provides doctoral students such as myself with an opportunity to research and work in a truly exceptional academic environment. I would also like to express my gratitude to those persons who have made it possible for me to reach the EUI in the first place, in particular Prof. Hildegard Schneider (Maastricht University).

Above all, I thank my mother for her unconditional support, my family at large, and especially Thac and Hue. Some things do not change, and I feel privileged to have met Dr Guilherme Vasconcelos Vilaça at a very early stage of the PhD and to remain friends despite years and distance. I am grateful to Dr Jana Warkotsch for her companionship during my PhD time and beyond; to Elmira Khadzhibaeva, Mina Andreeva, Dr Vicky Kosta and Dr Maren Frömel for their friendships; to my 'sister' Sarah Andres; and to my friends Maja Lethen, Anna Lytton, Dennis and Nina Sievert and Natalie Chatterjee for old friendships. Also, my thanks go to John, for his understanding and support in the often very busy times of manuscript writing.

Florence, Italy   Hanna Schebesta

Contents

Part II   The National Perspectives

Part IV   Conclusions and the Way Forward

Chapter 1
Introduction

Abstract "The EU Public Procurement Directives are hidden to most relevant actors behind the veil of the transposing national law. As a result the problem of unavailable damages remains defined by the national perspective. While considering the same problem, this book shifts the perspective to the point of view of EU law. What can EU law do in order to improve the effectiveness of damages for violations of public procurement breaches?"

1.1 Problem Discovery

The research for this book started out after the adoption of Directive 2007/66 on improving the effectiveness of review procedures concerning the award of public contracts, in order to examine the major changes to the existing secondary law remedies regime in the field of public procurement. The Directive introduced, for example, the remedy of ineffectiveness for unlawfully concluded contracts, and as such was quite a revolutionary intrusion into the Member States' remedial world in the field. The outcome of that research would, presumably, have been a rather straightforward comparative law overview of the legislative implementation measures undertaken in several Member States. During the precursory phase, it was quickly apparent that it was much more worthwhile to study what, in fact, had *not* been changed with the recent amendment: the damages provision, which was but a bare postulate that damages had to be made available to persons harmed.

The open nature of the damages provision has several institutional implications. The indeterminacy of the details of damages awards first affects national courts and then triggers cases demanding interpretation before the Court of Justice of the EU ('CJEU', also 'the Court'). This raises important questions of how the Court will use general doctrines in order to interpret the reach of the damages provision.

Further, damages adjudication must be understood as a legal process that encompasses the national and the European level. The damages provision is therefore used as a fix point to survey how EU law migrates to the national legal orders, and how ultimately it is realized in domestic courts. Simply put, while the law regulating public procurement procedures is highly harmonized at EU level, the enforcement in national courts of an identical EU right may be subject to very divergent modalities across the EU.

© Springer International Publishing Switzerland 2016

H. Schebesta, *Damages in EU Public Procurement Law*, Studies in European Economic Law and Regulation 6, DOI 10.1007/978-3-319-23612-4_1

For example, a tenderer in the UK is barred from claiming damages after 30 days, while this is 4 years in France. Whereas the underlying right is identical, these modalities seem to alter the nature of the right itself. A specific connection between the availability of damages and the violation of EU law exists, and has remained theoretically underdeveloped. Damages are a form of secondary protection of EU rights. Not only *whether* but also *the extent to which* damages may be claimed is a measure of the realization of EU-derived rights in national courts.

In this respect, bringing successful damages claims for violations is decried as notoriously difficult across Member States in the field of public procurement.

In the Netherlands, for example, the statistics show low degrees of compliance with public procurement rules, for example, at the level of local government and regarding services, it can be as low as 33 %.[1] Pervasive non-compliance means numerous breaches of EU procurement law are occurring, indicating an equally high number of potential damages claims to be filed. Yet, it is estimated that only approximately 3 % of tenderers have ever brought a dispute to court.[2] Among Dutch jurists, it is widely recognized that there is a reluctance to litigate on the merits of damages. Based on practitioners' experience, one cultural explanation may be that firms see litigation on the merits as more harmful than rapid litigation in interim procedures.[3] In a study, the authors observe a remarkably low number of aggrieved tenderers making use of that option and identify two important hinges, namely fixing the amount of damages and facilitating the burden of proof.[4]

In the UK, it has been remarked by some practitioners that even if this is not reflected in the number of actions brought, the strong stance taken by courts in delivering clear and authoritative rulings in favour of the aggrieved tenderer has had a significant deterrent impact on contracting authorities, and has strengthened the tenderers' position.[5] The present research did find that there is a steady rise in what was an initially low number of procurement actions being brought.[6] One of the most prominent recent actions was the attempt of Alstöm to claim damages.[7] The claim was ultimately unsuccessful, as the contract was not deemed to constitute a utility

---

[1] HAUTE CONSULTING, *Groei in rechtmatigheid, Onderzoek rechtmatigheid gemeenten 2006* (Zwanenburg, 2008).

[2] *Memorie van Toelichting aanbestedingswet*, TK 2005–2006, 30 501, nr 3 p 24.

[3] JM Hebly & FG Wilman, 'Damages for Breach of Public Procurement Law. The Dutch Situation', in D Fairgrieve & F Lichère (eds), *Public Procurement Law. Damages as an Effective Remedy* (Oxford, Hart Publishing, 2011), 87–88.

[4] JM Hebly, ET de Boer & FG Wilman, *Rechtsbescherming bij aanbesteding* (Paris, Uitgeverij Paris, 2007).

[5] As discussed among participants of the British Institute for International and Comparative Law conference 'Celebrating 20 Years of Francovich in the EU' held 17 November 2011.

[6] On litigation, Craig and Trybus report a change in the litigation attitude, attributing increasing awareness of the availability of procurement remedies as one of the reasons. P Craig & M Trybus, 'Angleterre et Pays de Galles/England and Wales', in R Noguellou et al (eds), *Droit comparé des contrats publics* (Bruylant, 2010), p 358.

[7] *Alstom Transport v Eurostar International & Siemens* [2011] EWHC 1828.

of the purposes of EU procurement law. Nevertheless, the case can be interpreted as a sign that, increasingly, big players are willing to litigate for damages.

Dissatisfaction with the varied and often unclear distribution of claims procedures is also pervasive in Germany. Most German commentators criticize the damages actions as they currently stand for reasons of legal uncertainty. The overall amount of damages is perceived as inadequate, since the general §126 GWB provision limits the amount of recoverable damages to the bid preparation costs. It is regarded as being of minor importance for legal practice.[8] Further reaching claims for lost profit are extremely rare.[9] Overall, judicial protection – as experienced by practicing lawyers – is perceived to be in need of a redesign in order to make it more efficient.[10] Successful damages claims against contracting authorities were assessed as 'rare' by practitioners.[11]

Of the surveyed jurisdictions, damages awards are regularly claimable only in France with a relatively high number of damages awards.[12] This is due to the way in which the lost chance doctrine is used in order to enable damages claims. As one of the most favourable legal regimes, the French system is of particular interest as a positive example.

The EU Public Procurement Directives are hidden to most relevant actors behind the veil of the transposing national law. As a result the problem of unavailable damages remains defined by the national perspective. While considering the same problem, this book shifts the perspective to *the point of view of EU law*. What can EU law do in order to improve the effectiveness of damages for violations of public procurement breaches?

1.1.1 What Does the Field Know?

The topic of damages claims for violations of EU public procurement law comes within the ambit of several branches of independent literatures. The perspectives on EU law can most broadly be divided into EU law generalist and public procurement

---

[8] C Alexander, 'Vergaberechtlicher Schadensersatz gemäss §126 GWB' (2009) *Wettbewerb in Recht und Praxis*, 28, p 29.

[9] HJ Prieß & FJ Hölzl, 'Id quod interest! Schadensersatz im Vergaberecht nach der neuesten Rechtsprechung des EuGH und BGH', in O Remien (ed), *Schadensersatz im europäischen Privat- und Wirtschaftsrecht* (Tübinger, Mohr Siebeck, 2012).

[10] HJ Prieß & FJ Hölzl, 'Drei Worte des EuGH: Schadensersatz ohne Verschulden! – Zur gemein-schaftsrechtskonformen Auslegung des §126S. 1 GWB' (2011) 1 *Neue Zeitschrift für Baurecht und Vergaberecht* 21, p 23. Not so Y Schnorbus, 'Der Schadensersatzanspruch des Bieters bei der fehlerhaften Vergabe öffentlicher Aufträge' (1999) *BauR* 77, p 106.

[11] See, eg Prieß & Hölzl, 'Drei Worte des EuGH: Schadensersatz ohne Verschulden!', above n 10, although the opinion of Prieß is that also aggrieved bidders are not *interested* in damages claims.

[12] N Gabayet in 'Damages for Breach of Public Procurement Law. A French Perspective', in D Fairgrieve and F Lichère (eds), *Public Procurement Law. Damages as an Effective Remedy* (Oxford, Hart Publishing, 2011), p 15.

specialist accounts. The generalists look at damages through a unified European outlook, most commonly focusing on the enforcement or remedies perspective, and rarely on damages in particular. Next to this is a large body of highly technical, and often national, procurement literature. Neither view communicates with the other. The book attempts to establish a bridge between the different circles of literature and to contribute to a European debate on the topic by reconciling general EU law assumptions with those of subject-specific procurement approaches at both national and EU levels.

At EU level, damages have most frequently been dealt with under the umbrella of remedies.[13] This literature does not deal with the particular nature of damages as opposed to other remedies. The literature on remedies has received increasing attention in the headlights of the notion of 'procedural autonomy', which has led to significant academic discussion on the topic.[14] Further, the literature on remedies overlaps significantly with enforcement literature, even though the former tends to be doctrinal in character, emphasizing the national/European competence dichotomy,[15] whereas the latter perspective focuses on the processes of enforcing EU law in terms of efficiency.

The topic of damages in EU law is comparatively lacking and largely descriptive. One notable contribution has been compiled by Oskierski, who provides a comparison of damages provisions in EU legal instruments and damages claims under the ECHR with the aim of studying common principles.[16] The remaining contributions fall into the two rather large substantive strands of literature: First, Member State liability[17]; and secondly, competition law.[18] In comparison to these, public procurement damages are less well researched from the point of EU law.

---

[13] Notably in the contribution of W van Gerven, 'Of Rights, Remedies and Procedures' (2000) 37 *Common Market Law Review* 501; A Ward, *Judicial Review and the Rights of Private Parties in EU Law* (Oxford, Oxford University Press, 2007); and most normatively in M Dougan, *National Remedies Before the Court of Justice: Issues of Harmonisation and Differentiation* (Oxford, Hart Publishing, 2004).

[14] HW Micklitz & B de Witte, *The European Court of Justice and the Autonomy of the Member States* (Intersentia, 2011).

[15] HW Micklitz, *The ECJ Between the Individual Citizen and the Member States: A Plea for a Judge-made European Law on Remedies* (Florence, European University Institute, 2011).

[16] JT Oskierski, *Schadensersatz im Europäischen Recht: Eine vergleichende Untersuchung des Acquis Communautaire und der EMRK* (Baden-Baden, Nomos, 2010). Another contribution is A Biondi & M Farley, *The Right to Damages in European Law* (Alphen aan den Rijn, Kluwer Law International 2009), but covering much fewer legal instruments.

[17] P Craig & G de Búrca, *EU Law: Text, Cases, and Materials* (Oxford, Oxford University Press, 2011), pp 241–254.

[18] As discussed in the relevant policy documents published by the Commission, see ec.europa.eu/competition/antitrust/actionsdamages/. See also V Milutinovic, *The "Right to Damages" Under EU Competition Law: From Courage v Crehan to the White Paper and beyond* (Alphen aan den Rijn, Kluwer Law International, 2010).

From a comparative point of view, public procurement damages have been dealt with by a number of SIGMA (OECD) studies.[19] In addition, several national articles have been published in the Public Procurement Law Review. A comparison of damages in public procurement has also been the topic of a dissertation by Pachnou.[20] Two edited books also deserve further attention, one concerning the enforcement of public procurement,[21] the other, a collection of articles on damages in public procurement.[22] The general EU public procurement literature itself is manageable, although several textbooks have been published.[23] The national perspective on public procurement, as one can imagine, is highly developed but idiosyncratic. The different national discourses remain isolated, which has thus far resulted in an inability to connect the EU law discourse with the EU legal orders in the plural, rather than with particular national systems. Where damages are discussed from the European point of view, the individual components often end up being mere parallel descriptions of damages claims at a rather superficial level.

1.1.2 Contribution of the Book

An overarching theory of the role of damages in EU law and the question of how particular damages regimes relate to the general EU legal framework can be identified as a gap in the literature. This book sets out to go beyond the existing body of knowledge in terms of the *theorization of damages from a general EU law perspective*. In this vein, the book explores the impact of general EU law on the specific field of public procurement.[24]

---

[19] SIGMA, *Public Procurement Review Procedures*, Sigma Paper No 30 (OECD 2000); SIGMA, *Central Public Procurement Structures and Capacity in Member States of the European Union*, Sigma Paper No 40 (OECD 2007a); and SIGMA, *Public Procurement Review and Remedies Systems in the European Union*, Sigma Paper No 41 (OECD 2007b).

[20] D Pachnou, *The Effectiveness of Bidder Remedies for Enforcing the EC Public Procurement Rules: a Case Study of the Public Works Sector in the United Kingdom and Greece* (Dissertation, University of Nottingham, 2003).

[21] S Treumer & F Lichère, *Enforcement of the EU public procurement rules* (København, DJØF Publishing, 2011).

[22] D Fairgrieve & F Lichère, *Public Procurement Law: Damages as an Effective Remedy* (Oxford, Hart, 2011).

[23] A confident authority in the field of EU public procurement is Arrowsmith, see S Arrowsmith, *The Law of Public and Utilities Procurement* (London, Sweet & Maxwell, 2005), updated volumes available in 2014/2015.

[24] The present book extrapolates the procurement-specific insights only to a limited degree to general observations on damages for breaches of EU law. In other publications, I have argued that damages are marked by a trans-substantive trend, meaning that they are transversally applied across substantive fields of law. First, most damages provisions are overarching general provisions. Secondly, and specifically within EU judge-made law, the Court has relied on cases rendered in other subject areas, so that there is an important spill-over between different areas of law. Lastly, this trans-substantive interpretation is reinforced through the increasing recourse to fundamental/

While embedding procurement within the broader framework, the research undertaken also goes further than previous accounts with respect to the *particular,* namely public procurement damages claims. The present book has a 'deeper' understanding of damages, as it goes beyond the study of constitutive criteria of damages liability, to include the quantification stage and comparisons of the net outcomes of damages claims.

To give an example of the importance of the quantification stage: In a famous case against the Dutch cadastre, the plaintiff made a rather enthusiastic estimate of the commercial success of the software licenses they would have sold and claimed € 22 million in damages. Apparently the defendant did not sufficiently rebut this allegation and the court was left without indication as to the actual losses sustained. *Ex aequo et bono,* the court awarded € 10 million. If we think about damages awards as pecuniary manifestations of rights, then without much ado the court 'halved' that right.[25]

EU law does not deal with one particular national legal system in a given case, but instead must make use of a fiction in order to connect with the EU legal orders *in the plural.* This presupposes a common conceptual base that is 'comprehensible' in all legal orders in the EU.

Therefore, for the purpose of examining the national perspective, a selection of national jurisdictions is presented in qualitative, in-depth, country studies that examine the possibility for aggrieved tenderers to claim damages for breaches of EU public procurement law. The internal and national point of view replicates the perspective of a national court.

One of the prime findings of the country studies is that damages claims are not a concept capable of unitary definition. Instead, several 'issues' define the overall availability of damages at the same time. Semantic theory discusses the relevance of relativity of terms, i.e. that the meaning of concepts derives from a relational understanding of their connected components. This approach can be equally applied to legal concepts. The initial research conducted in the country studies builds the network of issues which, on an abstract level, make up the structure of 'damages'. It is almost meaningless to see rules in isolation, for example to consider whether lost profits are available, without considering the wider modalities for such claims. It is, in reality, impossible to understand damages as 'unitary' constructs, as the comparative part makes clear.

The book therefore proposes to see damages claims as a bundle of rules and to study their constitutive and quantification criteria. A horizontal issue analysis places the different jurisdictions in dialogue with each other. However, as distinct from engaging in a closed comparison between the country studies, we look at the issues

human rights language. See H Schebesta 'Procedural theory in EU law' in K Purnhagen and P Rott (eds), *Varieties of European Economic Regulation* (New York, Springer, 2014).

[25] The judgment was later squashed, but because the higher court disagreed with the establishment of liability, not with the method of valuation.

from a defined and, more importantly, common perspective of EU law, and further to enrich this point of view with a wider theoretical framework.

On the basis of the results reached in the analysis on constitutive and quantification criteria of damages, the book closes with further-reaching recommendations, including the proposition to legislate on public procurement damages at EU level.

1.2   Outline of the Argument

The present book sets out the current EU law requirements on damages claims that derive from general EU law and the Public Procurement Directives. Based on a legal process point of view, the nature of damages claims integrates the national and European levels. The book therefore examines several national legal orders and their respective possibilities for damages claims in detail. From these concrete research findings, an abstraction is undertaken: damages claims are unbundled in the course of discussing different aspects such as time limits, causes of actions and so forth from a theoretical point of view. These findings are used to formulate points of critique on the current state of affairs of procurement damages at EU level. Ultimately, a refinement of the current EU law on public procurement damages is proposed.

1.2.1   Damages Claims in General EU Law and Public Procurement Specifically (Part I)

The book first provides an account of EU law requirements on damages claims for violations of EU public procurement rules. It exposes the current state of the law through an examination of public procurement legislation and damages claims in front of the CJEU with regards to both general EU law and public procurement law specifically.

This chapter sketches the development of the public procurement policy field in the EU. The substantive procurement directives are accompanied by a secondary legislative regime that specifically addresses remedies for public procurement violations, which is unusual. While damages are formally addressed in the Remedies Directives, over time that provision has remained opaque, even despite the amendments made by Directive 2007/66 that reformed the remedies legislation. Looking at the current procurement policy process, if the EU Commission does not address the damages gap further through legislation, the CJEU will increasingly be asked to provide interpretations of the requirements regarding damages stemming from EU law.

Chapters 2 and 3 adopt a court-centered perspective that focuses on adjudication and interpretation of damages by the CJEU. Chapter 2 features a discussion of general EU law doctrines that are pertinent to damages claims, such as 'procedural autonomy' and Member State liability. It is shown that the 'effectiveness' limb of the procedural autonomy doctrine has been applied by the CJEU in different forms, namely effectiveness as a standard, as a balancing exercise and the fundamental right to effective judicial protection. Member State liability equally emerges as an unstable doctrine, both from an internal point of view and with regards to its relation to parallel remedies at EU and national levels. Chapter 3 deals with EU public procurement law specifically. It presents the Remedies Directive and the way in which the amendments made by Directive 2007/66 indirectly affected damages claims by reshaping the surrounding remedial landscape. It further examines how, in the field of public procurement, the doctrines of Member State liability and Procedural Autonomy apply to damages claims. The current state of the law is very uncertain. The CJEU is shown to exhibit a tendency towards conflation, confounding the 'effectiveness' postulate with Member State liability. This book proposes to resort to a distinction between a public law of torts in the form of Member State liability, and damages for breaches of specific EU legislation under the effectiveness postulate (the 'separation thesis').

1.2.2 Damages Awards in National Courts (Part II)

In Part II, damages claims in four jurisdictions are discussed from an internal point of view. The chosen jurisdictions are the Netherlands (Chap. 5), the UK (Chap. 6), Germany (Chap. 7) and France (Chap. 7). The following criteria are explored: the general system, actions for damages, constitutive criteria, heads of damages, quantification of damages, and judges' discretion.

1.2.3 Transversal Issue-Based Discussion of Damages (Part III)

On the basis of the country studies, a horizontal discussion of the legal issues which structurally frame damages claims is provided in Part III. This is an abstraction based on the jurisdictions surveyed, and complemented by the relevant CJEU case law. In this discussion, comparative law serves to advance a conceptual analysis that refines the understanding of the structures of damages claims on a theoretical level. On a functional level, this part provides a tool for the identification of problematic issues and possible options for solutions. Chapter 9 covers the national public procurement policy space, the institutional framework, questions of jurisdiction and applicable law, causes of action, and the justiciability of norms. Chapter 10 covers quantification issues and comprises the heads of damages, the burden of proof and law of evidence, valuation methods for damages and the discretion of the judge. In all jurisdictions, the problem of causation emerges as particularly acute. Chapter 11 examines the loss of chance doctrine (as causality, burden of proof or head of damage) and discusses the lost chance as a functional solution capable of overcoming the particular difficulties encountered with regards to damages claims in public procurement situations.

1.2.4   Conclusions (Part IV)

The concluding Chap. 12 provides a brief summary of the book and a chapter-based overview of the findings. The book closes with a synthesis of recommendations that can help improve the effectiveness of damages for violations of EU public procurement rules and proposes a revision of the damages regime in the Procurement Remedies Directive.

Bibliography

Alexander, C (2009) 'Vergaberechtlicher Schadensersatz gemäss §126 GWB' *Wettbewerb in Recht und Praxis* 28.

Arrowsmith, S (2005) *The Law of Public and Utilities Procurement*, 2nd edition (London, Sweet & Maxwell).

Biondi, A & Farley, M (2009) *The Right to Damages in European Law* (Alphen aan den Rijn, Kluwer Law International).

Craig, P & de Búrca, G (2011) *EU Law: Text, Cases, and Materials* (Oxford, Oxford University Press)

Craig, P & Trybus, M (2010) 'Angleterre et Pays de Galles/England and Wales', in R Noguellou et al (eds), *Droit comparé des contrats publics* (Bruylant).

Dougan, M (2004) *National Remedies Before the Court of Justice: Issues of Harmonisation and Differentiation* (Oxford, Hart Publishing).

Fairgrieve, D & Lichère, F (eds) (2011), *Public Procurement Law. Damages as an Effective Remedy* (Oxford, Hart Publishing).

Gabayet, N (2011) 'Damages for Breach of Public Procurement Law. A French Perspective', in D Fairgrieve and F Lichère (eds), *Public Procurement Law. Damages as an Effective Remedy* (Oxford, Hart Publishing).

HAUTE CONSULTING (2008), *Groei in rechtmatigheid, Onderzoek rechtmatigheid gemeenten 2006* (Zwanenburg).

Hebly, JM, de Boer, ET & Wilman, FG (2007) *Rechtsbescherming bij aanbesteding* (Paris, Uitgeverij Paris).

Hebly, JM & FG Wilman, FG (2011) 'Damages for Breach of Public Procurement Law. The Dutch Situation', in D Fairgrieve & F Lichère (eds), *Public Procurement Law. Damages as an Effective Remedy* (Oxford, Hart Publishing).

Micklitz, HW (2011) *The ECJ Between the Individual Citizen and the Member States: A Plea for a Judge-made European Law on Remedies* (Florence, European University Institute).

Micklitz, HW & B de Witte, B (2011) *The European Court of Justice and the Autonomy of the Member States* (Intersentia).

Milutinovic, V (2010) *The "Right to Damages" Under EU Competition Law: From Courage v Crehan to the White Paper and beyond* (Alphen aan den Rijn, Kluwer Law International).

Oskierski, JT (2010) *Schadensersatz im Europäischen Recht: Eine vergleichende Untersuchung des Acquis Communautaire und der EMRK* (Baden-Baden, Nomos).

Pachnou, D (2003) *The Effectiveness of Bidder Remedies for Enforcing the EC Public Procurement Rules: A Case Study of the Public Works Sector in the United Kingdom and Greece* (Dissertation, University of Nottingham).

Prieß, HJ & Hölzl, FJ (2011) 'Drei Worte des EuGH: Schadensersatz ohne Verschulden! – Zur gemeinschaftsrechtskonformen Auslegung des §126S. 1 GWB' (2011) 1 *Neue Zeitschrift für Baurecht und Vergaberecht* 21.

Prieß, HJ & Hölzl, FJ (2012) 'Id quod interest! Schadensersatz im Vergaberecht nach der neuesten Rechtsprechung des EuGH und BGH', in O Remien (ed), *Schadensersatz im europäischen Privat- und Wirtschaftsrecht* (Tübinger, Mohr Siebeck).

Schebesta, H (2014) 'Procedural theory in EU law' in K Purnhagen and P Rott (eds), *Varieties of European Economic Regulation* (New York, Springer).

Schnorbus, Y (1999) 'Der Schadensersatzanspruch des Bieters bei der fehlerhaften Vergabe öffentlicher Aufträge' *BauR* 77, 106.

SIGMA (2000) *Public Procurement Review Procedures*, Sigma Paper No 30 (OECD).

SIGMA (2007a) *Central Public Procurement Structures and Capacity in Member States of the European Union*, Sigma Paper No 40 (OECD).

SIGMA (2007b) *Public Procurement Review and Remedies Systems in the European Union*, Sigma Paper No 41 (OECD).

Treumer, S & Lichère, F (eds) (2011) *Enforcement of the EU public procurement rules* (København, DJØF Publishing).

van Gerven, W (2000) 'Of Rights, Remedies and Procedures' 37 Common Market Law Review 501, 504.

Ward, A (2007) *Judicial Review and the Rights of Private Parties in EU Law* (Oxford, Oxford University Press).

Part I
The EU Perspective on Damages

Chapter 2
The EU Public Procurement Policy Field

Abstract This chapter briefly sketches the history of public procurement and how procurement procedures became increasingly regulated over time. Within the EU integration process, the policy area has always been an important cornerstone. As part of the creation of the internal market, several substantive procurement directives were adopted which were matched by a remedies regime. Although damages are explicitly addressed in the Remedies Directives, the provision remains but a vague obligation. The chapter argues that because the Commission has so far not shown its intention to take legislative action in this matter, the CJEU is coming under increasing pressure to clarify EU law requirements on damages in public procurement.

2.1 The Early Development of Public Procurement Regulation

Public procurement regulation is the body of rules that governs public purchases by the State or other regulated entities; it is part of the law of public contracts, laying down which procedures public authorities have to follow when they buy supplies (for example computers), works (such as a new bridge or building) or services (such as catering).

In the course of the EU integration process, public procurement became densely regulated by means of several directives. This legislation was introduced under an internal market logic with the aim of opening up the largely national procurement markets to companies from other Member States. However, public procurement is also an instrument of domestic governance and policy making as it lays down rules on how purchases that are financed through national budgets can be carried out. By regulating procurement, EU law not only controls how national budgets are spent, but – by prescribing permissible secondary considerations – defines how and whether domestic policies may be pursued through government spending. More than a mere administrative formality, public procurement rules incorporate many policy choices.

© Springer International Publishing Switzerland 2016   13
H. Schebesta, *Damages in EU Public Procurement Law*, Studies in European
Economic Law and Regulation 6, DOI 10.1007/978-3-319-23612-4_2

2.1.1   Historic Developments

Public procurement regulation governs the relations between the market and political entities,[1] it creates the framework for public purchasing and therefore presupposes some elements of a market society.[2] Where contracts are procured, a political entity is externalising its purchases, rather than producing necessities through internal processes. Additionally, by procuring, a political entity does not satisfy its demands through acquisition by force or duty, but through the market in a relationship of exchange. Public procurement regulation is political, in that it creates a specific allocating mechanism for resources and the satisfaction of its institutional demands. Also, purchases become governed by a formalized process, rather than a political entity's arbitrary means or through favoritism.

Public procurement has served as an instrument to satisfy 'public' demand in historically very different contexts. Over time, different types of political entities that exercise public authority deployed different public purchasing process designs. For instance, many domains of the Holy Roman Empire satisfied public demand through internal production or unfree labour (slavery), so that there was no contestable market. In medieval courts, purchases were often made through fixed agreements, for example in arrangements with so-called court suppliers. Here the public contract was simply not open to competition and, by consequence, there was no need to devise procedures for supplier selection.

Historically, procurement was also tied to the emergence of the nation state and codification movements. Public procurement regulation has a long tradition, for example in German law, where public contracts have been procured through private law since the beginning of the seventeenth century. Provisions on the regulation of government purchases were contained in the *Hamburgische Baulieferordnung* of 1617 and the *Preußische Bauregelement* of 1724.[3] In 1751, Frederick the Great ordered all works and reparations to be carried out through the procedure of licitation.[4] The spirit of the French Revolution, and the accompanying reconceptualization of the relationship between the State and the economy, also impacted on the regulation of

---

[1] Political entity here is meant to refer to a ruling body, in a weak rather than strong politically philosophical sense, in order to capture the fact that procurement is a form of organization not only in a nation state context, but also in other political entities, such as the Greek city state, the Roman Empire, or supranational organizations.

[2] This is contingent on the political system. A king will assign a contract, or take without reciprocal compensation. A planned economy, on the other hand, intrinsically denies the possibility of exchange. Similar effects can be achieved not by the political system as a whole, but through the way that 'purchasing' is regulated, i.e. the creation of legal duties. For example, under the German Third Reich, price controls were imposed obliging suppliers to deliver at the cost of production; similarly in the courts of kings who disposed of the power to impose purchasing prices on fixed court suppliers.

[3] C Riese, *Vergaberecht. Grundlagen - Verfahren - Rechtsschutz* (Berlin, Springer Verlag, 1998), p 2.

[4] M Martini, *Der Markt als Instrument hoheitlicher Lenkung* (Habilitationsschrift, Mohr Siebeck, 2008), fn 528.

public contracts. The institutional organization of public contracts through crown and court suppliers – that is, fixed contract awardees – were increasingly criticised.[5]

Special procedures for the awarding of public contracts were devised already in the classical antiquity: for example, in the Roman Empire, most infrastructural projects were undertaken not by public officials themselves, internally, but instead they were procured. For specific political positions, Roman law conferred the power to procure using the *auctio licitatio* – a reverse auction in which bids that spiralled downwards were put forward orally. One specification was the *leges locationes*, according to which the procuring entity could accept a bid under a reservation to accept subsequent lower bids.[6]

In the modern period, from the end of the seventeenth until the middle of the nineteenth century, the licitation procedure emerged as a very common purchasing mechanism by which public contracts were auctioned to the lowest bidder. The effect of the psychological dynamics in the momentaneous, oral, and publicly negotiated decision was to produce an undercutting spiral of bids, hence achieving a lower price for the contracting authority. 'Emotionality, craving for recognition, and irrationality'[7] characterized the dynamics of licitation, which often resulted in spontaneous, unrealistic and ruinous bids. This could be to the detriment of foresight, rational calculation, and ultimately the viability of the offers.

In view of its negative side effects, the licitation procedure gave way to the submission procedure. In response to a written invitation to express bids, those wishing to tender had to submit secret written offers. The Public Award Ordinances of Bavaria (1833) and Prussia (1834),[8] for example, laid down the principle of public and written procurement. The principle of submission, i.e. of handing in bids in writing, alleviated some but not all of the problems of the oral licitation procedure. For example, awards that were based on price alone often resulted in lower quality levels. Gradually, one acknowledged that the lowest is not necessarily the most economical bid. This new approach was, for example, enshrined in the *Circular Erlaß* of the Prussian Minister for Public works of 1885, which prohibited the awarding of tenders to anyone incapable of guaranteeing the 'efficient, timely and complete execution'[9] of an award.

Procurement is a formalization of purchasing relations between private parties and public authorities, and as such, closely bound to the emergence of the nation state and the centralization of public power. In order to remedy the fragmentation of procurement regulation across different levels of regulation in the German Reich, and to accommodate the harsh criticism on the procedure of submission, a unitary

---

[5] W Irmer, *Sekundärrechtsschutz und Schadensersatz im Vergaberecht* (Frankfurt, Peter Lang, 2004), p 55.

[6] Martini, *Der Markt als Instrument hoheitlicher Lenkung*, above n 4, p 274.

[7] M. MARTINI, 'Mit Hammer und Zunge', (2007) *Bucerius Law Journal* 68, p 77.

[8] For a concise historical overview, see Riese, *Vergaberecht. Grundlagen – Verfahren – Rechtsschutz*, above n 3, pp 1–7.

[9] Irmer, *Sekundärrechtsschutz und Schadensersatz im Vergaberecht*, above n 5, p 57 ('*tüchtige, pünktliche und vollständige Ausführung*').

approach for the German Reich was tabled in 1914. This suggestion was abandoned with the beginning of World War I,[10] but was followed up in 1921 by another attempt.[11] During the German Third Reich, procurement regulations remained in force. However, in 1936, the '*Verordnung über das Verbot von Preiserhöhungen*'[12] ordered prices and salaries to conform to the needs of an economy in service of war.[13] Thus, replacing the principles of competition with an obligation to supply purchases at production costs *de facto* put a hold on the application of the public procurement regulation.[14] Legally, post-war Germany went back to economic principles under the *Gesetz über Leitsätze für die Bewirtschaftung und Preispolitik*.[15] The '*zwangsweise Beschaffung*' (coercive acquisition or procurement) was again limited to situations of emergency and war, whereas public contracts generally fall under the considerations of private law.[16] This is in contrast to the ex-German Democratic Republic where, due to its characteristics as a planned economy, public procurement did not play a role.[17]

The historical observations illustrate the close link that exists between political entities (empires, kingdoms, nation states) and the regulation of procurement procedures. The way in which a society procures says a lot about the exercise of political power in that society.

2.2   EU Public Procurement Policy

For any governing entity, therefore, public procurement regulation is an important legal instrument of policy making. In a domestic setting, the underlying rationales of procurement can be diverse. The State acts as a buyer and satisfies its needs in a market transaction. Modern procurement regulation often focuses on budgetary policy aspects related to the minimization of costs and efficient public spending through competition. Additionally, in the EU Member States it was also an instrument for steering the economy and policy making, in the sense of directing public spending, for example, to encourage local businesses, employment schemes, 'buying green' and so forth.[18] The national policies across the Member States were

---

[10] ibid, p 58.

[11] For details on the political procedure leading to the adoption of the VOB and VOL, ibid, pp 58 ff.

[12] Verordnung über das Verbot von Preiserhöhungen vom 26. November 1936.

[13] '*Akriegsverpflichtete Wirtschaft*', Verordnung über das Verbot von Preiserhöhungen vom 26. November 1936, §22.

[14] Irmer, *Sekundärrechtsschutz und Schadensersatz im Vergaberecht*, above n 5, p 59.

[15] *Gesetz über Leitsätze für die Bewirtschaftung und Preispolitik nach der Geldreform*, 24. Juni 1948.

[16] Riese, *Vergaberecht. Grundlagen – Verfahren – Rechtsschutz*, above n 3, p 2.

[17] Irmer, *Sekundärrechtsschutz und Schadensersatz im Vergaberecht*, above n 5, p 60.

[18] See on the use of procurement as an instrument of social policy C McCrudden, *Buying Social Justice* (Oxford, Oxford University Press, 2007). Specifically on environmental considerations in

diverse, with different degrees of formalism in their respective systems of public purchasing. The creation of European rules instituted a specific economic approach which makes the choice of awarding contracts contingent on price considerations only, or on the economically most viable option. The rules allow for non-economic award criteria only to a limited extent, with narrow exceptions for environmental, employment and social considerations. Policy making *by means of* public procurement has moved largely from the national to the EU level.

Public procurement is a highly significant area of law for the EU integration process. Financially, it makes up almost one fifth of the EU Member States' combined gross domestic product.[19] This potentially contestable element of Member States' markets is traditionally subject to a high degree of protectionism, which is one reason why it became targeted through secondary EU legislation early on in the integration process. The design of public procurement regulation further has important structural and systemic implications in any political entity, especially when there are different levels of government, as in the EU. Whoever holds the competence over procurement regulation exerts ownership over budgets allocated under those rules. With the increase in procurement legislation, the control of the EU level over national spending has tightened. While national budgets are drawn up independently in national processes, the question of how national governments may spend their budgets is increasingly answered by EU procurement regulation. These procedures guarantee transparency and competition among bidders, to varying degrees, in terms of regulating access to public markets and the conditions of the 'playing field'. However, procurement regulation also sets out the substantive criteria which determine how public budgets may be spent. This defines the policy making space which is left to the Member States in instrumentalizing their national budgets for policy making purposes. EU public procurement is therefore a field of law constitutive of structural rules that govern the EU relationship with the Member States.

2.2.1 Public Procurement Policy: Governance, Competition Law, Budget Law, or Private Law?

By moving public procurement regulation to the European level, a new policy dimension was introduced – the creation of an internal market for public contracts. The legislation does not just guarantee non-discriminatory access to national procurement

---

tenderers, see H Schebesta, 'EU Green Public Procurement Policy Modernisation Package, Eco-Labelling and Framing Measures' in W Devroe, S Schoenmaekers, N Philipsen, *State Aid and Public Procurement in the European Union* (Cambridge, Intersentia, 2014). On fundamental (social) rights in procurement legislation, see V Kosta, *Fundamental Rights in EU Internal Market Legislation* (Oxford, Hart Publishing, 2015, forthcoming).

[19] The figure is quantified as over €2,100 billion public expenditure on goods, services and works, or around 19 % of EU GDP. See Commission Staff Working Paper Evaluation Report, Impact and Effectiveness of EU Public Procurement Legislation, SEC(2011) 853 final.

markets. It also pursues important competition law considerations.[20] Procurement regulation is itself highly harmonized, with the aim of creating an EU-wide level playing field, and guaranteeing equal competition for public suppliers. The European influence clearly strengthened the competition rationale of procurement law by stressing the role of procurement regulation in ensuring fair competition among bidders for public contracts. It is not meant merely to ensure fair competition in 'public markets': the opening of the European market, in theory, results in *structural* changes to the market. Monopolies of national operators that produce goods which traditionally could only be purchased by an entity as large as *the* national State are dissolved, because the demand side potentially has new entrants. Monopolistic providers are now subject to competition from providers from other Member States. The Court has confirmed the competition rationale in its case law: 'The principal objective of the Community rules in that field is the opening-up of public procurement to undistorted competition in all the Member States.'[21] Consequently, EU procurement procedures have a relatively weak budgetary underpinning. The optimal design of procurement procedures is studied by economists under the term 'auction design', a field that examines how different purchasing mechanisms influence the competitive conditions created for (potential) bidders and what the most efficient procedures for the selection of winners are. By contrast, public procurement regulation in the EU is much more pre-occupied with the creation of a common market than with optimal outcomes of procurement procedures.

2.2.2   The Opening Up of Public Procurement Markets: European and Plurilateral Efforts

At the inception of the European Community, the procurement domain was not specifically addressed and subjected only to the general internal market Treaty provisions. During the EU integration process, the sector was soon identified and framed by all major policy making processes (and still is, for example, the Single Market Act adopted in April 2011 to achieve the Europe 2020 Strategy). Consequently, public procurement regulation took the form of special secondary legislation. The legislative process has since been marked by an ever broadening scope of application by extending the coverage of industry sectors,[22] types of contracts,[23] levels of procuring bodies, thresholds and details of the procedures to be

---

[20] AS Graells, *Public procurement and the EU competition rules* (Oxford, Hart Publishing, 2011).

[21] C-450/06 *Varec* [2008] ECR I-581, para 34, confirming Case C-26/03 *Stadt Halle and RPL Lochau* [2005] ECR I-1, para 44.

[22] The defence sector is regulated by a special regime, Directive 2009/81/EC of 13 July 2009 on the coordination of procedures for the award of certain works contracts, supply contracts and service contracts by contracting authorities or entities in the fields of defence and security, and amending Directives 2004/17/EC and 2004/18/EC [2009] OJ L216, p 76.

[23] Public works, supply, different services, utilities and concessions.

followed both for procuring and for remedying violations of procurement rules are regulated at EU level. In contrast to European private contract law, EU public contracts have become so highly harmonized that one could legitimately speak of a European code of public contracts.

In 1971, the first procurement directive on public works was adopted, followed by a directive on public supply contracts in 1976. After several punctual amendments, a wave of new public sector directives was adopted in 1988 and 1989 and complemented by the first Utilities Directive. In 1992, a public service directive further extended the material scope of EU procurement rules to cover service contracts. Another modernization of the procurement rules followed in 1993, again this was subject to several amendments and a major reform in 2004 which consolidated the previous works, supplies and services directives.[24] The latter remain in force until 17 April 2016, when the new modernisation package will enter into force.[25]

Remarkably, EU substantive public procurement law was also matched by secondary legislation addressing the mechanisms of enforcement thereof. At the EU level, the review mechanisms were regulated first in 1989 for the public sector directives,[26] followed by a very similar legal framework for utilities in 1992.[27] This rather general remedies regime, on the other hand, remained largely unchanged until a major legislative overhaul under the amendments made by Directive 2007/66.[28] The new amendment introduced detailed provisions on interim relief, set-aside, and ineffectiveness of public contracts. While for the first time these remedies are spelled out in detail, the ability to claim damages in the Remedies Directive takes the form of a bare postulate. The conditions for claiming damages for violations of procurement rules remained only superficially addressed.

The EU rules on public procurement operate within an international legal framework. From the perspective of trade, procurement has been subject to WTO rules. Under the General Agreement on Tariffs and Trade, originally negotiated in 1947,

---

[24] Directive 2004/17/EC of 31 March 2004 coordinating the procurement procedures of entities in the water, energy, transport and postal services sectors and Directive 2004/18/EC of 31 March 2004 on the coordination of procedures for the award of public works contracts, public supply contracts and public service contracts [2004] OJ L134, p 114.

[25] The revision of the sector and the classical directives through Directive 2014/24/EU of 26 February 2014 on public procurement and repealing Directive 2004/17/EC and Directive 2004/18/EC [2014] OJ L94; and the new Directive 2014/23/EU of 26 February on the award of concessions contracts [2014] OJ L94.

[26] Directive 89/665/EEC of 21 December 1989 on the coordination of the laws, regulations and administrative provisions relating to the application of review procedures to the award of public supply and public works contracts [1989] OJ L395, p 33 [hereinafter 'Public Sector Remedies Directive'].

[27] Directive 92/13/EEC of 25 February 1992 coordinating the laws, regulations and administrative provisions relating to the application of Community rules on the procurement procedures of entities operating in the water, energy, transport and telecommunication sectors [1992] OJ L76, p 14 [hereinafter 'Utilities Remedies Directive'].

[28] Directive 2007/66/EC of 11 December 2007 amending Council Directives 89/665/EEC and 92/13/EEC with regard to improving the effectiveness of review procedures concerning the award of public contracts [2007] OJ L335, p 31.

government procurement was explicitly excluded, but plurilateral agreements followed in 1979.[29] In 1994, the Agreement on Government Procurement (GPA) was concluded as a plurilateral agreement under the auspices of the WTO,[30] which was last revised in 2011. EU procurement legislation in their broad structure encompass the rules agreed under the GPA. Disputes between parties to the GPA are to be submitted to the WTO dispute settlement mechanism (DSU), and so-called cross-retaliation must be allowed for. Article XX GPA lays down mandatory requirements for the establishment of a domestic bid challenge system.[31] Article XX 7(c) GPA provides that challenge procedures shall provide for 'correction of the breach of the Agreement or compensation for the loss or damages suffered, which may be limited to costs for tender preparation or protest'.

In addition to the GPA, many preferential trade agreements nowadays contain provisions concerning government procurement, with a highly varying degree of detail. The EU, as an important hub for such free trade agreements, pursues a policy of including procurement provisions (eg with Chile, Mexico, Switzerland, and others). Provisions in such agreements can be modelled on the detailed EU public procurement regime, thereby proliferating the EU rules far beyond its original geographic application. Additionally, the European Commission has tabled a proposal for a Regulation on access to international public procurement markets[32] which enables contracting authorities to exclude tenders from procedures, for example where they comprise more than 50 % non-covered goods and services originating outside of the Union. The proposal is essentially a protectionist measure and legally enables the foreclosure of EU markets to third country bidders. It shows that access to procurement markets has emerged as a central theme not only at supranational EU level, but equally so on the international plane.

2.3   Enforcing Public Procurement Policy Through Damages

The enforcement of EU law in public procurement is made up of two components, private and public enforcement. Private enforcement is pursued by individuals at Member State level, for example through damages claims or other remedies. As

---

[29] The first Agreement on Government Procurement was signed in 1979 and entered into force in 1981.

[30] Council Decision 94/800/EC of 22 December 1994 concerning the conclusion on behalf of the European Community, as regards matters within its competence, of the agreements reached in the Uruguay Round multilateral negotiations (1986–1994) [1994] OJ L336.

[31] A study on the correlation between the two legal regimes is beyond the scope of this book. A comparison between the revised GPA and the EU public procurement modernization package seems a promising area of future research.

[32] Proposal for a Regulation of the European Parliament and the Council on the access of third-country goods and services to the Union's internal market in public procurement and procedures supporting negotiations on access of Union goods and services to the public procurement markets of third countries Brussels, COM(2012) 124 final (21 March 2012).

noted above, public procurement is – next to Competition law – one of the few domains in which enforcement rules are laid down in detail at EU level. This regime is spelled out in secondary legislation in the Remedies Directives, which cover the public sector and the utilities sector. The public enforcement in procurement is carried out by the Commission under the regular 258 and 260 TFEU infringement proceedings. In addition, the Remedies Directive includes a specific 'corrective mechanism' that is a sharpened version of the Treaty's infringement proceedings.

2.3.1   Public and Private Enforcement of EU Public Procurement Rules

Public and private enforcement perform some identical functions: both processes can deter public authorities from committing procurement law violations ex-ante, and induce compliance ex-post. However, the mechanisms vary largely as do the protected underlying interests.

2.3.1.1   Public Enforcement Mechanisms

Under articles 258 and 260 TFEU, the Commission can bring an infringement action against Member States. Given that in most cases a contracting authority will be an entity of the Member State, this mechanism can be used in order to bring an infringement action against a Member State for violations of procurement rules. In addition to the infringement procedure, the Remedies Directives contain a specific provision[33] that is a correlative to the Treaty articles for bringing an expedite infringement mechanism.

For aggrieved tenderers, there are some advantages to public enforcement, for example the fact that it is essentially free of charge and risk, and that it guarantees the anonymity of complainants. However, at the very heart of it, the Commission infringement action is a political mechanism and the interest protected is not primarily that of the individual tender. The Commission has discretionary powers as to the cases it chooses to pursue, and the mechanism should not be mistaken as one that functions like an administrative appeal. The Commission political guidelines for enforcement proceedings do put particular emphasis on public procurement, a political strategy which is effectively pursued as the numerous cases against Member States for violations of public procurement rules illustrate. However, a large number of complaints reach the Commission on public procurement, all of which it is obliged to examine. Limited resources put severe limitations on the number of complaints that can be actively pursued. Increasingly, and not only for procurement policy, the

---

[33] The Commission possesses powers to intervene directly in the award procedure before the conclusion of a contract under a special procedure contained in Art 3 Public Sector Remedies Directive, above n 26 and Art 8 Utilities Remedies Directive, above n 27.

tendency is to pursue cases of general and systemic interest or manifest infringements over isolated single instances of violation. The immensely high number of complaints to the Commission in the procurement sector[34] has been taken to indicate that national proceedings are simply too unattractive to prevent complaints to the Commission. There are important limits to the enforcement of policy fields by means of Commission infringement actions as they are not intended to provide a regular enforcement mechanism for individuals, nor do they have the capacity to do so.

2.3.1.2   Private Enforcement

Enforcement through private claims pursues a twofold interest, namely the pure private interest in remedying the harm is pursued through litigation (compensation rationale) and the public interest in guaranteeing observance of the law (the rule of law). Moreover, the public has a vested interest in the financial situation of public authorities. Unlike in the competition sector, contracting authorities are not private companies disposing of their own capital, but public authorities spending public money. On one hand, private enforcement would induce compliance with procurement rules, and therefore theoretically contribute to safeguarding the public interest in prudent spending of public money. On the other hand, unfounded challenges to bid procedures and the resulting time delays are costs which are ultimately born by the public.

Looking at the economic effects of damages, the field of competition law has received the main attention. From the point of view of deterrence, damages are often discussed in terms of ineffectiveness versus over-deterrence in the 'optimal enforcement literature'.[35] The unwanted consequences of over-deterrence in competition law are ascribed to, for example, over-conservative investment behavior or marketing techniques of firms. Such considerations are less convincing in public procurement as, after all, public money is expected to be spent in prudent and low-risk ways. However, the cost-benefit effects of damages claims in public procurement in the EU context are largely unexplored from an economic point of view and an economic study thereof would make for a fruitful inquiry.

2.3.2   Private Enforcement in the Remedies Directive

There is a strong private enforcement component of public procurement law at EU level anchored in secondary legislation. The public procurement 'Remedies Directives', that is, the Public Sector Remedies Directive 89/665/EEC and the

---

[34] J Szychowska, Head of Unit, DG Internal Market and Services, European Commission Conference on 'Remedies in Public Procurement', Brussels (26 November 2012).

[35] WPJ Wils, *The Optimal Enforcement of EC Antitrust Law: Essays in Law & Economics* (London, Kluwer Law International, 2002).

Utilities Remedies Directive 92/13/EEC (as amended),[36] lay down the minimum conditions to be satisfied by the review procedures established in the national legal systems. It is rare for the EU legislator to make such distinct, explicit and detailed provisions regarding the enforcement side of an EU legislative instrument. The rules address the application of EU legislation by national courts, and as such, form part of the system of decentralized enforcement of EU law. Public procurement is a sphere in which the European legislative process has created procedural and remedial rules for judicial review. These are applicable only to contracts falling within the scope of the Public Sector and Utilities Directives.

The initial remedies regime instituted basic outlines of a system of review, an important counterpart to the substantive procurement rules. It consisted of a meagre six articles, aiming to create effective review procedures for decisions taken by contracting authorities. The Remedies Directive stresses effectiveness and rapidity (Art. 1(1)). Furthermore, it enshrines the equivalence principle, i.e. that there should be no discrimination between national rules implementing the Directive and national rules (Art. 1(2)). Any person having or having previously had an interest must be able to use such review procedures (Art. 1 (3)). Article 2 enumerates the available remedies, interim measures, set aside for decisions and damages, as well as the organizational features of the bodies having review powers. Article 3 grants specific powers of review to the Commission in cases of manifest infringement of the substantive Directives.

2.3.2.1   Damages in the Remedies Directives

Among the initially rather rudimentary provisions for remedies, damages in public procurement have long been identified as particularly difficult by the EU legislator. The memorandum of explanation for Commission proposals to the Remedies Directive of 1989 did contain several remarks on damages, see COM(87) 134[37] and COM(88) 733.[38] The subsequent and more detailed utilities proposal also mentions severe problems in claiming damages.[39]

---

[36] It would seem more appropriate to speak of Enforcement Directives, since it encompasses not only rules on remedies, but also on sanctions, as well as enforcement mechanisms granted to the Commission. The term 'Remedies Directive', however, is the most commonly accepted terminology.

[37] The explanatory memorandum mentions 'unequal opportunities for claiming damages' in the Proposal for a Council Directive coordinating the laws, regulations and administrative provisions relating to the application of Community rules on procedures for the award of public supply and public works contracts, COM(87) 134, p 2.

[38] The explanatory memorandum states that 'a few examples can be given to illustrate current differences and gaps in national systems … As regards remedies granted by the courts … the possibility of obtaining damages is subject in certain Member States to limits and uncertainties such that it is largely theoretical'. See Commission, Explanatory Memorandum for the revised 'Remedies Directive' COM(88) 733 (8 December 1988), p 9.

[39] Commission, Proposal for a Council Directive coordinating the laws, regulations and administrative provisions relating to the application of Community rules on the procurement procedures of

Later, the European Commission's Impact Assessment of 2006 reported that '*[t] here appears to be a particular problem with the use of damages as a remedies action – the figures collected, supported by the feedback from stakeholders during the consultation process, are so low as to be almost non-existent*'.[40] It identifies the following problems:

4.3. Inherent Limits of Damages Action
    An aggrieved supplier faced with a signed public contract, is often deterred from bring-ing a damages action for the following reasons:

- *actions in damages have **no real corrective effect**. Even if the public contract already signed is held to have been awarded illegally, in the great majority of cases it remains in force when it has already been signed. Hence, even if the damages action is successful and some (limited) financial compensation is granted, the eco-nomic operator will ultimately not win the public contract and may also feel that he has compromised his future business with the Awarding Authority. This also limits the deterrent effect.*
- *damages actions **are hampered by practical difficulties**. Actions are rarely success-ful as a result of the practical difficulty of needing to prove that the economic opera-tor was genuinely a tenderer who had a serious chance of winning the contract. If this is not proved, no compensation for lost business opportunities is awarded to the complainant and often, in practise, any financial award is limited to the reimburse-ment of costs incurred in bidding for the contract and may not even cover the legal costs of bringing the action. Such actions are even more difficult to bring for a potential tenderer who has not been able to participate in a public procurement procedure as a result of the lack of transparency.*
- *the **process is lengthy and costly**. In all Member States, damages is an action on the merits before ordinary Courts (and not by way of interlocutory procedures as in the case of interim measures) which may therefore last for years. Furthermore, given the requirements of proof, the process can be somewhat protracted, and may incur high litigation costs for both parties (economic operators and Awarding Authority).[41]*

In classifying the degree of importance of the overall weaknesses of the 1989 system (i.e. pre-2006/77 amendments), the 'threat' of damages not acting as a deterrent was classified as large, due to the burden of proof requirement, as well as restrictions on judicial action following the signature of a contract.[42] While precise cross-country statistics on damages claims were lacking, the total number for 8 countries out of the EU-15 countries amounted to only 28 damages actions. In addi-tion, external qualitative surveys indicate extremely low levels of practical consid-eration and impact in terms of damages claims.[43]

---

entities operating in the water, energy, transport and telecommunications sectors, COM(90) 297 (25 July 1990), p 3.

[40] Commission Staff Working Document, Annex to the Proposal for a Directive of the European Parliament and of the Council amending Council Directives 89/665/EEC and 92/13/EEC CEE with regard to improving the effectiveness of review procedures concerning the award of public contracts, Impact Assessment Report – Remedies in the field of public procurement, SEC(2006) 557 (4 May 2006), p 12 [hereinafter 'Impact Assessment Report on Remedies'].

[41] Impact Assessment Report on Remedies, ibid, p 12.

[42] ibid, p 21.

[43] See eg, JM Hebly, ET de Boer & FG Wilman, *Rechtsbescherming bij aanbesteding* (Paris, Uitgeverij Paris, 2007).

2.3.3   The Remedies Amendments by Directive 2007/66

20 December 2009 marked the end of the transposition period of Directive 2007/66, which was the first substantial amendment to both the Public Sector Remedies Directive 89/665/EEC and the Utilities Remedies Directive 92/13/EEC. As damages claims must be seen relative to the other available remedies, this chapter begins by surveying the changed remedies regime as has been in force since the amendments by Directive 2007/66.

The amendment of the Remedies Directive by Directive 2007/66 greatly strengthened the private enforcement of public procurement rules. Directive 2007/66 is entitled 'with regard to improving the effectiveness of review procedures concerning the award of public contracts'. The main thrust of the changes is clear. The review mechanisms of the 1989 Remedies Directive were perceived as weak, specifically as regards the possibility of aggrieved tenderers to challenge direct illegal awards of contract, also called *de facto* tendering, by which a contracting authority awards a public contract without opening the contract to public tender at all. Another weakness was the lack of time allowed for an effective review between the decision being made to award a contract and the conclusion of the contract in question.[44]

For the 2007/66 Directive, the Commission made a policy choice, based on the consideration that 'among the two types of Remedies [pre- and post-contractual], pre-contractual remedies are the more effective remedies in the context of public procurement'.[45] This policy consideration translated into a significant modification of the initial Remedies Directives targeting pre-contractual remedies and the specific post-contractual remedy of ineffectiveness. This left the existing damages provisions as they were: minimal.

The amendment to Directive 2007/66 changed the previous regime in mainly three ways[46]: by introducing a standstill clause between the award and conclusion of contract; providing for a new remedy, the ineffectiveness of illegally concluded contracts; and introducing automatic suspension of tender procedures when these are challenged in courts. In terms of available remedies, the main change is that in specific cases an additional post-contractual remedy is mandated, the ineffectiveness of *de facto* tenders. Article 2d requires the Member States to 'ensure that a

---

[44] Compare recital 3 of the preamble to Directive 2007/66/EC: 'Consultations of the interested parties and the case law of the Court of Justice have revealed a certain number of weaknesses in the review mechanisms in the Member States. As a result of these weaknesses, the mechanisms established by Directives 89/665/EEC and 92/13/EEC do not always make it possible to ensure compliance with Community law, especially at a time when infringements can still be corrected. Consequently, the guarantees of transparency and non-discrimination sought by those Directives should be strengthened to ensure that the Community as a whole fully benefit from the positive effects of the modernisation and simplification of the rules on public procurement achieved by Directives 2004/18/EC and 2004/17/EC.'

[45] Impact Assessment Report on Remedies, above n 40, p 23.

[46] For a thoughtful assessment of the amendment, see E Chiti, 'Directive 2007/66 and the Difficult Search for Balance in Judicial Protection Concerning Public Procurements' (2010) *Italian Journal of Public Law* 125.

contract is considered ineffective by a review body independent of the contracting authority or that its ineffectiveness is the result of a decision of such a review body' in case of specified violations.[47] Ineffectiveness is probably the most innovative remedy to address this 'most serious breach of Community law'.[48] For the first time, where a *de facto* contract has been concluded, the aggrieved tenderer might have access to a remedy other than the mere claiming of damages. However, 'ineffectiveness should not be automatic' but must be based on a decision of an independent review body.[49] The consequences of ineffectiveness are determined by national law, by providing for the retroactive cancellation of all contractual obligations (*ex tunc*) or, conversely, by limiting the scope of the cancellation to those obligations still to be performed (*ex nunc*).[50] All of these effects, however, are subject to the limitation of requirements of general interest.[51] The remedies are additionally subject to a public policy exception, which will predictably lead to some questions of interpretation in front of the CJEU. In cases where illegally awarded contracts have already been (partially) completed, Directive 2007/66 foresees sanctions of a punitive nature to be instituted by the Member State.[52]

For a large part, the amendments constitute a codification of the CJEU case law rendered in the field of procurement. The new Remedies Directive is an excellent example of the kind of dialogue taking place between the European legislator and the judiciary. EU law 'evolves'[53] through dynamic interpretation of existing legislation by the Court and subsequent codification by the EU legislator which in turn engages new preliminary reference procedures demanding the interpretation thereof. The Remedies Directive is both, codification and clarification. The *Alcatel* jurisprudence[54] is codified very clearly with regard to time limits. Also, regarding the 'most serious breach of Community law in the field of public procurement',[55]

---

[47] Art 2d(1)(a)–(c) of Directive 2007/66, above n 28.

[48] R 13, preamble of Directive 2007/66, above n 28.

[49] ibid.

[50] Art 2d(2) of Directive 2007/66, above n 28.

[51] Art 2d(3) of Directive 2007/66 reads: 'Member States may provide that the review body independent of the contracting entity may not consider a contract ineffective, even though it has been awarded illegally on the grounds mentioned in paragraph 1, if the review body finds, after having examined all relevant aspects, that overriding reasons relating to a general interest require that the effects of the contract should be maintained.' See ibid.

[52] Art 2e of Directive 2007/66, above n 28.

[53] Without entering into the intricacies of evolution in biology, the factors triggering evolution include recombination, mutation, selection, and drifting of genes (basically a shift of genes due to chance).

[54] Case C-81/98 *Alcatel Austria and others* [1999] ECR I-7671; and Case C-212/02 *Commission v Austria*, Judgment of 24 June 2004 (unpublished).

[55] R 13 of Directive 2007/66, above n 28.

the *Brunswick Waste Disposal* case law[56] has been processed in the Directive. However, the Directive goes further than mere codification, it is also reactionary and clarificatory to the rendered case law: issues such as the confusion over whether the *Brunswick Waste Disposal* case required *ex nunc* or *ex tunc* termination[57] of an illegally concluded contract were picked up and somewhat clarified through the detailed ineffectiveness provisions. In some aspects, the legislative actions therefore sets limits to broad interpretations of judgments rendered by the CJEU.

Significantly, the amendments made by Directive 2007/66/EC did not directly alter the damages provision in any way. As is apparent from the legislative history discussed above, this was a deliberate decision, and while damages claims were identified as a problematic area, the Commission decided not to include damages in the final proposal. However, the fact that the wording on damages has not changed does not mean that Directive 2007/66 has no significance for the interpretation of damages claims: first of all, it is an expression of the legislator's will. Damages were regarded as being too problematic and potentially beyond competence to legislate. On one hand, this provides some recognition on the part of the legislator that damages claims are problematic. On the other hand, a choice was made not to legislate. The omission can be interpreted as a perceived lack of political will on behalf of the Member States, competence or need. Secondly, the interpretation of the remedy of damages is influenced by the amendment since damages must be seen in the context of their interrelationship with other remedies. The fact that alternative remedies have changed means that damages claims must be reassessed in terms of their overall balance relative to other (newly available) remedies. Lastly, for violations other than *de facto* tenders, the post-contractual remedy of ineffectiveness is not mandatory. The only other post-contractual remedy then remains a damages action. In addition, the remedy of ineffectiveness may be waived in the public interest, thus potentially leaving an aggrieved tenderer with nothing but an action for damages. Damages actions therefore remain an important component of the private enforcement of EU public procurement law.

---

[56] In the first case of the Commission against Germany, the Commission brought infringement proceedings under Article 226EC against Germany, namely the municipality of Bockhorn for failure to tender, as well as the city of Brunswick for illegally using the privately negotiated procedure in contracting out the collection of waste water. The ECJ found that Germany had failed to fulfil its obligations under the respective public procurement provisions. See Joined Cases C-20/01 and C-28/01 *Commission v Germany* [2003] ECR I-03609. In the follow-up case, the Commission brought renewed action against Germany for failure to comply with the judgment rendered in 2003 which, since the Bockhorn contract had been annulled in the meantime, concerned only the waste disposal contract of the city of Brunswick. The contract concluded between Brunswick and Braunschweiger Kohlebergwerke remained in question, although at the time of judgment this was also rescinded, but only after the date of expiry of the period prescribed in the reasoned opinion. An important factor was that it was concluded for a period of 30 years. See Case C-503/04 *Commission v Germany* [2007] ECR I-06153.

[57] Ex nunc terminates the contract 'from now on', while ex tunc nullifies all effects of the contract 'from the outset'.

2.3.4 No Short-Term Legislative Intervention on Damages in Public Procurement

The EU legislators have recently passed a new modernization package, which included important changes to the substantive rules of public procurement.[58] Since this modernization concerns the recasting of the substantive public procurement directives, damages were not regarded as an issue. However, prior to the finalization of the modernization package, a conference was organized by the Commission on the Remedies Directives under the theme 'State of Play, Challenges and Opportunities'.[59] To anyone familiar with the policy making processes of the Commission, this initially raised the question of whether the conference was to be a preliminary and informal platform through which to assess a potential amendment to the Remedies Directive, perhaps in synchronization with the substantive modernization package. Stakeholders present voiced their opinion that the national legal systems needed more time in order to absorb the changes introduced by Directive 2007/66, the effects of which it was too early to assess. The panels considered the overall national review procedures, the Court of Justice of the EU, the division of tasks between review bodies and the Commission, and the question of whether the review systems suit the specificities of the procurement sector. The reactions of the Commission officials present indicated that the conference was a means of input for the outstanding 'impact assessment', but not a preparation for any future Remedies Directive amendment already in the pipeline. When confronted with the question of damages, the Commission officials showed definite awareness of the issues, but indicated that there was currently no willingness to table a political proposal in this regard.

2.3.5 What Is the Trouble with Public Procurement Damages?

A popular argument against legislative intervention in relation to damages is that, simply, aggrieved tenderers do not *want* to claim damages[60]; they 'do not want to bite the hand that feeds them'. When presented, the argument of the moot nature of damages mostly remains confined to the anecdotal, although some studies link the reluctant attitudes of aggrieved bidders to such 'behavioural' considerations.[61]

---

[58] The modernization process revised Directive 2004/17/EC and 2004/18/EC and adopted a directive on concessions.

[59] European Commission Conference on 'Remedies in Public Procurement', above n 34.

[60] ibid.

[61] P Craig & M Trybus, 'Angleterre et Pays de Galles/England and Wales', in R Noguellou et al (eds), *Droit comparé des contrats publics* (Bruylant, 2010), citing a UK business report in this respect. See also the findings of D Pachnou, *The effectiveness of bidder remedies for enforcing the EC public procurement rules: a case study of the public works sector in the United Kingdom and Greece* (Dissertation, University of Nottingham, 2003).

This book questions these assumptions. It puts forward a different explanation, namely that damages claims are not perceived as *claimable,* and so the reluctance of aggrieved bidders to engage in damages claims stems from a doctrinal problem rather than reasons founded in the behavior of firms. The fact that there are few damages claims could be a *result* of the difficulty in bringing damages claims, rather than an indicator for the superfluous nature thereof. The doctrinal problem, it seems, is that damages claims have remained what they were over 20 years ago, as described by the Commission: a mere theoretical possibility.

In the following chapters, several national systems are examined. The hypothesis pursued is that public procurement damages claims face inherent legal structural obstacles, which, if left unaddressed, will always make damages claims in the sector of public procurement difficult. Specific doctrinal legal criteria – as opposed to the behavioural reasons cited – regularly serve either to render the bringing of successful damages claims impossible, or to limit the damages claimable in a way that does not outweigh the risks inherent to litigation.

From an institutional perspective, the legislative vacuum necessarily leads to a focus on the Court of Justice of the EU as an actor. The indeterminate nature of the damages provisions contained in the Remedies Directives results in a greater number of cases requesting the interpretation and clarification of said provisions. With or without legislation, the Court will have to face these questions when adjudicating damages. Due to the current legislative inaction, the EU judge is faced with a lack of determinacy in law and hence enormous scope to maneuver – a judicial policy space within which it is forced to position itself, vis-à-vis both the EU legislator who has not acted, and the national courts. The Court is at the centre of the following two chapters, as it is the institution that is most immediately confronted with the interpretation and development of the EU law on damages in the field of public procurement.

Bibliography

Chiti, E (2010) 'Directive 2007/66 and the Difficult Search for Balance in Judicial Protection Concerning Public Procurements' *Italian Journal of Public Law* 125.

Craig, P & Trybus, M (2010) 'Angleterre et Pays de Galles/England and Wales', in R Noguellou et al (eds), *Droit comparé des contrats publics* (Bruylant).

Graells, AS (2011) *Public procurement and the EU competition rules* (Oxford, Hart Publishing).

Hebly, JM, de Boer, ET & Wilman, FG (2007) *Rechtsbescherming bij aanbesteding* (Paris, Uitgeverij Paris).

Irmer, W (2004) *Sekundärrechtsschutz und Schadensersatz im Vergaberecht* (Frankfurt, Peter Lang).

Kosta, V (2015, forthcoming) *Fundamental Rights in EU Internal Market Legislation* (Oxford, Hart Publishing).

Martini, M (2008) *Der Markt als Instrument hoheitlicher Lenkung* (Habilitationsschrift, Mohr Siebeck).

McCrudden, C (2007) *Buying Social Justice* (Oxford, Oxford University Press).

Pachnou, D (2003) *The Effectiveness of Bidder Remedies for Enforcing the EC Public Procurement Rules: A Case Study of the Public Works Sector in the United Kingdom and Greece* (Dissertation, University of Nottingham).

Riese, C (1998) *Vergaberecht. Grundlagen – Verfahren – Rechtsschutz* (Berlin, Springer Verlag).

Schebesta, H (2014) 'EU Green Public Procurement Policy Modernisation Package, Eco-Labelling and Framing Measures' in W Devroe, S Schoenmaekers, N Philipsen, *State Aid and Public Procurement in the European Union* (Cambridge, Intersentia).

Wils, WPJ (2002) *The Optimal Enforcement of EC Antitrust Law: Essays in Law & Economics* (London, Kluwer Law International).

Chapter 3
The CJEU's Approach to Damages Under General EU Law

Abstract In light of the considerable uncertainty inherent in the damages requirement in the current public procurement legislation, the CJEU is the institution that will have to delineate EU requirements on damages in this field. This chapter states the main general EU law doctrines developed to adjudicate damages by the CJEU. It first surveys the requirements of effectiveness and equivalence, effective judicial protection and the notion of procedural autonomy. Secondly, it examines the availability of damages under the doctrine of Member State liability.

3.1 Damages Under 'Effectiveness' & 'Equivalence' Requirements, Effective Judicial Protection and Procedural Autonomy

The previous chapter argued that there is considerable uncertainty regarding the damages provisions in the Remedies Directive, and that it is equally uncertain whether the EU legislature will take action in the immediate future. From an institutional point of view, the courts (national and EU) are the forum in which the question of damages for violations of EU procurement will have to be answered. National courts will be called upon to apply the damages provisions, and may turn for guidance to the CJEU (also 'the Court') through the preliminary reference procedure.

The Court as an actor is confined by doctrinal (EU law) and structural constraints (its institutional mandate in the Treaty). In its adjudication on damages, the Court is therefore framed by the body of general EU law. While public procurement damages are a specific problem, they cannot but be understood within the wider context of damages for breaches of EU law. In the EU legal order, damages have been examined under the 'effectiveness' and 'equivalence' requirements and therefore the 'procedural autonomy' doctrine[1]; from the fundamental rights point of view as

---

[1] Parts of this chapter are based on H Schebesta, 'Does the National Court Know European Law? A Note on Ex Officio Application after Asturcom' (2010) 18 *European Review of Private Law*, 847 and H Schebesta 'Procedural theory in EU law' in K Purnhagen and P Rott (eds), *Varieties of European Economic Regulation* (New York, Springer, 2014). The latter essay explores the effect of procedural autonomy on procedural justice in EU law.

© Springer International Publishing Switzerland 2016   31
H. Schebesta, *Damages in EU Public Procurement Law*, Studies in European
Economic Law and Regulation 6, DOI 10.1007/978-3-319-23612-4_3

'effective judicial protection'; and by the Member State liability doctrine as a 'remedial right'. These are briefly presented in the following.

3.1.1 Rewe/Comet *Effectiveness*

Even where the creation of rights is effected at EU level, their adjudication takes place in the national courts due to the decentralized enforcement of EU rights – the national judge becomes the 'juge de droit commun'.[2] On one hand, the division operates under a requirement of uniform application, expressed by the CJEU as follows: *'The executive force of Community law cannot vary from one State to another in deference to subsequent domestic laws, without jeopardizing the attainment of the objectives of the Treaty'.*[3] On the other hand, this 'executive force' of Community law remains located in the national courts, embedded in a national system of judicial organization, rules on procedure and actions in front of courts; rules that are fundamentally local.[4]

This functional distribution has been addressed in the famous *Rewe/Comet* rulings:

> In the absence of Community rules on the subject, it is for the domestic legal system of each Member State to designate the Courts having jurisdiction and to determine the procedural conditions governing actions at law intended to ensure the protection of the rights which citizens have from the direct effect of Community law, it being understood that such conditions cannot be less favourable than those relating to similar actions of a domestic nature.
> … The position would be different only if the conditions and time-limits made it impossible in practice to exercise the rights which the national courts are obliged to protect.[5]

The national legal systems are competent for procedural conditions, as long as these comply with the principles of equivalence (non-discrimination) and effectiveness (not rendering virtually impossible or excessively difficult the exercise of rights conferred by EU law).

The principle of equivalence precludes domestic claims from being treated more favorably than claims based on EU law.[6] This brings about the usual intricacies of discrimination-based tests, such as the necessity of finding a comparator.[7]

---

[2] K Lenaerts, 'The Rule of Law and the Coherence of the Judicial System of the European Union' (2007) 44 *Common Market Law Review* 1625, p 1645.

[3] Case C-6/64 *Flaminio Costa v E.N.E.L.* [1964] ECR 00585.

[4] JS Delicostopoulos, 'Towards European Procedural Primacy in National Legal Systems' (2003) 9 *European Law Journal* 599, p 599.

[5] Case C-33/76 *Rewe-Zentralfinanz AG and Rewe-Zentral AG v Landwirtschaftskammer für das Saarland* [1976] ECR 01989, para 5.

[6] It hence stipulates that EU law-based claims must be treated as favorably as national claims. Although it is basically a non-discrimination principle, one can read a more positive obligation into the requirement of equivalence than into the essentially negative assertion of non-discrimination. I am grateful to Prof. HW Micklitz for this remark.

[7] For a discussion, see M Dougan, *National Remedies Before the Court of Justice: Issues of Harmonisation and Differentiation* (Oxford, Hart Publishing, 2004), p 24.

The equivalence limb presupposes the context of a national legal order, and can be legally significant only with such a concrete setting to define the comparator. The principle of effectiveness (not rendering virtually impossible or excessively difficult the exercise of rights conferred by Community law) has been debated more, as the requirement is vague.[8] It sets out EU requirements on national rules that are not defined by reference or in relation to the national context. In order to crystallize the *EU requirements* on damages, this limb is the more relevant one. Overall, damages claims in national court must respect the requirements of equivalence and effectiveness.

3.1.2 Variations of 'Effectiveness'

The limitations of the 'effectiveness' and 'equivalence' tests have generated an enormous body of case law, and consequently scholarly discussion. The accounts of effectiveness are numerous and an attempt of classification thereof is undertaken below.

3.1.2.1 Descriptive Accounts

Historic accounts focus on the development of effectiveness and equivalence over time. This type of analysis mainly relates to the development of the principle of effectiveness[9] and the intensity of EU Law intervention in national legal orders distinguishing different waves, periods or generations. Most commonly, three stages are differentiated, which correspond to different degrees of intrusiveness of the CJEU[10] into what is now termed national procedural autonomy. The main insight to be drawn is that the CJEU's approach has varied over time. The historical account is not able to supply probable predictions, but it does draw attention to the fact that the case law has not yet steadied, and is therefore at a critical stage, prone to interpretation.

Topological accounts group the case law according to the procedural rules at issue and different functions within the legal process; that is, for example, the jurisdiction of courts, time limits for bringing claims, and the actual remedies (for example, in the form of damages).[11] Since it has often happened that case law clusters

---

[8] See for example S Seyr, *Der effet utile in der Rechtsprechung des EuGH* (Berlin, Duncker & Humblot, 2008); M Ross, 'Effectiveness in the European legal order(s): Beyond supremacy to constitutional proportionality' (2006) 31 *European Law Review* 476; and T Tridimas, *The general principles of EU law* (Oxford, Oxford University Press, 2006).

[9] V Trstenjak & E Beysen, 'European Consumer Protection Law: Curia Semper Dabit Remedium?, (2011) 48 *Common Market Law Review* 95, p 101 (noting that '[t]he case law of the ECJ has, however, been marked by an important evolution in the application of the effectiveness test.')

[10] A Ward, *Judicial Review and the Rights of Private Parties in EU Law* (Oxford, Oxford University Press, 2007).

[11] By way of example, Dougan, *National Remedies Before the Court of Justice*, above n 7, pp 32–33.

around claim types, these are also sometimes brought together; for example, in the form of recovery of illegal aid, or restitution of unlawfully levied charges.

3.1.2.2 Analytical Accounts

Analytical accounts examine the structure of the legal reasoning performed, and analyse the application of the 'effectiveness and equivalence' tests.

Regarding the sequence of the equivalence and effectiveness criteria, Ward proposes to first examine procedural rules under the equivalence principle. Once this is not violated, national procedural rules should be said to enjoy a *Keck*-style[12] presumption of compatibility, as long as they do not impede the essence of the right of access to court, pursuit of a legitimate aim, and proportionality.[13] This essentially likens the test to the internal market tests. It is argued that by putting 'equivalence' first in a sequence with effectiveness, the test would be able to deliver more legal certainty.[14] Bobek on the other hand disputes this potential and draws attention to the implications of the choice of comparator as in the equivalence limb of the test.[15]

One of the strongest structural differences can be found in the work of authors who separate the notion of judicial protection from the 'effectiveness' under the *Rewe/Comet* case law formulation. One could say that these are 'two limb' or 'three limb' accounts of 'effectiveness and equivalence', that is, consisting of either equivalence and effectiveness only; or equivalence, effectiveness, and judicial protection.[16] In addition, authors separate the question of effective judicial protection from whether the different limbs apply cumulatively or not. Timmermans, for example, advocates the distinction between the *Rewe/Comet*-effectiveness and judicial protection, but speaks out against the cumulative application of the criteria.[17]

---

[12] In *Keck*, the Court distinguished product requirements from selling arrangements. Under the internal market logic, product requirements would be subject to court scrutiny, while mere selling arrangements (such as opening hours and the like) would be accepted provided that the two conditions set out by the Court were met Cases C-267/91 and C-268/91 *Keck and Mithouard* [1993] ECR I-6097.

[13] A Ward, 'Do Unto Others as You Would Have Them Do Unto You: Willy Kempter and the Duty to Raise EC Law in National Litigation' (2008) 33 *European Law Review* 739.

[14] ibid, p 751.

[15] M Bobek, 'Why There is No Principle of "Procedural Autonomy" of the Member States', in HW Micklitz & B de Witte (eds), *The European Court of Justice and the Autonomy of the Member States* (Intersentia, 2011), the contribution is also notable for being outspokenly critical of the recent developments of procedural autonomy.

[16] C Timmermans, Presentation 'Limits Imposed by EU law to Member States' Freedom of Action in Fields not Regulated by EU law', Robert Schuman Centre for Advanced Studies, Florence (13 April 2011).

[17] Timmermans' conceptual understanding differentiates between (1) effet utile; (2) effectiveness under the Rewe/Comet formula in what we have called an objective and subjective right version; and (3) judicial protection. This position, in the light of the requirement of first entering the scope of EU law, seems untenable, as the autonomous application of principles of judicial protection is currently not possible. This distinction fails to account for the difference between (1) and (2).

Also Prechal, currently judge at the CJEU, suggests a distinction between effectiveness and the fundamental right to judicial protection.[18]

Instead of focusing on the legal reasoning deployed in the test, some authors stress the difference in outcome, which can be distinguished based on whether it is supposed to provide an adequate or only a minimum level of judicial protection.[19]

3.1.3 The Different Uses of Effectiveness

Effectiveness as a concept is elusive: is it a 'principle, arbiter, standard or result'?[20] From an analytical point of view, effectiveness has sometimes been considered as a standard, while sometimes the reasoning has drawn more attention to the balancing being undertaken.[21]

3.1.3.1 Effectiveness as a Standard[22]

Under the 'effectiveness' limb, the Court tests that a national rule must not render virtually impossible or excessively difficult either (i) *the exercise of rights* conferred by EU law or (ii) *the application of EU law*. These formulations differ from one another as one is geared towards the protection of a subjective right, and the other towards protection of the law itself. These two formulations exemplify a subjective and an objective approach respectively.[23] Subjective in this context refers to a specific interest of an individual or group right based test, whereas objective relates to the rule of law, which protects a wider common interest of society. Some scholars, for example former CJEU judge Timmermans, heavily stress the different rationales underlying the respective principles of effectiveness. Whereas effectiveness in

---

[18] R Widdershoven & A Prechal, 'Redefining the Relationship between "Rewe-effectiveness" and Effective Judicial Protection' (2011) 4 *Review of European Administrative Law* 31.

[19] See W van Gerven, 'Of Rights, Remedies and Procedures' (2000) 37 *Common Market Law Review* 501, p 504.

[20] M Ross, 'Effectiveness in the European Legal Order(s): Beyond Supremacy to Constitutional Proportionality' (2006) 31 *European Law Review* 476, p 479

[21] This is not to say that using effectiveness as a standard does not imply a certain trade-off between different values. However, the inherent *balancing* does not surface in a reasoned form.

[22] The principle of effectiveness is a relational term, expressing the relation between 'Ist-und Sollensleistung'.

[23] The acceptance of the terms subjective and objective for the indication that the protected interest can either be specific or general varies across legal traditions. The distinction is meant similarly to the French distinction between 'public policy rules designed to order society (*règles d'ordre public de direction*), adopted in the general interest and which the court may raise of its own motion, and public policy rules designed to protect specific interests (*règles d'ordre public de protection*), adopted in the interest of a particular category of persons and which may be relied upon only by persons belonging to that category'. See Case C-429/05 *Rampion and Godard* [2007] ECR I-08017, para 58.

an objective sense is concerned with the uniform application of the law, effectiveness in a subjective sense (of subjective rights) is concerned with the protection of rights. The third form of effectiveness of judicial protection can be phrased as effective 'access to justice',[24] as it mostly appears in cases in which an 'individual appears to be denied access to justice or an available remedy'.[25] Thus construed, the existence of such a maxim is connected to the principle of legal protection derived from, for example, Articles 6 and 13 ECHR, in the form of access to an independent and impartial (EU or national) court[26] and invokes the protection of fundamental or human rights.

'Effectiveness' is used as a standard against which to measure whether national rules sufficiently realize EU law/rights. The question of national procedural rules is framed as an instrumental one, in which national procedural law merely realizes substantive EU law.

3.1.3.2   Effectiveness as a Balancing Exercise

The classic formulation of 'effectiveness' was phrased slightly differently in the *van Schijndel/Peterbroeck* cases, in which the CJEU used additional and seemingly cumulative considerations when testing the 'effectiveness' of a national rule:

> …national procedural provisions … must be analysed by reference to the role of that provision in the procedure, its progress and its special features, viewed as a whole before the various national instances. [context part] In the light of that analysis the basic principles of the domestic judicial system, such as protection of the rights of the defence, the principle of legal certainty and the proper conduct of procedure, must, where appropriate, be taken into consideration [balancing part].[27]

In this instance, the analytical structure of the effectiveness test had changed[28] from that of a standard to place new emphasis of the national context ('contextualization'). In addition the CJEU took the purpose of the national rule into account ('purposive approach'), followed by a subsequent balancing of the two. Generally, the *van Schijndel/Peterbroeck* test is therefore referred to as a 'balancing

---

[24] Timmermans presentation 'Limits Imposed by EU law to Member States' Freedom of Action in Fields not Regulated by EU law', above n 16.

[25] J Engström, *The Europeanisation of Remedies and Procedures through Judge-made Law – Can a Trojan Horse achieve Effectiveness? Experiences of the Swedish Judiciary* (European University Institute, 2009), Tome I, p 48.

[26] van Gerven, 'Of Rights, Remedies and Procedures', above n 19, p 521.

[27] Joined Cases C-430/93 and C-431/93 *Van Schijndel / Stichting Pensioenfonds voor Fysiotherapeuten* [1995] ECR I-4705, para 19; Case C-312/93 *Peterbroeck, Van Campenhout & Cie / Belgian State* [1995] ECR I-4599, para 14.

[28] M Hoskins, 'Tilting the Balance: Supremacy and National Procedural Rules' (1996) 21 *European Law Review* p 376 (observing that the Court of Justice 'departed from the orthodox principle of procedural autonomy'). However, he criticizes the approach as being too vague and prefers effectiveness as a more useful standard in the national court.

approach'. In balancing, not only the purpose ('the role of that procedure') of the national rule is taken into account, but also the context, which is a wider notion including role, progress and various judicial instances. Moreover, the purpose is taken into account at both levels, EU and national. Accordingly, the rationale or purpose of a given procedural rule can justify a restriction of or limitation to the bringing of a claim based in EU law. The Court referred to rights of the defense, legal certainty, proper conduct of procedure, but one might also consider, for example, unjustified enrichment.[29] The basic principles upon which these national rules are based must *'be taken into consideration'*. Herein lays the truly fundamental importance of the contextual approach: the balancing aspect is a novelty, as for the first time the national procedural law receives 'standing'. By taking the national principles which justify the existence of these rules into consideration, *national* value judgments may enter into conflict with EU law requirements. The conflict is not automatically resolved by primacy as a rule but through a balancing exercise. However, this is not an alternative to effectiveness as a standard. In understanding the contextualized *van Schijndel/Peterbroeck* test as a balancing exercise, effectiveness as a standard is used to determine the EU law requirements on accuracy in the application of EU law, which are then justified and balanced against the contextualized national procedural provisions.[30]

To summarize, two uses of the principle of effectiveness are distinguished. The first is 'effectiveness as a standard', in which procedural law must meet a standard of accuracy[31] in the implementation of EU substantive law. Secondly, the 'balancing use'[32] of effectiveness – it allows a departure from the accurate or correct application of EU law and introduces a mechanism of justification. The justification raises questions in two dimensions. The first is the substantive question of how to balance the procedural values (such as legal certainty) against the postulates of an accurate application of law. Secondly, a constitutional dimension is inherent in the choice of source of the justificatory procedural values: do they derive from European/EU procedural justice values or from the national level?

---

[29] Joined Cases C-295/04 to C-298/04 *Manfredi and others* [2006] ECR I-06619.

[30] For strong criticism on the use of the 'effectiveness' limb in general, see Ward, 'Do unto others as you would have them do unto you', above n 13, p 753. According to her, effectiveness as a standard is too indeterminate, and the contextual approach too unstructured. She therefore proposes to streamline the CJEU's jurisprudence with Article 6(1) ECHR case law, according to which *'non-discriminatory temporal limitations to the enforcement of Community law, at national level, would only need to be disapplied, under EC law, if they struck at the "very essence" of right of access to a court, failed to pursue a legitimate aim, and were disproportionate.'* In my reading of the case, all of these elements are already implicit in the effectiveness under the *Peterbroeck* test, with the possible exception of the 'very essence' element.

[31] In procedural theory the merely 'servant function' of procedural law vis-à-vis substantive law is often described as the accuracy view. I discuss this aspect in greater detail in ch 14.

[32] P Haapaniemi, 'Procedural Autonomy: A Misnomer?' in L Ervo et al (eds), *Europeanization of Procedural Law and the New Challenges to Fair Trial* (Groningen, Europa Law Publishing, 2009), p 98.

While for some time the *van Schijndel/Peterbroeck* test was no longer regarded as pertinent, the CJEU has increasingly made use of the balancing formulation.[33] Probably as a consequence thereof, over the past ten years, the question whether 'procedural autonomy' is a normative claim on behalf of national rules has become increasingly polarizing. The effectiveness/equivalence test now could involve a weighing up of the procedural autonomy possessed by Member States *against* the effectiveness of EU law. This development is further discussed in section 3.1.4.

3.1.4   Judicial Protection as a Fundamental Right

Analytically, it is still open where judicial protection is situated systematically within this reasoning of the court. Effective judicial protection could be subsumed under the 'effectiveness and equivalence' test and therefore be treated either as a method of interpretation of effectiveness or a third limb of the test existing *in addition to* equivalence and effectiveness.

Effective judicial protection is based on subjective rights language and refers to an autonomous and concretizable set of sources of law (Charter of Fundamental Rights, the Convention of Human Rights and Member States' common traditions). It is also argued that the justifications that are accepted under effectiveness differs from those under fundamental right considerations.[34] Therefore, effective judicial protection should indeed be considered separately from traditional effectiveness.

Effective judicial protection has its roots in the ECHR, and is now also elaborated in the Charter of Fundamental Rights. Article 6(1) ECHR guarantees *a fair and public hearing* within a reasonable amount of time *by an independent and impartial tribunal* established by law. Article 13 ECHR guarantees the *right to an effective remedy* to everyone whose rights and freedoms as set forth in the Convention are violated.

In the EU legal order, the principle of judicial protection was enshrined by the CJEU in the *Johnston*[35] case, in which recourse was made to the common traditions of the Member States, as well as Articles 6 and 13 of the ECHR for authority (although, for example, Article 6 (1) ECHR concerns fair trials, confined to civil law disputes, granting overall procedural rights). *Steffensen* concerned the admissibility of evidence in a procedure, and the Court of Justice stated that parties '*must be afforded a real opportunity to comment effectively on it in order for the*

---

[33] Case C-246/09 *Bulicke* [2010] ECR I-7003.

[34] See S Prechal and K Cath, 'The European Acquis of Civil Procedure: Constitutional Aspects' (2014) 19 *Uniform Law Review*, pp 179–198 (arguing that the test for justifications for 'restrictions on the principle of effective judicial protection is stricter than the more lenient test of the 'procedural rule of reason' employed to justify restrictions on "Rewe effectiveness"'. This remains to be seen in practice.)

[35] Case 222/84 *Johnston v Chief Constable of the Royal Ulster Constabulary* [1986] ECR 1663.

proceedings to reach the standard of fairness required'.[36] Since *Johnston*, the importance of the effectiveness of judicial protection has been continuously stressed.[37]

Since the entry into force of the Lisbon Treaty in 2009, the Charter of Fundamental Rights of the EU enjoys the same legal value as EU treaties (taking into account the respective protocols). The application of the Charter is contingent on the scope of application of EU law to a case – Charter rights are thus not self-standing. The wider implications of the change of legal status of the Charter still largely depends on its future interpretation. Although Article 6 TEU and Article 51(2) of the Charter restrict the Charter from extending the competences of the EU, it remains to be seen how the Charter will inform the case law, in particular on judicial protection regarding the right to an effective remedy and a fair trial enshrined in Article 47 of the Charter.[38] Article 52(3) provides that the corresponding Charter and ECHR rights shall be given the same meaning and scope, although EU law can go beyond the minimum levels enshrined in the ECHR. Additionally, the level of protection of human rights shall not be adversely affected by the Charter according to Article 53. Article 47 provides for the right to an effective remedy and a fair trial:

> Article 47 Right to an effective remedy and to a fair trial
>   Everyone whose rights and freedoms guaranteed by the law of the Union are violated has the right to an effective remedy before a tribunal in compliance with the conditions laid down in this Article.
>   Everyone is entitled to a fair and public hearing within a reasonable time by an independent and impartial tribunal previously established by law. Everyone shall have the possibility of being advised, defended and represented.
>   Legal aid shall be made available to those who lack sufficient resources in so far as such aid is necessary to ensure effective access to justice.

The first sentence enshrines Article 13 ECHR on an effective remedy. The EU offers more extensive legal protection since it requires a recourse in front of a court rather than merely a national authority. The second sentence mirrors Article 6(1) ECHR and provides for the right to a fair hearing. This right is more extensive in the EU as it is not limited to civil law rights and obligations but regardless of the type of dispute at issue. The third sentence codifies ECHR case law on the availability of legal aid.[39]

The CJEU's rulings so far have been inconclusive on the relationship between effective judicial protection and 'effectiveness and equivalence' (and the notion of

---

[36] Case C-276/01 *Steffensen* [2003] ECR I-3735, para 77.

[37] One of the most important recent cases being Case C-432/05 *Unibet (London) Ltd. and Unibet (International) Ltd. v Justitiekanslern* [2007] ECR I-2271.

[38] For a discussion of Article 47 in relation to private law, and discussing the relevance of 'prohibitions to interfere' and 'positive claims to protection' with respect to fundamental rights, see C Mak, 'Rights and Remedies: Article 47 EUCFR and Effective Judicial Protection in European Private Law Matters' in HW Micklitz (ed), *Constitutionalization of European Private Law* (Oxford, Oxford University Press, 2014), pp 236–258.

[39] See for an 'official' comparison of the texts of the ECHR and the Charter Praesidium of the European Convention, *Explanations relating to the Charter*, OJ C 303 (14.12.2007), pp 29–30.

procedural autonomy): in *Alassini*,[40] *Pontin*,[41] and *Impact*[42] for example the Court stated that '*the requirements of equivalence and effectiveness* **embody** *the general obligation on the Member States to ensure judicial protection of an individual's rights under EU law*'. By contrast, in *Mono Car Styling*,[43] the Court stated that effective judicial protection is *in addition to* effectiveness and equivalence. However, the bracket over all three elements was still 'whilst it is in principle for national law to determine…', which is the formulation of the procedural autonomy test. In the light of this case law, effective judicial protection could be described as the third limb of the 'effectiveness and equivalence' doctrine.

Importantly, the values which these rights incorporate are not national, but inherently inter/supranational since they derive from the Member States' common traditions, the Charter or the ECHR. However, the judicial protection rights are, as of yet, not self-standing and serve only as interpretative tools, and would represent a common EU-wide denominator.

The role that the fundamental right to an effective remedy is going to play in the development of the CJEU's approach to damages is open to speculation, but it is likely to be increasingly important in interpreting remedies.

3.1.5 *'Procedural Autonomy' Results in Considerable Uncertainty for the Court*

Initially, the CJEU constructed the *Rewe/Comet* formula, which was only later dubbed the principle of procedural autonomy. The notion of procedural autonomy is often based on a negative conception: procedural autonomy is what is left between the boundaries of demands of equivalence and effectiveness. In this sense, it is nothing more than a result and procedural autonomy is but the *consequence* of the absence of Community rules. It is thus characterizable as 'just another label'[44] for the *Rewe/Comet* formula, as mere 'shorthand for the fact that where (and as long as) there are no Community rules, Community law has little choice but to rely on national rules'.[45]

The notion of 'procedural autonomy' becomes legally relevant only once the area delimited by 'equivalence' and 'effectiveness' can also make claims independently, therefore deserving a positive description. Is procedural autonomy a prescriptive concept, a positive prohibition of interference with national procedural

---

[40] Joined Cases C-317-320/08 *Alassini* [2010] ECR I-2213.

[41] Case C-63/08 *Pontin* [2009] ECR I-10467, para 44.

[42] Case C-268/06 *Impact* [2008] ECR I-2483, paras 47-48

[43] Case C-12/08 *Mono Carstyling*, ECLI:EU:C:2009:466.

[44] S Prechal, 'Community Law in National Courts: The Lessons from Van Schijndel' (1998) *Common Market Law Review* 681, p 682, fn 3.

[45] Also defended by Prechal, ibid, p 681.

law? The Member States' claim to procedural autonomy is then capable of being weighed against demands of effectiveness and equivalence.

Opinions are highly divided on this point. Some deny the existence of procedural autonomy, while others rely on it unreflectedly, as though it were a natural obstacle to EU law interference. It has been referred to as 'more apparent than real',[46] and it has been argued that in any case, autonomy does not equal independence.[47] The creation of the term 'procedural autonomy' was credited to the commentator Joel Rideau in 1972 and a subsequent textbook.[48] In 1996, Tonne was able to write that only the older literature spoke of procedural autonomy as a limitation to Community competence.[49] In 1998, Judge Kakouris questioned the very existence of procedural autonomy,[50] a call which was echoed by van Gerven in 2000, who referred to the procedural competence, rather than autonomy, of the Member States.[51] All of these observations reflect the same sentiment, namely skepticism in relation to the normative powers of the principle, and the validity thereof as a whole.

Originally, the contours of the 'principle' of procedural autonomy, namely effectiveness and equivalence, were what shaped the concept. The lack of normative significance of procedural autonomy *itself* was underscored by the attitude of the Court. It continued to refine the *Rewe/Comet* formula but for the longest time did not use the notion of procedural autonomy as such.[52] It was mainly Advocate Generals, especially AG Darmon and Jacobs (and from time to time, parties in their submissions), that started referring to a principle of procedural autonomy. In 2004, for the first time, the CJEU used the terminology 'procedural autonomy' in the *Wells*[53] case. It then appeared in a string of consumer law cases, and is now commonly encountered in CJEU judgments. Until 2004 the Court itself had *never* used 'procedural autonomy'. Nowadays a search on the Court's database yields above 100 results,[54] this is next to those judgments which use the effectiveness/equivalency formulation but without calling it procedural autonomy. In many ways the reception of the concept as such is a clear 'success'. Although there is no single way of reasoning which could justify all of the case law rendered, it can be stated that

---

[46] Advocate General Tesauro CN Kakouris, 'Do the Member States Possess Judicial Procedural "Autonomy"?' (1997) *Common Market Law Review* 1389.

[47] Statement by Cavallini, quoted in Kakouris, ibid.

[48] Haapaniemi dates the term back to the commentator Joel Rideau in 1972 and a textbook released thereafter. See Haapaniemi, 'Procedural Autonomy: A Misnomer?', above n 32, 89.

[49] M Tonne, *Effektiver Rechtsschutz durch staatliche Gerichte als Forderung des europäischen Gemeinschaftsrechts* (Köln, Heymanns, 1997), p 315.

[50] Kakouris, 'Do the Member States Possess Judicial Procedural "Autonomy"?', above n 46, p 1389.

[51] van Gerven, 'Of Rights, Remedies and Procedures', above n 19, p 501.

[52] In 1997 Kakouris was still able to write that the Court had never used the notion. See Kakouris, 'Do the Member States Possess Judicial Procedural "Autonomy"?', above n 46, p 1389.

[53] Case C-201/02, *The Queen on the application of Delena Wells and Secretary of State for Transport, Local Government and the Regions* [2004] ECR I-723.

[54] Curia website, search for text 'procedural autonomy' in the category of judgments only (published and unpublished) produced 114 results, retrieved April 2015.

procedural autonomy moved from being a descriptive to an increasingly prescriptive concept with the potential to shield national rules against requirements of effectiveness from European law.

Of the contributions on procedural autonomy, Pekka Haapaniemi captures the *use* of the principle of procedural autonomy very well by drawing attention to the dangers of the 'nominalist fallacy':

> …when we speak of procedural autonomy, we suppose that there must somewhere be procedural autonomy. So, by speaking of it we, in fact, tend in some way to create it at least in our minds. The danger is that we draw a conclusion that there is procedural autonomy, because we speak about it. By contrast, we should examine what is behind the expression we use i.e. analyze the contents of the legal phenomenon.[55]

Procedural autonomy is a doctrine that has gradually manifested. While we can affirm its existence, its meaning remains open. As the doctrine stands so far, the existence of such a claim to autonomy and the precise nature thereof are disputed. In applying procedural autonomy, the CJEU faces significant uncertainties: is procedural autonomy descriptive or prescriptive, and if the latter is the case, what does it prescribe?

Procedural autonomy, and in particular the effectiveness limb of the test, constrains judicial reasoning when damages are involved: the CJEU has fully subjected damages claims to the use of the procedural autonomy doctrine. In the area of public procurement, even the legislator has refrained from legislative action on damages on grounds of the Member States' procedural autonomy.[56] The relevance of this framework for the specific area of damages public procurement is explored in the following chapter.

3.2   Damages as a Remedy (Member State Liability)

Under procedural autonomy, in the absence of EU law requirements, damages are governed by the domestic national legal system. The absence of regulation through secondary legislative instruments does not mean, however, that there are no requirements emanating from the European level. In cases of breaches of EU law, the effectiveness of EU law must be ensured. Additionally, under the general principles of the Treaty, the CJEU created a remedy for violations of breaches of EU law by the Member States: damages claims are possible under Member State liability.[57]

---

[55] P Haapaniemi in A Rösenkotter & T Wuersig, *The Impact of the Lisbon Treaty in the Field of Public Procurement* (European Parliament, 2010), p 114.

[56] Commission Staff Working Document, Annex to the Proposal for a Directive of the European Parliament and of the Council amending Council Directives 89/665/EEC and 92/13/EEC CEE with regard to improving the effectiveness of review procedures concerning the award of public contracts, Impact Assessment Report – Remedies in the field of public procurement, SEC(2006) 557 (4 May 2006), p 12 [hereinafter 'Impact Assessment Report on Remedies'].

[57] And potentially, through the bridge of the *Bergaderm*-judgment, Institutional liability also, see Case C-352/98 *P Bergaderm and Goupil/Commission* [2000] ECR I-5291.

3.2.1   The Constitutive Criteria of Member State Liability

In *Francovich*, the Court founded an obligation to make good the damage resulting from breaches of Member States' obligations under Community law.[58] *Francovich* lays down the conditions for liability as regards a Member State's failure to take all the measures necessary to achieve the result prescribed by a directive, holding that there must be a rule intended to confer an individual right, ascertainability of the right's content, and causality between the breach and the loss suffered. In *Brasserie du Pecheur*,[59] an individual's right to claim damages for violations of Community law was extended to 'whatever … organ of the State whose act or omission was responsible for the breach'.[60] The material conditions giving rise to Member State liability as substantiated in *Brasserie* are the following: (1) a breach of a European rule intending to confer individual rights, (2) a breach of a sufficiently serious nature, and (3) causality between the breach and the damage sustained.

3.2.1.1   Breach of a Rule Intended to Confer Individual Rights

Whether or not a Community rule is intended to confer rights on individuals is determined solely by the EU Courts, as that determination exclusively concerns the interpretation of the content of an EU legal instrument.[61] A distinction between the creation of an individual right on one hand and the direct effectiveness of a provision on the other exists.[62] The Court has regularly interpreted the 'individual right' criterion to mean that an EU provision must protect an individual interest, without, however, requiring enforceability of an individual right in the strict sense. By contrast, it is argued that some provisions only extend to the protection of for example 'the market' or other broader/general interests, and therefore do not confer

---

[58] C-479/93 *Andrea Francovich v Italian Republic* [1995] ECR I-03843, para 35 (concerning the failure of the legislature to act: 'It follows that the principle whereby a State must be liable for loss and damage caused to individuals as a result of breaches of Community law for which the State can be held responsible is inherent in the system of the Treaty.').

[59] In contrast to *Francovich*, *Brasserie* concerned a positive violation of Community law rather than an omission.

[60] Joined Cases C-46/93 and C-48/93 *Brasserie du Pêcheur v Bundesrepublik Deutschland* and *The Queen v Secretary of State for Transport, ex parte Factortame and others* [1996] ECR I-1029, para 31. In this respect European law resembles international law whereby the State is taken as a unitary legal entity which is liable as a whole, rather than the liability resting with any of its constituent parts. Compare also Art 27 of the Vienna Convention on the Law of Treaties.

[61] A Biondi & M Farley, *The right to damages in European Law* (Alphen aan den Rijn, Kluwer Law International, 2009), 32. Due to the national variations regarding rights and interests, one must keep in mind that Community law operates on an assumption of rights that is not contingent upon national law interpretations thereof.

[62] S Prechal, *Directives in EC Law* (Oxford, Oxford University Press, 2005).

individual rights. Confirmation of this approach may be read into *Peter Paul*.[63] A German national law obstructed individual claims for deficient banking supervision as required by a banking directive. While depositors enjoyed individual rights for their deposit guarantees, the national law did not consider the (EU) prudential banking supervision requirement at hand to confer individual rights, as it protected the market. The CJEU upheld the national law. The case raised much attention and criticism in the literature,[64] and the distinction between subjective liability schemes (which require the violated norm to protect the interest of an individual) and objective liability schemes[65] (according to which the mere violation of a rule is enough to ground a claim for damages)[66] is still disputed. However, the Court has not made reference to *Peter Paul* in any subsequent judgment.[67]

3.2.1.2 Seriousness of the Breach of Community Law

A second condition is the quality of the breach of EU law. Case law strongly supports that the seriousness of a breach[68] is differently qualified for different types of conduct of Member States.[69] Liability for judicial action[70] has been accepted, and

---

[63] Case C-222/02 *Peter Paul, Cornelia Sonnen-Lütte and Christel Mörkens v Bundesrepublik Deutschland* [2004] ECR I-09425.

[64] For example M Tison, 'Do not attack the watchdog! Banking supervisor's liability after Peter Paul' (2005) 42 *Common Market Law Review*, pp. 639–675. See also N Reich, 'The Interrelation between Rights and Duties in EU Law: Reflections on the State of Liability Law in the Multilevel Governance System of the Union: Is There a Need for a More Coherent Approach in European Private Law?' (2010) 29 *Yearbook of European Law*, pp 112–163.

[65] Regarding objectivity of liability one may distinguish the following dimensions – objectivity in terms of a protected interest is not necessary, a mere breach suffices. However, also regarding the dimension of fault and subjective liability, the term of objective liability is sometimes used to denote the difference in relation to fault between an objective legal fault perspective and a subjective moral fault perspective. The question of fault is examined at a later stage.

[66] MP Granger, 'National Applications of Francovich and the Construction of a European Administrative Jus Commune' (2007) 32 *European Law Review* 157.

[67] As of April 2015.

[68] The differences in linguistic versions in this respect have been used in order to cast doubt regarding the nature of this condition – the literal English translation of the concepts used in French and German (violation suffisamment characterise, hinreichend qualifiziert) would be a sufficiently qualified breach. For details see J Beatson & T Tridimas, *New Directions in European Public Law* (Oxford, Hart Publishing, 1998), p 43, referring to D Edward & W Robinson, 'Is there a Place for Private Law Principles in Community Law?', in T Heukels & A McDonnell (eds), *The Action for Damages in Community Law* (The Hague, Kluwer Law International, 1997). It is tempting to follow the distinction under English national law giving this condition an inherent connection with legal factual situations. However, from a formal point of view all linguistic versions are equally authentic. The legal concept of a sufficiently serious breach is filled with European, rather than national meaning.

[69] A discussion on the merits in relation to immunities for particular parts of the State is omitted here.

[70] Which was clearly established in Case C-224/01 *Gerhard Köbler v Republik Österreich* [2003] ECR I-10239.

may be limited by national law to cases of 'manifest infringement' of EU law.[71] Legislative and administrative action on the other hand has been found by the Court also for less severe breaches. The Court has re-iterated that it is for the national court to ascertain whether an infringement is characterized as a sufficiently serious breach of EU law.[72] At the same time, where the Court has all the information necessary to judge whether the facts presented are to be characterised as a sufficiently serious breach of EU law, it will do so.[73]

At the very least, Member State liability results where a State has manifestly and gravely disregarded the limits to the exercise of its powers.[74] Factors which the competent court may take into consideration include:

> the clarity and precision of the rule breached, the measure of discretion left by that rule to the national or Community authorities, whether the infringement and the damage caused was intentional or involuntary, whether any error of law was excusable or inexcusable, the fact that the position taken by a Community institution may have contributed towards the omission, and the adoption or retention of national measures or practices contrary to Community law.[75]

Liability for a legislative act was addressed in the *British Telecommunications* case[76]; incidentally a case arising in the utilities sector, therefore falling under (the old) Utilities Directive 90/531. The Court stated that a restrictive approach to liability is justified for Member States exercising their legislative function in order that they not be '*hindered by the prospect of actions for damages whenever the general interest requires the institutions or Member States to adopt measures which may adversely affect individual interests*'.[77] The case concerned a Member State's legislative action, and the Court found that Article 8(1) was imprecisely worded and could reasonably have borne the interpretation that Britain had given to it in its implementation. In general, therefore, good faith in the implementation of directives precludes Member State liability during legislative action.[78]

---

[71] Case C-173/03 *Traghetti del Mediterraneo SpA v Italy* [2006] ECR I-5204.

[72] C-318/13 *X* [2014] ECLI:EU:C:2014:2133.

[73] C-429/09 *Fuß v Stadt Halle* [2010] ECR I-12173, para 45.

[74] Judgments in Joined Cases 83 and 94/76, 4, 15 and 40/77 *Bayerische HNL Vermehrungsbetriebe GmbH & Co. KG and others v Council and Commission of the European Communities* [1978] ECR 01209, para 6; *Brasserie*, above n 60; and *Factortame*, above n 60, para 55.

[75] See *Brasserie* and *Factortame*, above n 60.

[76] Judgment in *The Queen v Secretary of State for Trade and Industry, ex parte British Telecommunications plc*, Case C-302/94, ECLI:EU:C:1996:485.

[77] ibid, para 40.

[78] See also the *Brinkmann* case, in which Denmark had classified tobacco roles erroneously as a 'cigarette' in its implementation. Since other Member States had followed the same interpretation, Denmark was said to have acted in good faith, and was not found liable. See Case C-319/96 *Brinkmann Tabakfabriken GmbH v Skatteministeriet* [1998] ECR I-05255. See also Biondi & Farley, *The right to damages in European law*, above n 61, p 50.

It has been argued that the seriousness of the breach of Community law is a disguised fault criterion, or something akin to it.[79] For example, in *Hedley Lomas*,[80] the Court referred to the failure of the breaching Member State to produce any evidence regarding the justification which it had advanced (concerning the non-compliance of slaughterhouses with a Directive on the stunning of animals). The failure to substantiate the justification for the refusal to grant the license was taken into account by the Court within the argument on seriousness of the breach. Implicitly, the seriousness criterion could thus include an element of fault on behalf of the Member State to aggravate the breach.[81] In *X*, the Court carved out conditions for the national court to take into consideration, in this case (a legislative action), the fact that the CJEU had not previously ruled on the legality on a specific provision in a directive.[82]

Initially, Member State liability was granted for wrongful or missing implementation of EU law – it served to overcome the lack of direct effect of directives when Member States failed to implement them by not passing legislation. From granting individuals protection against non-implementation, the doctrine was extended to cover the application of law or situations involving administrative law. Operational mistakes in the application of the law, for example, were regarded as fulfilling the qualification of the 'sufficiently serious' breaches since they were characterized as breaches with 'no discretion'.[83] Such conduct was at issue in *Hedley Lomas*. *Hedley Lomas*[84] found the United Kingdom to be obliged to make reparations for the damage caused to an individual on the basis of a Member State's refusal to issue an export licence in breach of Article 34 of the Treaty. When examining the 'seriousness of the breach' criterion, the Court ruled that where '*the Member State in question was not called upon to make any legislative choices and had only considerably reduced, or even no, discretion, the mere infringement of Community law may be sufficient to establish the existence of a sufficiently serious breach*'.[85] Due to the lack of consideration and choice which characterize legislative actions, an administrative action involves less discretion, and consequently may more readily constitute a 'sufficiently serious' breach. Admittedly, *Hedley Lomas* concerned a direct breach of a Treaty provision, rather than merely a breach of the terms of a directive. On the other hand, one may argue that rules contained in directives are often more readily ascertainable and clear, consequently leaving the Member State without discretion. In this respect it is

---

[79] IB Lee, 'In Search of a Theory of State Liability in the European Union' (1999) 9/99 *Harvard Jean Monnet Working Paper*; Biondi & Farley, The right to damages in European law, above n 61, pp 53–55; and Granger, 'National applications of Francovich', above n 66, p 157.

[80] Case 5/94 *R. v Ministry of Agriculture, Fisheries, and Food (MAFF), ex parte Hedley Lomas Ltd* [1996] ECR I-02553.

[81] Ward, *Judicial Review and the Rights of Private Parties in EU Law*, above n 10, p 230.

[82] C-318/13 *X* [2014] ECLI:EU:C:2014:2133.

[83] Biondi & Farley, The right to damages in European law, above n 61, p 47.

[84] *Hedley Lomas*, above n 80.

[85] ibid, para 28.

also worthwhile to compare the argument of the Court in *COS.MET*,[86] which concerned liability for a statement of a public official and therefore factual conduct of the Member State rather than an administrative decision. The Court similarly held that the obligations set out in the directive did not give Member States discretion, and therefore that a breach thereof would be sufficiently serious to give rise to liability.[87] However, uncertainty persists regarding the interpretation of the 'sufficiently serious' criterion deployed by the Court, for example, in considering the threshold to be reached regarding operational breaches only.

Through the open characterization of a sufficiently serious breach, *all types* of actions emanating from the State are caught by the criterion. The act of implementation – perhaps better: giving effect to EU law – includes legislating, executing and adjudicating. The criterion is only shaped by the degree of discretion incumbent on a Member State based on a norm it is supposed to effectuate.

3.2.1.3   Causality/Causation

In principle, the notion of causality is left mostly untouched by requirements set at EU level. It is notorious that in many instances whereby cases have been 'won' successfully in the CJEU, the national courts have in the end found against the individual applications on the grounds of a lack of causality.[88] Especially in countries establishing objective liability,[89] more emphasis is put on the requirement of the chain of causation.[90] Nevertheless, there are instances in which the CJEU scrutinized causality more closely, for example in *Rechberger*. The Court held that once a direct causal link was established it could not be limited *in casu* by the imprudence of a travel organizer or by the 'occurrence of exceptional or unforeseeable events', since such circumstances do not preclude the existence of a causal link.[91] Similarly, in *COS.MET*, a statement which was made by a government official on the lacking security of elevators produced by a company, a statement which was in violation of the product safety directive's procedures, was indicated

---

[86] Case C-470/03 *A.G.M.-COS.MET Srl v Suomen valtio and Tarmo Lehtinen* [2007] ECR I-02749, para 82.

[87] Similarly, in Larsy II, Belgium was held liable for the simple misapplication of a social security regulation despite being in possession of all the relevant information. Case C-118/00 *Gervais Larsy v Institut national d'assurances sociales pour travailleurs indépendants (INASTI)* [2001] ECR I-05063.

[88] Both *Francovich* and *Brasserie* under German law failed to give the claimant a right to compensation on grounds of lacking causality. Contrary to this, consider the Factortame judgment, in which causality was easily established, leading to a settlement of GBP 55 million, see Biondi & Farley, The right to damages in European law, above n 61, p 57; and Granger, 'National applications of Francovich', above n 66, p 157.

[89] Objective liability in the sense of independence no-fault liability.

[90] Granger, 'National applications of Francovich', above n 66, p 157.

[91] See, eg Case C-140/97 *Walter Rechberger, Renate Greindl, Hermann Hofmeister and Others v Republik Österreich* [1999] ECR I-03499.

by the Court to potentially be sufficient to establish causation in relation to the fall in turnover and decreasing profit margins. The facts were then left to the verification of the national courts.[92]

3.2.1.4   Ambiguities of the Member State Liability Doctrine

Member State liability is unclear in several respects: in the first instance, there is *internal uncertainty* – for example, discord regarding the definition of the 'sufficiently serious' criterion, particularly in relation to what extent operational measures by a State are covered. The personal scope of the liability is also ambiguous, that is, in relation to whether and in what form a public-private divide applies. In addition, there is the *external or structural uncertainty* that results from the fact that the relation to *parallel* remedies granted by EU law is ambiguous, as is its relation to additional domestic remedies in the application of Member State liability at the national level.

3.3   Conclusion

The enforcement standard which national law must meet is set only partly by the public procurement Remedies Directives themselves, since many aspects of enforcement either remain untouched by them, or are not exhaustively regulated. This chapter demonstrated the relevance of general EU law to the procurement field.

In adjudicating damages claims for breaches of EU law, the CJEU is constrained by several doctrinal boundaries which are embedded in the emerging system of EU law. EU law *as it presently stands* formulates certain requirements which must be met by national damages claims. Procedural autonomy is a doctrine in which damages as a remedy of enforcement of EU law must meet effectiveness requirements (the doctrine as actually applied implies the procedural *and* remedial autonomy of the Member States). Member State liability requires the provision of damages for violations of EU law, as a specific remedy. Under the doctrine, a remedy – namely damages – can be postulated at EU level.

Several uncertainties and gaps in the way in which these doctrines can be applied with regard to damages were highlighted. The following chapter looks at damages for violations of EU public procurement rules in particular and examines how this can be fitted with the general framework presented in this chapter.

---

[92] *COS.MET*, above n 86, para 84.

Bibliography

Biondi, A & Farley, M (2009) *The right to damages in European Law* (Alphen aan den Rijn, Kluwer Law International).

Beatson, J & Tridimas, T (1998) *New Directions in European Public Law* (Oxford, Hart Publishing).

Bobek, M (2011) 'Why There is No Principle of "Procedural Autonomy" of the Member States', in HW Micklitz & B de Witte (eds), *The European Court of Justice and the Autonomy of the Member States* (Intersentia).

Delicostopoulos, JS (2003) 'Towards European Procedural Primacy in National Legal Systems' 9 *European Law Journal* 599.

Dougan, M (2004) *National Remedies Before the Court of Justice: Issues of Harmonisation and Differentiation* (Oxford, Hart Publishing).

Edward, D & Robinson, W (1997) 'Is there a Place for Private Law Principles in Community Law?', in T Heukels & A McDonnell (eds), *The Action for Damages in Community Law* (The Hague, Kluwer Law International).

Engström, J (2009) *The Europeanisation of Remedies and Procedures through Judge-made Law – Can a Trojan Horse achieve Effectiveness? Experiences of the Swedish Judiciary* (European University Institute), Tome I.

Granger, MP (2007) 'National Applications of Francovich and the Construction of a European Administrative Jus Commune' 32 *European Law Review* 157.

Haapaniemi, P (2009) 'Procedural Autonomy: A Misnomer?' in L Ervo et al (eds), *Europeanization of Procedural Law and the New Challenges to Fair Trial* (Groningen, Europa Law Publishing).

Haapaniemi, P (2010) in A Rösenkotter & T Wuersig, *The Impact of the Lisbon Treaty in the Field of Public Procurement* (European Parliament).

Hoskins, M (1996) 'Tilting the Balance: Supremacy and National Procedural Rules' 21 *European Law Review* 376.

Kakouris, CN (1997) 'Do the Member States Possess Judicial Procedural "Autonomy"?' *Common Market Law Review* 1389.

Lee, IB (1999) 'In Search of a Theory of State Liability in the European Union' 9/99 Harvard Jean Monnet Working Paper.

Lenaerts, K (2007) 'The Rule of Law and the Coherence of the Judicial System of the European Union' 44 *Common Market Law Review* 1625.

Mak, C (2014) 'Rights and Remedies: Article 47 EUCFR and Effective Judicial Protection in European Private Law Matters' in HW Micklitz (ed), *Constitutionalization of European Private Law* (Oxford, Oxford University Press).

Prechal, S (2005) *Directives in EC Law* (Oxford, Oxford University Press).

Prechal, S and Cath, K (2014) 'The European Acquis of Civil Procedure: Constitutional Aspects' 19 *Uniform Law Review* 179.

Reich, N (2010) 'The Interrelation between Rights and Duties in EU Law: Reflections on the State of Liability Law in the Multilevel Governance System of the Union: Is There a Need for a More Coherent Approach in European Private Law?' 29 *Yearbook of European Law* 112.

Ross, M (2006) 'Effectiveness in the European Legal Order(s): Beyond Supremacy to Constitutional Proportionality' 31 *European Law Review* 476.

Schebesta, H 'Does the National Court Know European Law? A Note on Ex Officio Application after Asturcom' (2010) 18 *European Review of Private Law* 847.

Schebesta, H (2014) 'Procedural theory in EU law' in K Purnhagen and P Rott (eds), *Varieties of European Economic Regulation* (New York, Springer).

Seyr, S (2008) *Der effet utile in der Rechtsprechung des EuGH* (Berlin, Duncker & Humblot).

Timmermans, C (2011) Presentation 'Limits imposed by EU law to Member States' Freedom of Action in Fields not Regulated by EU law', Robert Schuman Centre for Advanced Studies, Florence.

Tison, M (2005) 'Do not attack the watchdog! Banking supervisor's liability after Peter Paul' 42 *Common Market Law Review* 639.

Tonne, M (1997) *Effektiver Rechtsschutz durch staatliche Gerichte als Forderung des europäischen Gemeinschaftsrechts* (Köln, Heymanns).

Tridimas, T (2006) *The general principles of EU law* (Oxford, Oxford University Press).

Trstenjak, V & Beysen, E (2011) 'European Consumer Protection Law: Curia Semper Dabit Remedium?' 48 *Common Market Law Review* 95.

van Gerven, W (2000) 'Of Rights, Remedies and Procedures' 37 *Common Market Law Review* 501.

Ward, A (2007) *Judicial Review and the Rights of Private Parties in EU Law* (Oxford, Oxford University Press).

Ward, A (2008), 'Do Unto Others as You Would Have Them Do Unto You: Willy Kempter and the Duty to Raise EC Law in National Litigation' 33 *European Law Review* 739.

Widdershoven, R & Prechal, A (2011) 'Redefining the Relationship between "Rewe-effectiveness" and Effective Judicial Protection' 4 *Review of European Administrative Law* 31.

Chapter 4
Sources of EU Procurement Law and Damages

Abstract This chapter assesses the damages provision in the Remedies Directives. It discusses the judicial interpretation thereof and the application of the general court-developed doctrines of EU law, notably 'procedural autonomy', effective judicial protection and Member State liability. It provides a critique of the Combinatie Spijker Infrabouw CJEU case and presents an argument in favour of a separation thesis of effectiveness and Member State based damages.

4.1 Damages as Regulated by the Public Procurement Remedies Directives

According to its title, the objective of the Remedies Directives is mere coordination. Or, as the Court held: '*Since Directive 89/665 does no more than coordinate existing mechanisms in Member States in order to ensure the full and effective application of the directives laying down substantive rules concerning public contracts, it does not expressly define the scope of the remedies which the Member States must establish for that purpose.*'[1] This statement certainly belies the significance of the Directives in the face of judicial developments and the amendments made by Directive 2007/66/EC. Whether referred to as coordination or harmonization, the rules contained are detailed requirements on procedural aspects and remedies which Member States are under a duty to implement.

Although the damages provisions have not been directly altered, there can be implications – the overall level of regulation of remedies has increased, where other elements of the remedial systems have become more refined; questions of hierarchy of the remedies have arisen, and to a certain extent these have been addressed. For example, since it is expressly regulated, ineffectiveness as *lex specialis* takes precedence over damages claims. The 'penal' aspect of damages, on the other hand, has been expressed in a separate provision on sanctions and administrative fines. The place of damages is thus to be determined relative to other available remedies. Without modifying the damages provision, Directive 2007/66 modified the balance of remedies and therefore impacts on a systemic interpretation of the Remedies Directive.

---

[1] Case C-92/00 *Hospital Ingenieure Krankenhaustechnik Planungs-Gesellschaft mbH (HI) v Stadt Wien* [2002] ECR I-05553, para 58.

© Springer International Publishing Switzerland 2016 51
H. Schebesta, *Damages in EU Public Procurement Law*, Studies in European
Economic Law and Regulation 6, DOI 10.1007/978-3-319-23612-4_4

Although leaving the damages provision untouched, the *overall* remedies regime has become more intensely regulated. This can be seen as a reason for which procurement damages, as integral part of the remedial system, ought to be determined at EU level as well. As we will see in the following, the Court has taken an ambivalent position in this respect. It has intervened, also under the influence of effective judicial protection, and struck down national rules which limited the effectiveness of damages claims. On the other hand, it has been shy of stating positive requirements with respect to damages claims, notably with a reference to the lack of amendments to the damages provision through Directive 2007/66. Notably, the significance of the so-called doctrine of procedural autonomy is contentious.

4.1.1   Damages as Largely Unregulated by the Remedies Directives?[2]

To claim that damages themselves are 'regulated' by the Remedies Directive is to go too far. The 'heavy mists'[3] surrounding damages in the Remedies Directive have not been lifted by the amendments made by Directive 2007/66. The Directive is limited to providing that the review procedures must include the power to 'award damages to persons harmed by an infringement'[4]:

> Article 2 Directive 89/665/EEC
>
> 1. The Member States shall ensure that the measures taken concerning the review procedures specified in Article 1 include provision for the powers to:
> ...(c) award damages to persons harmed by an infringement.
>
> 2. The powers specified in paragraph 1 may be conferred on separate bodies responsible for different aspects of the review procedure.
>
> 5. The Member States may provide that where damages are claimed on the grounds that a decision was taken unlawfully, the contested decision must first be set aside by a body having the necessary powers.
>
> 6. ...

Furthermore, except where a decision must be set aside prior to the award of damages, a Member State may provide that, after the conclusion of a contract following its award, the powers of the body responsible for the review procedures shall be limited to awarding damages to any person harmed by an infringement.

---

[2] This Chapter is partially based on H Schebesta, 'Community Law Requirements for Remedies in the Field of Public Procurement: Damages' (2010) *European Procurement & Public Private Partnership*.

[3] H Lefler, 'Damages Liability for Breach of EC Procurement Law: Governing Principles and Practical Solutions' (2003) *Public Procurement Law Review* 151.

[4] Directive 89/665/EEC of 21 December 1989 on the coordination of the laws, regulations and administrative provisions relating to the application of review procedures to the award of public supply and public works contracts [1989] OJ L395, Art 2(1)(c) [hereinafter 'Public Sector Remedies Directive'].

Unchanged and unelaborated from its original version, this formulation remains confined to the mere duty of providing a cause of action for damages. In legislative terms, the regulation of the existence of damages in public procurement has not intensified and the crucial question regarding possible heads of damages is omitted. One of the most important heads to discuss in terms of efficiency of a remedy for an aggrieved tenderer would be, for example, the award of loss of profit, but also the recuperation of bidding costs.[5] The procedural modalities are other crucial aspects that ultimately define the effectiveness of a remedy, and the specific procedural conditions such as the burden of proof in claiming damages are not touched upon by the black letter of the Directive.

It is important to note that, surprisingly for two regimes that are otherwise close to identical, on the point of damages there is an important difference between the general Remedies Directive 89/665/EEC and the Utilities Remedies Directive 92/13/EEC. The latter contains a more specific damages provision in Article 2(7):

> Where a claim is made for damages representing the costs of preparing a bid or of partici- pating in an award procedure, the person making the claim shall be required only to prove an infringement of Community law in the field of procurement or national rules implement- ing that law and that he would have had a real chance of winning the contract and that, as a consequence of that infringement that chance was adversely affected.

The meaning of this article is underlined by the recitals to Directive 92/13/EEC, which read:

> Whereas claims for damages must always be possible;
> Whereas, where a claim is made for damages representing the costs of preparing a bid or of participating in an award procedure, the person making the claim is not be required, in order to obtain the reimbursement of his costs, to prove that the contract would have been awarded to him in the absence of such infringement;

In the utilities sector, therefore, bid preparation costs must be made available on the basis of the real chance. The aggrieved bidder does not need to prove that a contract would have been awarded to him or her. The Directive 92/13 provision is particularly interesting because it invokes the vocabulary of the lost chance. Because of that, there are several ways of interpreting the reach of the provision itself. It can be qualified as being an evidentiary rule distributing the burden of proof. At the same time, it could be interpreted as stipulating the availability of specific heads of damages or, on the other hand, as a true chance in the sense of a departure from the general causation rule of the 'but for' test.

From the point of view of systemic interpretation, it is open how the more detailed damages provision in the Utilities Remedies Directive relates to the inter- pretation of damages available under the Public Sector Remedies Directive. It raises the question why the directives are not identical on the point of damages. The regime in the Utilities Remedies Directive grants a more precise right to bid costs, and ensures that the availability thereof is not linked to proving that a contract would

---

[5] Lost profits can be claimed in a number of Member States; however, a comparative analysis of the domestic legal systems is postponed until later chapters.

have been awarded to the aggrieved bidder. Such clarity is lacking in the Public Sector Remedies Directive.

4.1.2   Judicial Interpretation in Case Law

In the meantime, the Court was repeatedly asked to interpret the Remedies Directive, including on aspects related to damages claims.

For instance, it was asked to rule on time limits in *Uniplex*,[6] in which the Court held that a limitation period, the duration of which was at the discretion of the competent court, was precluded by EU law as it was not predictable in its effects. In *Aktor/Club Hotel Loutraki*,[7] the Court struck down a national rule which limited standing by prohibiting actions brought individually by a member of the consortium. The discovery of documents was at issue in *Varec*, a judgment cited widely even beyond the public procurement field.[8]

In the Portuguese case line, the Court ruled on the burden of proof regarding fault for damages claims.[9] This case law was subsequently strengthened in *Strabag*,[10] in which the Court held that the right to damages may not be subject to a fault requirement at all. The Court also struck down a rule on intervening causes: in *GAT*,[11] it held that the Remedies Directive precluded a national judge from denying damages on the ground that the award procedure was in any event defective owing to the unlawfulness, raised *ex proprio motu*, of another (possibly previous) decision of the contracting authority.

However, the case in which the damages question was directly asked was *Combinatie Spijker Infrabouw*.[12] The referring national court wanted to know whether there are any EU requirements on the availability of damages and what these were. The Court interpreted the damages provision to be an expression of the

---

[6] Case C-406/08 *Uniplex (UK)* [2010] ECR I-00817.

[7] Judgment in *Aktor A.T.E./Club Hotel Loutraki and Others*, Joined Cases C-145/08 and C-149/08, ECLI:EU:C:2008:306 /ECLI:EU:C:2010:247.

[8] Case C-450/06 *Varec* [2008] ECR I-581.

[9] In the Portuguese case line: Case C-275/03 *Commission of the European Communities v Portuguese Republic* (14 October 2004), which was an unpublished 226 EC action. Details of the case derive from the follow-up action by the Commission under 228 EC in C-70/06 *Communautés européennes contre République portugaise* [2008] ECR I-00001 (not published in English); Commission Decision of 25 November 2008 requiring payment of the penalty payments under the C-70/06 judgment, C(2008) 7419 final; C-33/09 *Portugal v Commission* [2011] ECR II-1429, which is the application of annulment of that Commission Decision. The General Court case was subject to appeal in front of the CJEU in Case C-292/11 P, but the appeal was rejected and the case confirmed in Judgment in *Commission v Portugal*, C-292/11, ECLI:EU:C:2014:3.

[10] Judgment in *Strabag and others*, Case C-314/09, ECLI:EU:C:2010:567.

[11] Judgment in *GAT*, C-315/01, ECLI:EU:C:2003:360.

[12] Judgment in *Combinatie Spijker Infrabouw-De Jonge Konstruktie and Others*, C-568/08, ECLI:EU:C:2010:751.

principle of State liability, thereby providing for a right to damages were loss and damage was caused to individuals as a result of breaches of EU law for which the State can be held responsible. The judgment is discussed below in Sect. 4.2.2.

Several other court cases deal with damages more incidentally, as a remedy of last resort. For example, in *Fastweb*,[13] a preliminary reference questioned an exception to the remedy of ineffectiveness. Would the provision, which resulted in an illegal contract not being declared ineffective under Directive 89/665, violate the principle of effective judicial protection? The Court answered (among other reasons), that because damages would be available as a remedy of last resort, an exception to the remedy of ineffectiveness did not violate the principle of effective judicial protection.

The substantive issues raised in the cases are discussed in greater detail in the issue-based analysis of procurement damages (Part III). In the following we are concerned with the judicial tools used by the Court to interpret damages actions.

4.2   Legal Reasoning of the CJEU

The purpose of this section is to reach a better understanding of the legal reasoning deployed by the CJEU in the adjudication of damages in EU law. It therefore discusses the methodological relevance of cases to the interpretation of the Remedies Directives, specifically in relation to general EU law principles on damages discussed in the previous chapter.

4.2.1   Interpreting Damages Claims Under the 'Effectiveness' Paradigm

In several judgments, the CJEU interpreted the Remedies Directive and the damages provision under the preliminary reference procedure.[14] In the name of 'effectiveness', it has not been reluctant to interfere with procedural and remedial rules,

---

[13] Judgment in *Ministero dell'Interno v Fastweb S.p.a.*, C-19/13, ECLI:EU:C:2014:2194.

[14] The CJEU has 'dodged' detailed questions on the damages article at earlier times. For example, in the GAT case, the referring administration (*Bundesvergabeamt*) had included a question on whether ' … *Article 2(1)(c) of Directive 89/665, if necessary considered in conjunction with other principles of Community law,*[is] *to be interpreted as meaning that if the breach committed by the contracting authority consists in imposing an unlawful award criterion, the tenderer will be entitled to damages only if he can actually prove that, but for the unlawful award criterion, he would have submitted the best tender?*'. The CJEU declared this specific question inadmissible because the body was not competent to award damages at all: '*On the other hand, the Bundesvergabeamt, which is not directly competent to award damages to persons harmed by unlawfulness, is not entitled to refer to the Court for a preliminary ruling questions relating to the award of damages or the conditions for awarding them*' in *GAT*, above n 11, para 38.

and has struck down national legislation on time limits, standing, discovery of documents, fault requirements and intervening causes.

In doing so, it has consistently used the 'effectiveness' and 'equivalence' paradigm, on rare occasions clothed in the notion of procedural autonomy. Further, the Court has sometimes referred to the principle or right to effective judicial protection. It is apparent that the CJEU's approach to damages in relation to effectiveness and procedural autonomy is far from uniform, even in a confined area such as procurement law.

4.2.1.1   Interpreting Effectiveness Through Procedural Autonomy

In interpreting the Remedies Directives, the Court in the past has avoided to use the words 'procedural autonomy', while reference to the concept was made relatively often in the corresponding opinions of Advocate Generals. However, the Court did mention procedural autonomy in *Strabag*:

> Although, therefore, the implementation of Article 2(1)(c) of Directive 89/665 in principle comes under the procedural autonomy of the Member States, limited by the principles of equivalence and effectiveness, it is necessary to examine whether that provision, **interpreted in the light of the general context and aim of the judicial remedy of damages, precludes a national provision** such as that at issue in the main proceedings from making the award of damages conditional, in the circumstances set out in paragraph 30 of this judgment, on a finding that the contracting authority's infringement of the law on public contracts is culpable.[15]

The Court makes a rather passing reference to procedural autonomy, but proceeds to scrutinize the national measure. The Court, in fact, specifies two additional criteria according to which the national measure can be judged: *the general context* and the *aim of the judicial remedy of damages*. This specific judgment is worded very closely to the *van Schijndel/Peterbroeck* case law on effectiveness and may be interpreted as a first step into the direction of stronger differentiation between different areas of law. The assessment of the general context and aim of the judicial remedy of damages therefore had to be carried out on the basis of the specific purposes of Directive 89/665. The Court found that the Directive particularly recognizes the need for rapidity. Further, the Court held that the remedy damages was seen as a procedural alternative which is compatible with the principle of effectiveness underlying the objective pursued by that directive of ensuring effective review procedures. In finding that damages claims cannot be made dependent on culpability, the CJEU did little but pay lip-service to the principle of procedural autonomy.

---

[15] *Strabag*, above n 10, para 34, which concerned proceedings between the City of Graz and Strabag and Others following the unlawful award of a public procurement contract by Stadt Graz.

4.2.1.2   Going beyond Procedural Autonomy: The Procedural Independence of Member States?

In *Simvoulio*, a case interpreting Article 2(8) of Directive 89/665 on the right to seek judicial review, the Court went a step further and spoke about 'the procedural independence enjoyed by the Member States'.[16] Additionally, the Court brought up the non-harmonizing nature of the Directive, in stating, '[t]*he argument that such an interpretation would be likely to lead to a lack of uniformity in the application of European Union law cannot be accepted, in so far as Directive 89/665, as is apparent, in particular, from Article 1(3) thereof, does not seek to completely harmonise the relevant national legislation.*'[17] This terminology is new, and bears witness to a self-restraining court. At the same time, one might wonder whether the doctrine of 'procedural autonomy' is solidifying into one of 'procedural independence'. In this judgment, the CJEU relied on the nature and intensity of the degree of harmonization envisaged and refrained from striking down a national rule on the basis of effectiveness requirements.

However, this case may appear in a different light when considering the national rule that was at issue. The case concerned the question whether Member States were required to provide, *also for contracting authorities*, a right to seek judicial review of the decisions of non-judicial bodies responsible for review procedures. The most hands-off judgment was therefore rendered in a case that did not concern the interests of aggrieved bidders, but rather the required protection for contracting authorities.

The oscillating approach of the Court in public procurement mirrors the legally indeterminate nature of the procedural autonomy doctrine under general EU law.

4.2.1.3   Effective Judicial Protection

Similarly, public procurement law reflects the general rise of a recourse to human/ fundamental rights language.[18] The Court has included references to the principle of effective judicial protection in its procurement case law. In *Aktor/Club Hotel Loutraki,* the Court stated that effective judicial protection is a general principle of

---

[16] Case C-570/08 *Simvoulio Apochetefseos Lefkosias* 2010 ECR I-10131, para 36. According to a search conducted through the curia.eu search engine, so far it is the first and only time that the 'procedural independence' wording has been used by the Court itself. Whether this is a negligible translation deviation or the manifestation of an incrementally changing understanding of the Court as to the competence of Member States regarding their procedural law cannot be determined by reference to the wording of a single case. Nevertheless, a change in phrasing, if recurring, is certainly noteworthy as a proxy for changing meaning.

[17] ibid, para 37.

[18] See on the issue of the interaction between public procurement and the area of human rights more generally A Georgopoulos, 'EU Accession to the ECHR: An Attempt to Explore Possible Implications in the Area of Public Procurement', in V Kosta, N Skoutaris & V Tzevelekos (eds), *The EU Accession to the ECHR* (Oxford, Hart Publishing, 2014).

EU law, which precluded a national rule on standing that deprived individual members of a consortium of the possibility of seeking compensation for the loss suffered. In particular, it held that effective judicial protection was not granted, because the applicant was deprived of 'any opportunity to claim, before the competent court, compensation for any damage it has suffered by reason of a breach of EU law'.[19] In this case, the Court interpreted effectiveness in the light of effective judicial protection; the principle was breached since standing in this case had acted as a total obstacle to the applicant's access to justice.

The effect of the Charter of Fundamental Rights is likely to amplify the attention paid to effective judicial protection also in the field of public procurement. For example, a reference by the Italian Consiglio di Stato questioned the validity of the provision on ineffectiveness in the Remedies Directive 89/665 in the light of Article 47 of the Charter.[20] The request was made in proceedings between the Ministry of the Interior and Fastweb SpA, concerning the award to Telecom Italia SpA of a public contract for the supply of electronic communications services under a negotiated procedure without prior publication of a contract notice. The Court held the Directive not to be in violation of Article 47 on the right to an effective remedy under the Charter. The requirements of effective judicial protection was defined on the basis and the context of the Directive much more so than by reference to an autonomous understanding of effective judicial interpretation as a fundamental right. In substantive terms, effective judicial protection here proved no more than a rhetorical tool.

Perhaps more importantly, the Court explained its reasoning as a reconciliation of the various interests at play:

> … is to reconcile the various interests in play, that is to say, the interests of the undertaking that has been adversely affected, to which it is important to make available the remedies of pre-contractual interim relief and of annulment of the contract unlawfully concluded, and the interests of the contracting authority and the undertaking selected, which entails the need to prevent the legal uncertainty that might be engendered by the ineffectiveness of the contract.[21]

As in other cases, the Court made a highly contextualised interpretation, taking into account the other available remedies under Directive 89/665, and the specific need for rapidity and legal certainty in the field of procurement procedures.

4.2.1.4   Overview

In the field of procurement, the Court consistently subjects cases on enforcement rules to the effectiveness and equivalence tests. However, even in a confined area of law, the use of this doctrine is extremely divergent. In *Simvoulio* the CJEU went so far as to speak (for the first time) of procedural independence of the Member States,

---

[19] *Aktor/Club Hotel Loutraki*, above n 7, para 78.

[20] Judgment in *Ministero dell'Interno v Fastweb S.p.a.*, C-19/13, ECLI:EU:C:2014:2194.

[21] ibid, para 44.

while in *Strabag* procedural autonomy did not preclude the Court from striking down a fault requirement. Effective judicial protection is becoming more important, but it is questionable whether and in how far it provides substance to the Court's interpretation.

Although sometimes clothed in the right to effective judicial protection, and sometimes paying lip-service to the principle of 'procedural autonomy', it is probably more accurate to describe the Court's approach to effectiveness with its own formulation in *Fastweb*, namely that it tries to "reconcile the various interests in play".[22] On the basis of the case law rendered so far, one might suspect that much like consumers, aggrieved bidders are a specially protected group, to which the Court will be inclined to grant protection.

4.2.2   Member State Liability and Effectiveness in Combinatie Spijker Infrabouw

A most far-reaching judgment on damages has been rendered in the *Combinatie Spijker Infrabouw* case. In the long reference, the national Court asked several questions, among which the question whether EU law sets criteria for determining and estimating damages, and if so, what they were.

The CJEU clearly pointed out that Directive 89/665 does not contain a '*detailed statement either as to the conditions under which an awarding authority may be held liable or as to the determination of the amount of the damages which it may be ordered to pay*'.[23] In other words, it held that the wording of the Directive did not contain either constitutive criteria, or criteria for the quantification of damages.

However, after this deferring passage, the judgment continued: '*That provision* [Article 2(1)(c)] *gives concrete expression to the principle of State liability for loss and damage caused to individuals as a result of breaches of EU law for which the State can be held responsible.*'[24] After remarking in passing that although the principle of Member State liability was only developed in 1991 in *Francovich*,[25] ie that it did not exist at the time of drafting of the Directive, the '*right of reparation*' was now '*consistent*', and as a '*principle is inherent in the legal order of the Union*'.[26] The judgment continues '[a]*s matters stand at present, the case-law of the Court of Justice has not yet set out, as regards review of the award of public contracts, more detailed criteria on the basis of which damage must be determined and estimated.*'[27]

---

[22] ibid.

[23] *Combinatie Spijker Infrabouw*, above n 12, para 86.

[24] ibid.

[25] Joined Cases C-6/90 and C-9/90 *Francovich and Others* [1991] ECR I-5357, para 87.

[26] *Combinatie Spijker Infrabouw* , above n 12, para 87.

[27] ibid, para 88.

Accordingly, the criteria used for Member State liability should inform the interpretation of the damages article. The Court rejected the idea that, in any form, the CJEU had elaborated more detailed criteria for damages that were valid for the specific area of law, ie the review of the award of public contracts specifically. At the same time, the judgment leaves that possibility open for the future by stressing the fact that this is 'for the moment', and 'not yet' the case.

On the point of damages, the judgment proceeded to mention the principles of equivalence and effectiveness ('procedural autonomy'), but did not test or apply them. It simply repeated the *Rewe*-formula, stating that 'damages arising from an infringement of EU law' (para 90) and the 'detailed procedural rules governing actions for safeguarding an individual's rights under EU law' (para 91) are for the internal legal order of each Member State to be determined in the absence of any provisions of EU law in that area. Further, the judgment specifically states that in Directive 2007/66, the EU legislator chose not to alter the damages provision. It is rare for the CJEU to base an interpretation on the legislative will so explicitly. The implicit argument seems to be that this fact provides evidence of the "absence of EU law" under which effectiveness and equivalence operate.

To sum up the argumentative steps performed, first, the CJEU stated that the Directive itself contains no precise conditions for damages. Second, it proceeded to equate the damages article with a specific expression of Member State liability. Third, it stated that specific criteria have not yet been developed in relation to Member State liability in the field of public contracts. Fourth, it found that national rules must comply with the principles of effectiveness and equivalence (referring to the relevant case law, but without using the term 'procedural autonomy').

In many ways, the judgment is disappointing. Overall, the CJEU showed itself to be extremely reluctant to engage with the question in substantive terms.[28] However, the structural implications of the ruling are immense, as it 'imports' Member State liability as a source of law through which the Remedies Damage provision may be interpreted.

The ramifications of this, albeit isolated, case could well go beyond the field of public procurement. The impact for the area of procurement are, however, clearly far reaching. Below, the example of public procurement is used as a thought experiment to illustrate why this conflation of Member State liability and secondary legislation damages is doctrinally highly questionable.

---

[28] This may in part be due to the wording of the referred questions, which asked, in a highly abstract manner that was almost entirely detached from the particular circumstances of the case and its factual situation, whether '*Community law set*[s] *criteria for determining and estimating those damages*'.

4.2.2.1 Member State Liability Applied in Public Procurement: A Thought Experiment

In *Combinatie Spijker Infrabouw*, the Court did not proceed to apply the Member State criteria, or to flesh them out. Already prior to the judgment, it had been argued that the case law on Member State liability under *Francovich* and *Brasserie* could be pertinent to damages claims for breaches of EU law.[29] What place Member State liability would then occupy in relation to damages claims arising from secondary instruments, such as the public procurement directives themselves, was less apparent. Would there be a minimum threshold, or a hybridization[30] of remedies? With its ruling in *Combinatie Spijker*, it seems that, at least for the public procurement sector, the Court has furnished an answer which conflates the secondary damages article with damages under Member State liability. This is a plausible argument at first sight, but one which, as argued below, ought to be rejected.

Generally speaking, procurement damages claims are likely to satisfy the criteria of Member State liability (a sufficiently serious breach of a provision intended to confer rights and causality between the breach and the loss sustained).

With regards to a breach of a provision intended to confer rights, the Court has held that the provisions on the right to have decisions which have been made by the contracting authorities reviewed effectively, and as rapidly as possible (Articles 1(1) of Directive 89/665) and the right to have unlawful decisions set aside (Article 2(1)(b)) are directly effective.[31] As the obligations contained in 2(1)(a) and (c) on damages are similarly precisely worded, they must be seen as likely to dispose of direct effect as well.[32]

So far, it has not been determined as to which violations of the public procurement rules are to be regarded as 'sufficiently serious' to entail Member State liability.[33] The Court distinguished between areas of broad and little discretion in order to

---

[29] See, eg Lefler, 'Damages Liability for Breach of EC Procurement Law', above n 3, pp 151 and 154 who draws attention to the ECJ's wording (eg case C-92/00 *Hospital Ingenieure Krankenhaustechnik Planungs-Gesellschaft mbH (HI) v Stadt Wien* [2002] ECR I-05553) and demands that it is foremost a strengthening of the remedies in public procurement specifically. He therefore (although not very insistently so) pleads for a more nuanced view of the general principles and public procurement-related cases, stating that public procurement should 'colour the decision in the concrete case' (p 154).

[30] N Reich, 'Horizontal Liability in EC Law: Hybridization of Remedies for Compensation in Case of Breaches of EC Rights' (2007) 44 *Common Market Law Review* 705.

[31] To this effect, see Case C-15/04 *Koppensteiner GmbH v Bundesimmobiliengesellschaft mbH* [2005] ECR I-04855, para 38.

[32] Case C-222/02 *Peter Paul, Cornelia Sonnen-Lütte and Christel Mörkens v Bundesrepublik Deutschland* [2004] ECR I-09425. The situation differs in this respect from the situation giving rise to the preliminary question on Member State liability in Peter Paul. In Peter Paul, the Court held that the Member State could not be liable because the Directives did not confer directly effective rights onto individuals. It is here contended that Directive 89/665 does create a directly effective right for individuals to receive damages under certain circumstances.

[33] S Treumer, 'Damages for Breach of the EC Public Procurement Rules – Changes in European Regulation and Practice' (2006) *Public Procurement Law Review* 159.

establish whether there were grounds for State liability and what their precise respective conditions were. The question is whether a breach of a directive would constitute a 'sufficiently serious' breach,[34] which is contingent on the question of whether it concerns an area in which the Member State enjoys broad or little discretion. Again, in public procurement one can think of two distinct Member State violations, one of which would be the actual law enacted, which would indeed be a 'classic' case of Member State liability for legislating. Member States can also incur liability for mere administrative acts, that is, for decisions taken by a contracting authority. In the very detailed provisions contained in the public procurement directives, this lack of discretion is manifest.[35] A simple breach of the Directives could then be 'sufficiently serious', thus amounting to a liability closely approaching strict liability.

The last requirement of causation might be regarded as problematic since procedural law violations may amount to mere technicalities.[36] In the field of public procurement, one of the advantages is that the breach of the rules on how to award a contract makes the awarding of the contract unlawful. In particular causation as a requirement is usually left to the determination of the national courts.

Following the *Combinatie Spijker Infrabouw* ruling, we observe that damages were subject to a 'conflationary' trend of interpretation, which imposed the case law of general Member State liability on the damages provision in the Remedies Directive. This tendency does not stop here, but is amplified when considering the possible extension through the Institutional liability of the EU.

4.2.3   The Role of Institutional Liability in Interpreting Member State Liability

Member State liability has often been read in conjunction with the conditions for the liability of EU institutions under 340 TFEU, as some argue that the liability of Member States and that of the EU converge (or at least should do so).[37] To a certain

---

[34] To the opposite effect, see ibid, Treumer, p 159 (arguing that it is not of great practical importance). It is here submitted that whether a breach is sufficiently serious is important in order to determine whether there is a requirement flowing from Community law, rather than grounding a praxis by means of a comparative overview of the Member States' legislation on damages in order to then reintroduce it at the European level via principles as generally recognized in the Member States' legal orders.

[35] A Ward, *Judicial review and the rights of private parties in EU law* (Oxford, Oxford University Press, 2007), p 230 (also in favor of liability for the mere breach of a directly effective Community rule). See also A Biondi & M Farley, *The Right to Damages in European Law* (Alphen aan den Rijn, Kluwer Law International 2009), p 45.

[36] G Anagnostaras, 'Not as Unproblematic as You Might Think: The Establishment of Causation in Governmental Liability Actions' (2002) 27 *European Law Review* 663.

[37] W van Gerven, 'Of Rights, Remedies and Procedures' (2000) 37 *Common Market Law Review* 501. The reason most commonly cited is that there should be no difference in the rights of an indi-

degree, this trend towards convergence is supported by the case law, namely the *Brasserie* and the *Bergaderm* judgment. In *Brasserie,* the Court held that 'liability for damage caused to individuals by a breach of Community law cannot, in the absence of particular justification, differ from those governing the liability of the Community in like circumstances'.[38] This statement was repeated in *Bergaderm*, wherein the Member State liability conditions were applied to the liability of the EU.[39] If one accepts the *Combinatie Spijker Infrabouw* ruling that the damages provision in the Remedies Directives is an expression of Member State liability, this case law by consequence also becomes pertinent.

The case law rendered by the General Court in the field of Institutional liability on damages has been discussed specifically within the field of public procurement, in the context of tendering procedures undertaken on behalf of the European Union. This is in the framework of 340 TFEU procedures.[40] The General Court had to decide on the amount of damages and the different heads of damages which an aggrieved tenderer should be able to claim. There is a tendency in the literature to look at damages claims rendered by the General Court and those in preliminary reference proceedings as identical. For example, on the basis of jurisprudence rendered in the field of Institutional liability, it has been argued that the Court's scrutiny amounts to a 'relaxed review standard'[41] only, based on the *Embassy Limousines* line of cases.[42]

However, it is false to assume that these cases are only interpretations of the Public Procurement Directives. While to many of the EU's tenders, the procurement directives are applicable, they are often governed additionally by a distinct set of

---

vidual when faced with different institutions violating its rights.

[38] Joined cases C-46/93 and C-48/93 *Brasserie du Pêcheur SA v Bundesrepublik Deutschland and The Queen v Secretary of State for Transport, ex parte: Factortame Ltd and others* [1996] ECR I-01029, para 42.

[39] Case C-352/98 P *Bergaderm* [2000] ECR I-5291, para 41ff.

[40] Case T-203/96 *Embassy Limousines & Services v European Parliament* [1998] ECR II-04239.

[41] Lefler, 'Damages Liability for Breach of EC Procurement Law', above n 3 (who is also critical, but cites Arrowsmith).

[42] *Embassy Limousines*, above n 40, para 56, also often cited as authority T-13/96 *TEAM v Commission* [1998] ECR II-4073; T-160/03 *AFCon Management Consultants, Patrick Mc Mullin and Seamus O'Grady v Commission of the European Communities* [2005] ECR II-00981, para 98 which granted no compensation for bid preparation, based on an exemption therefrom in the contract: 'Article 24 of the General Regulations for Tenders and the Award of Service Contracts financed from Phare/Tacis Funds provides that in the event of closure or annulment of a tendering procedure, the tenderers are not entitled to compensation. It follows that the charges and expenses incurred by a tenderer in connection with his participation in a tendering procedure cannot in principle constitute damage which is capable of being remedied by an award of damages. However, the provision in question cannot, without potentially undermining the principles of legal certainty and of protection of legitimate expectations, apply in cases where an infringement of Community law in the conduct of the tendering procedure has affected a tenderer's chances of being awarded the contract'.

rules.[43] In the interpretation of damages claims, the General Court has further recourse to administrative law principles and financial regulations as they apply to the EU. It is therefore important to insist on distinguishing the characteristics of the tendering procedure of the EU from those of a contracting authority in a national Member State.[44] Recourse to the Institutional liability case law can only be made by means of analogy, not by straight application.

In *Embassy Limousines & Services v European Parliament,*[45] the Parliament's liability was alleged on different grounds, one based on the Directive, the other on general principles of European administrative law. The claim regarding infringement of the Directive was rejected, and the Parliament was found to be in breach of having invoked legitimate expectations which were not rectified early enough. It is correct that the Parliament was held liable, however not for infringement of the Directive. This influenced the Court's judgment on the damages claim, since they were specific damages claimed relying on the legitimate expectations invoked, which therefore resulted in the Court granting damages for reliance as well as bidding costs. Re-iterating the argument against the generalizability of the 340 TFEU jurisprudence, it is here submitted that *in casu* it was the special circumstances of the trust induced by Parliament rather than an automatic breach of public procurement rules which resulted in these heads of damages. The judgment as such is therefore not easily transferred to regular damages for a breach of the EU Public Procurement Directives.

Significant inconsistencies in the Courts approach to both forms of liability persist.[46] From the point of view of the legal process, the actions are entirely different ones, with different roles for the CJEU in Member State liability and the General Court under Institutional liability. The General Court acts as a court of law and as a court of fact. Therefore, when faced with damages claims, it is required to rule on all aspects of the case, and particularly apply the law to the factual situation. The Member States' common traditions are then the relevant sources of law. We can see, however, the magnitude of the bridge which is created by importing Institutional liability into Member State liability: it is likely to open a gate for the interpretation and make the Institutional liability case law a source of law for public procurement damages.

---

[43] Such as the general principles of the EU, such as the principle of sound administration, principle of equal treatment in the award of public contracts, concern for sound financial management of Community funds and the prevention of fraud. See, eg *AFCon Management Consultants, Patrick Mc Mullin and Seamus O'Grady v Commission of the European Communities*, ibid, paras 74ff. In the relevant case, the tendering procedure was said to be governed under the General Regulations for Tenders and the Award of Service Contracts financed from Phare/Tacis Funds.

[44] T Gruber, 'Public Procurement in the European Union', in G Gruber, T Gruber, A Mille & M Sachs, *Public Procurement in the European Union* (Cambridge, Intersentia, 2006). It seems at least to suggest the applicability of the principles enunciated in the cases on the Community liability for damages in relation to contracting authorities.

[45] *Embassy Limousines*, above n 40.

[46] For a very recent and pointed comparison between the two forms of action, see Biondi & Farley, *The Right to Damages in European Law,* above n 35.

4.3 Member State Liability and Effectiveness Damages: The Separation Thesis

This section criticises the conflation of Member State liability and effectiveness damages which results from the judgment in *Combinatie Spijker Infrabouw*. It presents a separation thesis and justifies Member State liability as a third, distinct level of liability – a tertiary form of protection of EU law conferred rights. Member State liability should be understood as a constitutional instrument that specifically enforces Member States' *implementation duties* to *transpose, give effect to* and *apply* EU law. Effectiveness of EU law on the other hand, is the enforcement of specific EU obligations, which burden particular actors, not Member States as international actors, with specific enforcement duties. Especially in the field of public procurement, enforcement has been endowed with a highly specific regime in which the available remedies are matched to the particular context of the area of law.

4.3.1 An Implementation Duty Based View of Member State Liability

The first step in constructing the justification for Member State liability concerns looking at *upon whom* EU law provisions impose *which obligations*.

Member States are generally under a duty to implement legislation in order to provide the necessary legal interface between EU law obligations and the individual; there is a duty of transposition. While implementation can, for example, be understood as the simple transposition of an EU directive into national law, it can also be given a much wider meaning which comprises duties of effectuating a legal text in a larger sense. Here, implementation also covers compliance and enforcement. The CJEU has in several judgments exhibited this wider understanding of implementation duties, for example in the *Spanish Strawberries*[47] case, in which a favourable 'implementation environment' was required. Such duties to effectuate a functioning legal system in order to enable effective enforcement are duties implied in a Treaty, but they are incumbent on the Member State and not the individual.

To capture the different types of implementation obligations on Member States, one can distinguish between transposing (legislative duties), effecting (facilitative duties) and applying (operational or executive duties) EU law. These obligations encompass both implementation as a one-off duty as well as a compliance aspect in the sense of continuous observance and enforcement – implementation thus constitutes a process. The implementation duties (transposition, effecting and applying) result in different margins of discretion and standards of review which nuance the 'sufficiently serious' test.

---

[47] Judgment in Commission v France (Strawberries Case), Case C-265/95, ECLI:EU:C:1997:595

Member State liability is correlative to these structural implementation duties. In this sense, Member State liability is explored as a 'liability [that] can become a way to enforce federalism'.[48] This interpretation can be aligned with the 'process towards the constitutionalization of remedies'.[49] Along the same lines, Member State liability was described as a 'high point in the evolution of the principle of supremacy'.[50] All of these descriptions express the underlying supranational justice type considerations – ensuring treaty compliance, by means of guaranteeing the invocability of individual rights for Member States' nationals. Member State liability is a constitutional remedy, the judicial guardian of the Treaty.

This reading results in a distinction between Member State liability damages and damages available under the effectiveness of EU law, presented hereafter.

4.3.2   A 'Separation Thesis' of Member State liability and Effectiveness Damages

In the following section, a separation thesis will be defended, according to which Member State liability and effectiveness damages should not be read as one and the same type of liability. The case of public procurement provides an excellent example to illustrate the dangers of conflation regarding the personal scope, types of duties and justifications, extent of the remedy, sources of law and the institutional process legitimacy of the latter.

4.3.2.1   Personal Scope

Member State liability and the procurement directives have different personal scopes. For Member State liability the scope of the meaning of the word 'State' is blurred. Whether or not the *Foster*[51] definition in State aid of emanations from the State can and should be accepted has been debated. It is clear from case law that the notion of the State in liability cases is drawn widely, including decentralized authorities and bodies.[52] There is thus a rather large intersection between a contracting authority and State body under liability but the two concepts are not congruent with each other. However, not all contracting authorities are public in this sense and there

---

[48] ibid, 29.

[49] T Tridimas, *The General Principles of EU Law* (Oxford, Oxford University Press, 2006), p 441.

[50] ibid, p 323.

[51] Case C-188/89 *A Foster and Others v British Gas plc* [1990] ECR I-03313.

[52] See for a discussion M Dougan, *National Remedies Before the Court of Justice: Issues of Harmonisation and Differentiation* (Oxford, Hart Publishing, 2004), pp 252–255. See also G Anagnostaras, 'The allocation of responsibility in State Liability actions for breach of Community law: A modern Gordian knot' (2001) 26 *European Law Review* 139. See also Biondi & Farley, *The Right to Damages in European Law*, above n 35, pp 61–63.

will be a certain degree of incongruence between the personal scopes of the two provisions. Regarding the question on whom EU law imposes which obligations, the case of public procurement is especially telling. The personal scope of application of the procurement directives is highly positively defined. Although broadly speaking there is a large overlap between procurement authorities and State entities, there is no congruence. Within the applicability of the Remedies Directives, it is the contracting authority which is liable for damages. Under Member State liability on the other hand, one of the implicit conditions is first and foremost that a given act has been carried out by the State. Not every contracting authority is necessarily an organ of the State. Public and private partnerships are a case in point. In addition, under the utilities public procurement directives, explicitly private law entities are covered by the legal regime as well.[53] The question of which State instance a liability action has to be brought against is on the other hand for the internal organization of national law to answer,[54] whereas under public procurement law it would be the contracting authority.

4.3.2.2 Correlating Breach of a Duty and Justifications

The justifications under Member State liability are different from those for breaches of EU law under effectiveness considerations. Under Member State liability, the justifications allowed are based on the intention of the Member State; they are not substantive reasons found in the specificities of the underlying legislation. The Member State liability justifications corroborate the argument that the underlying obligations against which these justifications may be invoked are implementation obligations. The common definition of a 'sufficiently serious' breach relies on:

> clarity and precision of the rule infringed and the measure of discretion left by that rule to the national authorities, whether the infringement or the damage caused was intentional or involuntary, whether any error of law was excusable or inexcusable, and the fact that the position taken by a Community institution may have contributed towards the adoption or maintenance of national measures or practices contrary to Community law.[55]

On one hand, the legal obligation at the basis of an implementation duty is assessed against the standard of determinacy (clarity) of the EU norm. Implementation is rather seen to constitute a process and for example actions of EU institutions supporting a particular interpretation of a legal text exculpate a Member State for mis-implementation. In addition, the '*mens rea*' or intention of a Member State is taken

---

[53] For an analysis of the State or non-State identity of utilities, see PA Trepte, 'When is a Utility not a "Utility"?', in LW Gormley (ed), *Gordian Knots in European Public Procurement Law: Government Procurement Agreement: Standards, Utilities, Remedies* (Koln, Bundesanzeiger, 1997), and the cited jurisprudence.

[54] Biondi & Farley, *The Right to Damages in European Law*, above n 35, p 66.

[55] Case C-278/05 *Robins and others* [2007] ECR I-1053, para 77; *Brasserie and Factortame*, above n 38, para 56; and Case C-224/01 *Gerhard Köbler v Republik Österreich* [2003] ECR I-10239, para 55.

into account. All of these justifications refer to duties of implementation and, in a wider sense, supranational loyalty and solidarity in relation to the implementation of EU law among Member States. They are not based on the particular relationship between the individual and the Member State.

By contrast, the type of duty and the connected justifications under the public procurement regime are those contained in the legislative regime. Strict observance of the rules is necessary, and finding a breach may not be made contingent on the finding of fault in the field of public procurement. The public interest exception, which would allow a national court not to pronounce the remedy of ineffectiveness even though ordinarily required, is also a specific kind of justification. It is valid only in an autonomous procurement related interpretation, and it is a justification available to the national court (not the contracting authority) for not granting a specific remedy.

4.3.2.3   Extent of the Remedy

Member State liability limits and defines the liability incurred to a pecuniary remedy. In the case law, Member State liability has been limited to pecuniary damages. Those damages at the moment seem confined to compensation damages. The CJEU held that from an enforcement point of view, the imposition of State liability pursues different goals than the imposition of penalties. Look at *COS.MET*, for example: "*the purpose of a Member State's liability under Community law is not deterrence or punishment but compensation for the damage suffered by individuals as a result of breaches of Community law by Member States.*"[56] Yet deterrence as such is to some extent factored into the constitutive criteria and whether liability is incurred. The deterrence rationale disappears after liability has been affirmed. Compensation damages become the measure and extent of Member State liability.

Member State liability is limited to the remedy of damages; it is abstract in nature, and hence more general. By contrast, damages articles in secondary legislation and the corresponding liability are relative to their substantive reasons. Secondary law accords liability based on more specific and connected reasons whereby a different kind of balancing is carried out. The constitutive criteria differ as do the respective consequences: effectiveness asks which heads of damages (material condition) are available, whereas in Member State liability the consequences are arguably limited to compensation.[57] In the case of public procurement, the general remedies must first be interpreted in accordance with the specific legal regime. For example, in the case of public procurement, the ineffectiveness of

---

[56] Case C-470/03 *A.G.M.-COS.MET Srl v Suomen valtio and Tarmo Lehtinen* [2007] ECR I-02749, para 88.

[57] M Dougan, 'What is the point of Francovich', in T Tridimas & P Nebbia (eds), *European Union Law for the Twenty-First Century: Rethinking the New Legal Order* (Oxford, Hart Publishing, 2004). Dougan for example argues that the choice of remedy granting reparation is up to the Member State. In any case, compensation is always among the sanctioned remedies to put right the wrong caused.

contracts might be required under the 2006/77 Remedies Directive and have priority over the damages remedies (specific 'hierarchization' of remedies). To what extent a remedy is sufficient is for the EU level to judge in relation to the specific 'effectiveness' requirements. However, Member State liability is based on compensation as a measure, and they are damages in tort. In the context of procurement, there is often a contractual or statutory element to damages awards. By equating the damages available under the Remedies Directive with those for Member State liability purposes, the specificity of the public procurement context is neglected. Other rationales become suppressed, such as the pre-contractual/*culpa in contrahendo* action for damages. In addition, it is problematic in legal orders which have not transposed the damages article by means of one single cause of action. In many legal orders, tort provisions sit alongside specific statutory damages actions for violations of public procurement rules or strong pre-contractual doctrines. Heads of damages which are not commonly granted under tort may well be granted in contractual damages. On the other hand, Member State liability usually grants lost profits. In a public procurement context, this may be excessive in several factual constellations.

4.3.2.4 Sources of Law and Legitimacy

The sources of law which are cited by the Court differ. Member State liability was regarded as implicit in the Treaty, echoing the fact that certain duties are incumbent upon Member States in their capacity as signatories and parties to a Treaty. Therefore, the Court has relied on the Member States' traditions as a common denominator, sometimes reinforced by an analogy to the non-contractual liability of the EU as a source of law either national law, or comparative law as a common tradition of the Member States. Effectiveness in interpreting EU law provisions directly does not benefit from this source of law. The Directive's damages notion is an autonomous one. Unless one were to accept a 'comparative law based' interpretation of secondary law,[58] it is not possible to rely on the common traditions of Member States in an interpretation of the damages article.

Member State liability has the status of Treaty law, while secondary legislation can be changed by EU amendments to secondary legislation taking place through the EU legislative procedure. Principally, secondary law cannot reduce the impact of primary law, as has also been held in relation to damages in the field of public procurement.[59] If one were to take the statement of the CJEU in *Combinatie Spijker Infrabouw* at face value, the national political forces of the EU legislative process would dispose of the power to curb their own liability for violations of EU law. To follow the separation thesis is therefore also a constitutional guarantee that preserves

---

[58] As is argued in the comparative law methodology part, in the CJEU such a comparative law informed interpretation is the standard practice of judges coming to terms with cases. However, the common traditions of Member States are not a recognized 'source of law' as such, in the same way as is the case for Member State liability that strives to promulgate general principles of law.

[59] Joined Cases C-20/01 and C-28/01 *Commission v Germany* [2003] ECR I-03609, para 37–39.

a separation and balance of power in the EU legal order by isolating Member State liability from the interference of the EU political process.

The separation between effectiveness and Member State liability is confirmed in Competition law, where damages are based on the direct effect of Treaty articles 101 and 102 TFEU. Effectiveness is fully applied to private law persons, while *Francovich* states the instances in which the State is specifically protected (for example, when legislating, the State enjoys special immunities and a "presumption of benevolence").[60] Mainstream opinion holds *Francovich* to be separate from direct effect *Courage* damages.[61]

4.3.3   Effectiveness of EU Law and Member State Liability Ought to Operate in Sequence

In line with the proposal to see Member State liability as a tertiary protection of rights, it makes sense that it be not applied as a hybrid or minimum floor, but sequentially.

A successful claim for damages under the Remedies Directive would probably preclude a claim under Member State liability because, *prima facie, Francovich* is a tool to make the Member State comply with EU law, which under these circumstances a Member State would arguably have done. Where a breach has occurred, but effective remedies are made available, the Member State should not be liable for a claim under Member State liability. Providing effective remedies for a breach of EU law addresses the compliance default and a violation of an implementation duty no longer persists. We can imagine an action of an aggrieved tenderer against a procurement authority, claiming damages for the violation of the procurement directives. Assuming the public authority to be a State entity, the State has not complied with EU law. The non-compliance would be addressed by the national court through the granting of damages or an ineffectiveness remedy, as required to give secondary protection to the EU right.

Interpreted in the way that the Court proposed in *Combinatie Spijker Interbouw*, the Remedies Directive would serve a purpose exactly opposite to that for which it was created, in conjuring a loophole through which the Member State might escape liability by retreating safely into national law. In order to incur Member State liability, the obligation against which the remedy would be measured is not the constitutive right itself – it would be determined by the failure of the Member State to implement. Did the Member State have broad discretion? Could it have reasonably

---

[60]V Milutinovic, *The "Right to Damages" Under EU Competition Law: From Courage v Crehan to the White Paper and Beyond* (Alphen aan den Rijn, Kluwer Law International, 2010).

[61]This was the consensual opinion among the participants of the British Institute for International and Comparative Law conference 'Celebrating 20 Years of Francovich in the EU' held 17 November 2011 which discussed extensively the role of competition law damages in relation to Francovich damages.

failed to understand the exigencies of EU law? Taking the example in the case of the damages article in the procurement directives and given the meager wording, it is legitimate for any Member State to argue that the provision is too indeterminate. The conduct of a Member State can serve to immunize it against liability claims, resulting in a complete dependence on the national system of damages – which may very well grant the aggrieved tenderer no damages at all. The paradoxical result would be that although the remedies regime is more concrete and elaborate than in other areas of law, the Court would be forced into the abstract generalities of Member State liability, rather than considering the specificities of the procurement sector.

By interpreting the damages provision as an expression of Member State liability, the national courts are effectively dissuaded from applying for a preliminary ruling to interpret the exigencies of EU law on the matter. This is to be deplored as not every clarification of EU law would necessarily amount to a violation of the Member State's implementation duty. The traction of Member State liability in domestic courts is notoriously low; keeping the effectiveness of EU law separate has the advantage of providing a greater incentive for national courts to ask for guidance and would equally guarantee a better reception.

4.4 Conclusion

Overall, in the field of public procurement law, the Court of Justice of the EU is placed in a particular position with regards to damages: legislative inertia regarding damages claims in public procurement exerts systemic pressure on the Court to interpret the relevant legislation. The pressures of the preliminary reference procedure put the CJEU in the position of having to determine the interpretation of damages because the Court is held to give an answer to all national cases.

In coming to terms with the interpretation of damages, the Court has mostly used the 'effectiveness' paradigm, sometimes in combination with the notion of procedural autonomy, and sometimes taking into consideration the principle of effective judicial protection. While procedural autonomy does not seem to deter the Court from ruling on remedial and procedural aspects of damages claims, the principle of effective judicial protection so far has not been very important substantively. The Court therefore in practice relies on a contextual interpretation of the Remedies Directive's specific requirements, such as rapidity, efficiency, and a balance of interest between the aggrieved bidder, third parties, the contracting authority and the general public interest.

The *Combinatie Spijker Infrabouw* judgment contrasts this approach, as the Court stated that the Remedies Directive's damages provision is an expression of Member State liability. Doctrinally, the general damages available are assimilated with Member State liability damages and therefore, as argued above, also those stemming from non-contractual liability of the EU (340 TFEU).

The chapter aimed at carving out a specific purpose and function of Member State liability by vesting Member State liability *with a normative framework based on considerations of supranational justice, in which it provides a 'tertiary protection' of EU integration through the protection of EU rights.* Thus conceived, damages awarded under the doctrine of Member State liability are distinct from other types of damages awarded under EU law (the 'separation thesis').

Bibliography

Anagnostaras, G (2001) 'The allocation of responsibility in State Liability actions for breach of Community law: A modern Gordian knot' 26 *European Law Review* 139.

Anagnostaras, G (2002) 'Not as Unproblematic as You Might Think: The Establishment of Causation in Governmental Liability Actions' 27 *European Law Review* 663.

Biondi, A & Farley, M (2009) *The Right to Damages in European Law* (Alphen aan den Rijn, Kluwer Law International).

Dougan, M (2004a) *National Remedies Before the Court of Justice: Issues of Harmonisation and Differentiation* (Oxford, Hart Publishing).

Dougan, M (2004b) 'What is the point of Francovich', in T Tridimas & P Nebbia (eds), *European Union Law for the Twenty-First Century: Rethinking the New Legal Order* (Oxford, Hart Publishing, 2004).

Georgopoulos, A (2014) 'EU Accession to the ECHR: An Attempt to Explore Possible Implications in the Area of Public Procurement', in V Kosta, N Skoutaris & V Tzevelekos (eds), *The EU Accession to the ECHR* (Oxford, Hart Publishing).

Gruber, T (2006) 'Public Procurement in the European Union', in G Gruber, T Gruber, A Mille & M Sachs, *Public Procurement in the European Union* (Cambridge, Intersentia).

Lefler, H (2003) 'Damages Liability for Breach of EC Procurement Law: Governing Principles and Practical Solutions' *Public Procurement Law Review* 151.

Milutinovic, V (2010) *The "Right to Damages" Under EU Competition Law: From Courage v Crehan to the White Paper and Beyond* (Alphen aan den Rijn, Kluwer Law International).

Reich, N (2007) 'Horizontal Liability in EC Law: Hybridization of Remedies for Compensation in Case of Breaches of EC Rights' 44 *Common Market Law Review* 705.

Schebesta, H (2010) 'Community Law Requirements for Remedies in the Field of Public Procurement: Damages' *European Procurement & Public Private Partnership*.

Trepte, PA (1997) 'When is a Utility not a "Utility"?', in LW Gormley (ed), *Gordian Knots in European Public Procurement Law: Government Procurement Agreement: Standards, Utilities, Remedies* (Bundesanzeiger).

Treumer, S (2006) 'Damages for Breach of the EC Public Procurement Rules – Changes in European Regulation and Practice' *Public Procurement Law Review* 159.

Tridimas, T (2006) *The General Principles of EU Law* (Oxford, Oxford University Press).

van Gerven, W (2000) 'Of Rights, Remedies and Procedures' 37 *Common Market Law Review* 501.

Ward, A (2007) Judicial Review and the Rights of Private Parties in EU Law (Oxford, Oxford University Press).

Part II
The National Perspectives

This part provides an overview of selected Member States' systems with respect to the availability of damages actions for violations of EU public procurement law. The purpose is to compare the damages available at national level in order to study whether and how the realization of European (public procurement) rights differs across Member States.

The case studies were selected on the basis of the legal families approach. Central exponents of these jurisdictions were chosen, these being the UK for the common law approach, Germany for the Germanic tradition, France for the Roman tradition, and the Netherlands as an example of a modern and mixed jurisdiction.

The case studies provide an in-depth qualitative analysis of procurement damages adjudication at national level and include the legislative frameworks as well as courts' jurisprudence.

The focus of the comparison is on the constitutive criteria for damages claims, but also provides a more detailed analysis of the quantification phase of damages. The country studies look at the different countries in isolation, outlining (i) the general system; (ii) actions for damages; (iii) constitutive criteria; (iv) heads of damages; (v) quantification of damages; and (vi) discretion of judges.

Chapter 5
Case Study: The Netherlands

Abstract This chapter presents public procurement damages claims in the Netherlands, with a particular emphasis on jurisprudential developments. It covers the causes of action, in particular the constitutive criteria for pre-contractual liability and tort law, as well as the justiciability of claims. It further examines the quantification aspects of damages claims, notably the recoverable losses (bid costs, lost profits and the compensation for lost chances) and judges' quantification methods.

5.1 Systemic Features of Procurement Claims

While damages claims were touched upon in the legislative debate surrounding the Dutch implementation process for Directive 2007/66, no explicit provision regulating damages claims in public procurement was passed. This is understandable in the light of Directive 2007/66, which refrained from further addressing damages. The legislative history to the new Dutch procurement legislation makes clear that the legislator regarded the general tort liability scheme as sufficient. Damages claims in the Netherlands are therefore brought under the overarching tort liability regime.

5.1.1 The Implementation of the Amendments Made by Directive 2007/66

The new substantive public procurement rules at EU level have been implemented in the Netherlands by means of the *Aanbestedingswet 2012*, which entered into force on April 1 2013.[1] Due to the layered structure of administrative law in the Netherlands, there is a multitude of legal instruments which regulate the procuring

---

[1] The previous European substantive public procurement Directives 2004/18 and 2004/17 had been implemented in the Netherlands through the Raamwet EEG-voorschriften aanbestedingen (the 'framework law') and two ministerial decrees based on this framework law: Besluit aanbestedingsregels voor overheidsopdrachten (decree tendering rules for public procurement, 'BAO') and Besluit aanbestedingen speciale sectoren (decree tendering in special sectors, 'BASS').

© Springer International Publishing Switzerland 2016   75
H. Schebesta, *Damages in EU Public Procurement Law*, Studies in European
Economic Law and Regulation 6, DOI 10.1007/978-3-319-23612-4_5

behavior of different government bodies. These may differ according to the object of a contract (e.g. works[2]), contracting authorities (e.g. *Rijksoverheid*), or else for specific areas of law (e.g. transport law).[3]

A separate act of implementation for the original Procurement Remedies Directives 89/665 and 92/13 was not regarded as necessary at the time, since effective and fast procedures for legal protection were already in place within the general Dutch framework of judicial protection. These included the possibility of interim measures and suspension of contract (*voorlopige voorziening* and *opschorting*), as well as the possibility to claim damages.[4] The amendments introduced by Directive 2007/77 led to the adoption of Dutch implementing legislation, namely the *Wet implementatie rechtsbescherming bij aanbesteding* ('Wira'). The law was later repealed and the provisions integrated in the *Aanbestedingswet 2012*. It includes no specific damages provision.

5.1.2 Jurisdictional Questions

The Netherlands is one of the systems in which arbitration is an important feature of procurement litigation. For example, the standard terms of contract for works and technical installations mandate that disputes arising between contracting authority and contractor are subject to arbitration by the *Raad van Arbitrage voor de Bouw* (Arbitration council for the construction sector, 'RvA').[5] Arbitration, as an institutionalised extra-judicial track of litigation, is still an important feature of procurement practice.[6] The RvA decides public procurement disputes that fall within the

---

[2] The first European substantive Directive 71/305 for works was implemented in the Netherlands by means of the Uniforme Aanbestedingsreglement (Uniform public procurement regulation, 'UAR') 1971. The intensification of regulation of public procurement at the European level was subsequently transposed by the 'UAR 1986', the 'UAR-EG 1991', and then the 'UAR 2001'. The latter was then replaced by the Aanbestedingsreglement Werken 2004 (Public procurement regulation for works, 'ARW' 2004) which was in turn replaced by the 'ARW 2005', and now 'ARW 2012'. For the utilities sector, this was the Aanbestedingsreglement Nutssectoren 2006 (Public procurement regulation for utilities sectors, 'ARN 2006'), now 'ARN 2013'.

[3] The Dutch substantive public procurement rules are not discussed in this work. Regarding the Netherlands, see EH Pijnacker Hordijk, WH Van Boom & JF Van Nouhuys, *Aanbestedingsrecht. Handboek van het Europese en het Nederlandse Aanbestedingsrecht* (Den Haag, Sdu Uitgevers, 2009).

[4] See the explanatory memorandum to the Dutch implementing proposal of Directive 2007/66, Tweede Kamer 2008–2009, 32 027, nr 3, p 3.

[5] Uniforme administratieve voorwaarden voor de uitvoering van werken en van technische installatiewerken 2012 (Uniform administrative conditions for the execution of works and technical installation works, 'UAV 2012').

[6] In 2013, the RvA arbitration tribunal handled around 1000 construction cases. See Raad van Arbitrage van de Bouw, 'Raad van Arbitrage voor de Bouw (RvA)', www.raadvanarbitrage.nl. These are not all cases in which the public procurement rules are applied, as many are contractual claims.

scope of application of the EU procurement rules in accordance with the rules of law.[7] In light of the fact that the RvA has become less important and that its adjudication was methods were changed when applying EU procurement law,[8] one needs to consider in how far older cases can still be regarded as pertinent. Since then, the law of damages is increasingly determined by the Dutch judicial system.[9]

Judicial proceedings can be in front of administrative or civil courts because public procurement disputes can arise under private and/or administrative law. In most public tenders the contracting authority acts in a private capacity. For these, administrative appeals are precluded[10] and the administrative judicial branch is foreclosed. The major part of public procurement disputes are therefore brought in front of a civil judge. Additionally, the Dutch system of legal protection under civil jurisdiction is characterized by a split system of judicial protection, granting both the possibility of bringing a claim in front of an interim judge in a *kort geding* (summary/interim procedure), and/or bringing a fully fledged *bodemprocedure* (full court procedure). Damages claims are regularly brought in full court procedures and not in interim proceedings.[11]

5.2   Causes of Action

In the Netherlands, a claim by an aggrieved tenderer against the unlawful tendering procedure of a contracting authority could theoretically be based in both contract and tort. The contractual liability would arise trough a form of pre-contractual liability, specifically good faith and fair dealing (*redelijkheid en billijkheid*) in contract negotiations. Tort-based damages claims arise from the general tort provision. In the legislative history of the implementation of the Remedies Directives, the Dutch legislator presumed that an action in tort would be the regular cause of action for procurement damages claims.[12] It has been observed that substantively it makes no

---

[7] This means that parties cannot agree not to apply the EU procurement rules. Such a specific rule for EU procurement disputes has been in force since 1 September 1995. It is now contained in Art 12(2) of the RvA Arbitragereglement from 1 January 2015.

[8] Whereas the RvA principally adjudicated based on the principle 'good men in all fairness', the statutes of the RvA were changed in 1995 in relation to the requirements of European public procurement claims, so as to provide for adjudication 'according to the law'. See Art 18 (2) of the RvA statutes, ibid. The date of entry into force of that alteration was 1 September 1995. Only since 2015 does the RvA generally adjudicate according to the rules of law unless otherwise agreed between the parties.

[9] MA Van Wijngaarden and MAB Chao-Duivis, *Hoofdstukken Bouwrecht: Aanbestedingsrecht* (Den Haag, Kluwer, 2008).

[10] Algemene wet bestuursrecht ('Awb', General administrative law), Art 8:3.

[11] It is usually assumed by interim judges that interim procedures are not suitable for determining damages claims.

[12] This is the vision defended by the legislator, which, in the written preparations for the *Wira*, stated several times that the damages provisions are to be implemented by means of the tort law

difference whether an action for damages is based in contract or torts.[13] This is true for the stage of the quantification of damages, which is done according to an identical article in the Dutch civil code for both actions. The constitutive criteria for an action, on the other hand, differ under contract and torts.

5.2.1 *Pre-contractual Liability and* **Redelijkheid en Billijkheid**

The doctrine of pre-contractual liability is well developed in the Netherlands. A number of authors therefore defend the position that a pre-contractual relationship arises between a contracting authority and a tenderer. The general doctrine of pre-contractual liability in the Netherlands was developed in case law, which established that the pre-contractual relationship between parties is governed by the principle of good faith.[14] In *Plas/Valburg*,[15] the court held that where the pre-contractual relationship is governed by a requirement of *redelijkheid en billijkheid* (fair dealing), a right to damages can arise. Accordingly, three different situations of negotiations are distinguished[16]: the negotiations can be terminated without any costs to the parties; the negotiations are at such an advanced stage, that the costs incurred by the parties must be reimbursed; or the termination of the negotiations is considered to be contrary to good faith and fair dealing. Where termination is unlawful, both the negative and positive interest (lost profits) must be reimbursed. The degree of pre-contractual commitment in the negotiations is therefore intrinsically linked to the types of damages which are recoverable through pre-contractual liability.

The main principle is that contractual negotiations can be terminated without consequences unless this is 'unacceptable'. In order to prove that a termination of the negotiations was unacceptable, the party must have had legitimate expectations that the contract would have been concluded. This assessment takes account of the actions of parties, of the legitimate interests of the terminating party, and other unforeseen circumstances. Another element is whether there was agreement on all

---

provision contained in 6:162 BW. See for example in the conversion table between Directive and the *Wira* implementation act attached to the proposal TK 2008–2009, 32027, nr 3, p 24.

[13] WJ Slagter, 'Aanbestedingsaansprakelijkheid: grondslagen en knelpunten', in WH van Boom et al (eds), *Aanbesteding en aansprakelijkheid* (Schoordijk Instituut Centrum voor aansprakelijkheid, 2001), p 14. See, also JM Hebly & FG Wilman, 'Damages for Breach of Public Procurement Law. The Dutch Situation', in DR Fairgrieve & F Lichère (eds), *Public Procurement Law. Damages as an Effective Remedy* (Oxford, Hart Publishing, 2011), p 77.

[14] Hoge Raad, 15 November 1957, NJ 1958, 67 (*Baris/Riezenkamp*).

[15] Hoge Raad, 18 June 1982, NJ 1983, 723.

[16] There is considerable discord among legal academics concerning the question whether the pre-contractual stage is made up of three phases, or less, or as the author suggests one ought rather to speak of different negotiation situations. See MR Ruygvoorn, 'Bestaat de "tweede fase" uit Plas/Valburg nog?' (2011) 2 *Contracteren*, 39, p 40.

essential elements of a contract. In 2005, the *Hoge Raad* rendered an important judgment which re-iterated that the standard of whether termination in pre-contractual stage is unacceptable or not is one of strict scrutiny and to be given a restricted interpretation.[17] This restricted interpretation was confirmed in later cases. For example, in *TPN/Aalten,* real estate developers tried to claim damages from the municipality Aalten for terminating negotiations on a land development project. TPN had repeatedly contacted the municipality and presented a proposal for developing a piece of property. This was not deemed sufficient to have created legitimate expectations on their behalf. The municipality had stated that the developers' presumption of having concluded a contract was erroneous, in particular given the fact that the plans for the specific location in question had not been finalized.[18] The court held that in this situation no legitimate interest arose.

In general, the doctrine of pre-contractual liability is highly casuistic and marked by legal uncertainty. It has been applied – mainly unsuccessfully – in public procurement disputes. The *ARW 2012* now contains a reference to the *Slibintegratie* case[19] and a note stating that, due to the pre-contractual duty of fair dealing, a decision not to award a contract may result in a right to damages.

In the *Slibintegratie* case, the court defined the standard for pre-contractual liability in public procurement procedures more closely.[20] The case concerned a tender for a sludge disintegration unit through a restricted procedure based on the lowest price award criterion. Party A subscribed with the lowest bid, but the contracting authority decided not to award the contract. In the notification, the contracting authority stated that the economic feasibility of the project was no longer warranted. The court held that the *ARW 2005* does not require the contracting authorities to award contracts for which a tendering procedure was organised. Further, public procurement law does not contain a duty for the contracting authority to compensate the bid costs incurred by tenderers. However, under special circumstances a claim to damages may arise either under tort or precontractual liability. In such case, the burden of proof is with the claiming party. Had the contracting authority known that it would under no circumstances proceed to award a contract, the conduct of a tendering procedure would be clearly unlawful. Whether it *ought* to have known was to be examined based on the standard whether there was fault so reckless as to border intention.[21] In case of the sludge disintegration unit, the municipality had taken out a loan of 19 million, while Party A's bid (the lowest bid) in the tendering procedure

---

[17] Hoge Raad, 12 August 2005, ECLI:NL:HR:2005:AT7337 (*CBB/JBO*). The case is less clear on the application of the test to the facts of the negotiations as the Hoge Raad only struck down the (lack of) reasoning of the lower court.

[18] Rechtbank Zutphen, 29 December 2010, ECLI:NL:RBZUT:2010:BO9733.

[19] This note is included in the ARW 2012 explanations, p 242 with a reference to Rechtbank' s-Hertogenbosch, 5 November 2008, ECLI:NL:RBSHE:2008:BW2949 (*Van der Horst/De Dommel*).

[20] ibid.

[21] Literally, the court said that the attitude of the contracting authority would have to be one along the lines of: 'We zien het eigenlijk niet zitten, maar laten we toch maar een aanbesteding houden, je weet nooit hoe een koe een haas vangt'. See ibid, para 4.4.2.

was around 22 million. The court held that this was insufficient to demonstrate that the municipality knew or ought to have known that it would never have been able to award the contract. In principle, therefore, no damages claims arise simply because a contracting authority does not proceed to award a contract after a procurement procedure, unless its decision to conduct a procedure were reckless.

However, a less far-reaching duty for compensation can arise where the negotiations have reached a stage in which it is still possible for a party to terminate negotiations, but where some compensation is due for costs incurred by the other party. This type of compensation was awarded in *woonzorgcentrum Odendael*.[22] The municipality carried out a tendering procedure for a new work. It appeared that the original design was not feasible, and therefore the municipality invited bidders to come forward with other solutions. Nautilius presented a solution, and made an offer to the municipality. Later, the municipality rejected the offer stating that it had received a much lower offer by the competitor Bavro. However, Nautilius had provided the modified design of the construction, which was undisputedly used as a model for the contract to be awarded. The court held that the municipality was no longer free to terminate the negotiations with Nautilius without compensating for the damage resulting from the termination of the negotiations. Within the doctrine of pre-contractual liability, this corresponds to the 'second phase' of negotiations. The court examined whether the work carried out by Nautilius in the bidding procedure are the kind of work for which consideration is in order. This did not result in Nautilius having a right to being awarded the contract, but to receive damages from the municipality for the work that it had actually carried out, namely the development of the work model. The total costs of €40.000 included work time, travel costs, general business costs (including applied know-how), and the costs for legal counsel. The court required further substantiation of some of the items, as well as the fact that several items might have been counted twice. Generally, the loss itemization was done concrete, costs had to be evidenced, and were calculated in order to reflect the actual bid costs.

Only the actual bid costs were awarded because the court held (on the basis of the *JBO* jurisprudence[23]) that Nautilius did not have legitimate expectations to be awarded the contract ('phase 3' of pre-contractual liability). The competitor Bavro had a 30 % lower bid. The court therefore accepted that even if Nautilius had been granted the possibility to revise its bid, it would not have lowered it sufficiently in order to match that price. Under such circumstances, the pre-contractual principles did not preclude the municipality from awarding the contract to someone else than Nautilius.[24]

Although casuistic in nature, it follows from above examples that contractual claims are an integral part of the current procurement litigation landscape, and must be considered an important basis for damages next to tort.

---

[22] Gerechtshof' s-Hertogenbosch, 3 November 2009, ECLI:NL:GHSHE:2009:BK7579.

[23] Hoge Raad, 12 August 2005, ECLI:NL:HR:2005:AT7337, (*CBB/JBO*).

[24] Gerechtshof' s-Hertogenbosch, 3 November 2009, above n 22.

5.2.2   Tort Law

Next to damages claims based in contract, public procurement damages actions are possible under the general tort provision of 6:162 *Burgerlijk Wetboek* (Civil Code, 'BW'). These were the claims primarily envisaged by the legislator.

5.2.2.1   Constitutive Elements

The Netherlands is characterized by a two-tiered tort liability scheme, meaning that the finding of liability is distinct from the quantification of damages. The constitutive elements are enumerated in a general provision of the Dutch Civil Code:

Dutch Civil Code 6:162

1. Whoever commits a tortuous act, which is attributable to him, against another is under a duty to compensate the damage which the other consequently sustains.
2. Regarded as tortuous acts are a violation of a right, an act or omission in breach of a statutory duty or with whatever according to unwritten law as determined by common dealing, both safe the existence of a justification.
3. A tortuous act can be attributed to the tortfeasor if it is imputable to his fault or a cause which according to the law or under common opinion are imputable to him.

6:162 (1) BW contains the constitutive conditions for tort liability, according to which liability is established in the first place. The quantification of the extent of quantifiable losses is carried out in a second stage according to 6:95 BW and following.

The overarching principle in the Dutch Law of damages is the principle of full compensation,[25] even though this is not explicitly laid down by law. The aim of Tort law is primarily compensatory. In addition, a preventive or deterrent purpose is also recognized, but not a penalizing or retributive one. Tort requires the following elements: (i) a tortuous act, (ii) attributability thereof to the tortfeasor, (iii) damage, (iv) causality, and (v) relativity.

5.2.2.2   Tortuous Act and Attributability (Fault)[26]

A tortuous act is defined in Article 6:162(2) BW as 'the violation of a right, an act or omission in breach of a statutory duty or under unwritten law in *maatschaapelijk verkeer betaamt* (as determined by societal convention)' save if a justification exists.

---

[25] J Spier, T Hartlief, GE Van Maanen & RD Vriesendorp, *Verbintenissen uit de wet en Schadevergoeding* (Deventer, Kluwer, 2006) write about the 'principle of full compensation', 'a principle with many exceptions… not absolute'.

[26] This is attributability in the narrow sense. The fault criterion is here used to determine whether it is attributable to a specific person. The case law is sometimes ambiguous in using the 'fault' criterion in cases which qualify the tortuous act, rather than using attributability as such. See Spier et al, ibid.

In principle, upon the breach of a statutory duty, an act is qualified as tortuous.[27] This has evident advantages for a plaintiff, since the burden of disproving liability in cases of a statutory breach shifts to the defendant (e.g. in order to demonstrate that the tort was justified). A breach of the *Aanbestedingswet 2012* will count as a breach of statutory duty and satisfy the requirements of a tort action rather easily. Similarly, broader principles of transparency and equality are likely to count as breach of unwritten societal norms.

The tortuous act must be attributable to the tortfeasor, based on fault or causes which according to the law or by societal convention are regarded as attributable.[28] Attribution is generally easily accepted in procurement situations; for example in a case in which the municipality outsourced the procurement procedure, the ultimate responsibility for the procedure and decisions relating to it were attributed to the contracting authority.[29]

5.2.2.3 Damage and Causality

The tort provision does not define damage. However, it is understood to comprise three elements: '(i) a causal element, i.e. damage occurs as a result of a certain event; (ii) an element of comparison, i.e. comparison between the situations with and without the damage causing event; and (iii) a hypothetical element.'[30]

Article 6:162 BW provides that a certain (in the sense of ascertainable) link between the wrongful act and the loss needs to be sustained. Whether this is indeed the case is judged according to the same criterion as that for heads of damages, i.e. the extent to which damages can be imputed to the tortfeasor. The theoretical two stage distinction between establishing and quantifying liability is blurred on this point.

In principle, therefore, an aggrieved bidder has to prove that the 'conditio sine qua non' condition of 6:162 BW is fulfilled, i.e. that the tortuous event was a necessary condition for the damage to occur. For the aggrieved bidder this may involve the onerous proof that it would indeed have been awarded the contract.[31] This stringent approach to causality has on some occasions been disregarded by the courts in favour of a proportional liability approach in cases where causality could not clearly be established.[32]

When establishing liability, the problem of causality is a problem of evidence. According to the regular rules of procedure, the injured party as the person relying

---

[27] ibid.

[28] See Art 6:162, para 3 of BW.

[29] Gerechtshof' s-Hertogenbosch, 3 November 2009, above n 22.

[30] MH Wissink & WH Van Boom, 'The Netherlands. Damages under Dutch Law', in U Magnus (ed), *Unification of Tort Law: Damages* (The Hague, Kluwer, 1996), p 146.

[31] Rechtbank Amsterdam, 23 April 2014, ECLI:NL:RBAMS:2014:3456 (*Lingotto*).

[32] See also AJV Heeswijck, *Rechtsbescherming van ondernemers in aanbestedingsprocedures* (Dissertation, University of Groningen, 2014), 116–118.

on the rule also has to prove causality (Article 150 *Wetboek van Burgerlijke Rechtsvordering* ('Rv')).[33]

Several justifications can break causality. Due to the private law approach to contracting authorities' awarding of contracts, the party autonomy doctrine obstructs the presumption that in an unlawfully conducted procedure the contracting authority would have necessarily awarded a contract to the second lowest bidder. This precludes the claiming of damages for the positive interest of the contract unless the contracting authority has indeed awarded the contract, in which case the justification is discarded.[34]

In terms of admissible justifications, one of the practically most relevant questions is whether the fact that an aggrieved tenderer's bid submission was invalid breaks the chain of causation. It seems to be assumed (and often criticized) in the literature[35] that invalidity does not break causation. This statement is questionable. In several interim proceedings, lower courts have discarded cases as having no prima facie basis for assuming that a claimant which had not submitted a valid tender would indeed have suffered any loss.[36] Also at the level of appeal it was held that without a valid submission an aggrieved tenderer has no claim for damages.[37]

5.2.2.4 Relativity (6:163 BW)

The last condition is a requirement of relativity between the norm and the claimant. Despite the breach of a statutory norm, 6:163 BW can preclude the attribution of liability as '[t]*here is no duty of compensation, whenever the norm that was breached does not serve to protect against losses as the injured party has sustained them*'. In principle, the article is an expression of a limitation of liability through testing of the objective and purpose of a statutory norm regarding the protected person/entity and protected losses. It is by definition a concrete – that is, factual – rather than an abstract test. In order to test relativity, the Dutch courts have referred to the goal and

---

[33] Certain exceptions to this rule have been granted, like a rule of reversal, which means that in specific areas of tort law, notably traffic law and risk norms, the mere breach of a rule thereof switched the burden of proof requirement. In principle, the possibility of alleviating the burden of proof could also be considered for public procurement disputes. However, this is clearly not the direction that the Supreme Court is taking at the moment, as it is narrowing down the rule of reversal concerning norms for specific dangers (in the sense of risk). Public procurement disputes do not fulfill these criteria developed in the more recent case law and therefore do not fall under risk liability and the reversal of proof that it can provide. See HR 29 November 2002, NJ 2004, 304 and 305 (DA), on the reversal of proof rule in general. Further, see Spier et al, above n 25.

[34] Hebly & Wilman, 'Damages for Breach of Public Procurement Law. The Dutch Situation', above n 13, p 79, citing the authority of Rechtbank Rotterdam, 8 October 2008, LJN BG3796, ECLI:NL:RBROT:2004:AS3395 and Gerechtshof' s-Hertogenbosch, 26 November 1990, BR 1991/641.

[35] ibid. Gerechtshof' s-Gravenhage was later appealed in Hoge Raad, 9 May 2008.

[36] Rechtbank' s-Gravenhage, 7 August 2006, ECLI:NL:RBSGR:2006:BA4384; and Rechtbank' s-Gravenhage, 7 August 2006, ECLI:NL:RBSGR:2006:BA4390.

[37] Gerechtshof' s-Hertogenbosch, 23 November 2010, ECLI:NL:GHSHE:2010:BO5839.

scope of the rule, namely to which persons, which losses and which ways of forma-
tion of loss it extends.[38] The public procurement norms are clear as to the fact that
they serve to protect aggrieved tenderers once these can be singled out. In circumstances of an unpublished illegal contract, an argument could be made to the effect
that it is impossible for any entity to prove that they would indeed have benefited
from the scope of the public procurement rules in that specific tender.

5.3   Justiciability of Claims

The justiciability of claims is in part defined by the requirements of relativity
(discussed above). For the public procurement context, relativity does not stand in
the way of bringing damages claims as the procurement rules are seen to be designed
to protect the interests of aggrieved bidders. Standing requirements and the lack of
a demonstrable interest are more likely to impede the bringing of a successful claim.
Time limits are the regular time limits and therefore do not pose a particular obstacle. The protracted duration of damages as full proceedings may be an indirect
obstacle that negatively influences a tenderer's decision of whether or not to bring
a claim.

5.3.1   Standing

Standing is regulated by Article 3:303 BW and requires sufficient interest. As such,
the rule is widely drawn, as a theoretical interest is sufficient. The interest does not
need to have been manifested, for example, through a claimant expressing interest
in a tendering procedure.

However, some Dutch courts have required aggrieved bidders to have been suitable and submitted a valid bid in order to demonstrate sufficient interest in order to
receive standing.[39] When unable to demonstrate actual loss, a claimant can be
regarded as enjoying insufficient self-standing interest.[40] This precluded the court
from entering the dispute on the merits of a claim: the municipality Steen had started
a procurement procedure with a lowest price award criterion, but later decided not
to proceed with the award and instead start a new procedure. The aggrieved bidder
Kanters brought an action in tort claiming that the municipality had acted wrongfully.

---

[38] The Dutch Supreme Court elaborated sub-questions to determine the condition of relativity and
on the basis of which the extent of the intended protection of the statutory norm should be examined. See HR 7 May 2004, NJ 2006, 281 (*Linda*) in Spier et al, above n 25.

[39] Rechtbank' s-Gravenhage, 8 May 2009, ECLI:NL:RBSGR:2009:BI3892.

[40] Rechtbank Maastricht, 28 August 2003, ECLI:NL:RBMAA:2003:AI1604.

Kanters claimed lost profits for the works of the procurement procedure, as well as profits for other works for which it could now, lacking the work experience with the municipality, not tender. Before considering the actions of the municipality and whether they had indeed been illegal, the court turned directly to the demonstration of damage. Regarding the lost profits, the court considered that Kanters had submitted the lowest bid and that the second ranked had a 40 % higher price. Kanters claimed that it would have made around 15 % profit, but the district court found that it regarded the submission of Kanters so low that it would not have made any profit. Further, it found Kanter's claim that it suffered damage by being deprived of the procurement experience as insufficiently probable. Kanters therefore could not demonstrate to have suffered any loss, and was not regarded to have sufficient interest in bringing the claim for illegality of the procurement procedure. The reasoning in this case seems to be unusual in that it enters the quantification of profits in detail already at the stage of answering the preliminary question whether an aggrieved tenderer had standing. It demonstrates that sufficient interest can limit the justiciability of damages claims.

5.3.2   Time Limits

The prescription period for damages claims in the Netherlands remains at the standard level of limitation for legal claims of five years, according to Article 3:310 BW. These standard limitation periods was deviated from under the old Dutch standard public procurement regulations,[41] although this provision has now disappeared.

5.3.3   Duration

Overall, damages actions, as actions on merit (and not awardable in interim proceedings[42]), have an average duration estimated at about 18 months in first instance.[43] Including a phase in appeal, a judgment takes around 4–5 years. Between the bringing of a claim and a final judgment by the Supreme Court around 7 years would pass.

---

[41] Art 2.33.2 of the 'ARW 2005' provided for a 90 day period, while Art 67(3) of the 'UAR-EG 1991' provided for a 3 month period after the award. See above n 2.

[42] See Hebly and Wilman, 'Damages for Breach of Public Procurement Law. The Dutch Situation', above n 13, p 76.

[43] ibid, p 87 (admitting variations).

5.4   The Quantification of Damages

The Dutch system draws a rather clear distinction between the question of the existence of a duty to compensate damage and the quantification of the value of compensation for the damage.[44] Regardless of the cause of action for the breach, be it in tort or for breach of contract,[45] the same provisions on the quantification of damage apply. In a dispute, the plaintiff does not initially claim the exact extent of the losses s/he wishes to recover; it is sufficient to prove the likelihood of the tortuous act having caused damage in order to start the court proceedings.[46]

In regular (full) court procedures granting a claim for damages, the judge quantifies the damage to the extent that this is possible. Where quantification is impossible, s/he orders the damage compensation to be determined by the court. If juridically determined, this is done in the damage factoring procedure (*schadestaatprocedure*[47]) in order to quantify the amount of the damage to be compensated. Procedurally, this split mirrors the substantive distinction between finding and determining the extent of a duty to compensate for damage. In practice, the procedure for establishing liability for compensation in the first place and the procedure for the quantification of damage compensation are often collectively referred to as the 'procedure for establishing damage'.[48] The purpose of the *schadestaatprocedure* lies only in determining the extent of the damages to be compensated; the basis for establishing damage liability[49] is not reopened – the parties are bound by the finding in the main procedure on that point.[50] The aggrieved tenderer must at that stage merely demonstrate that the probability of damage exists.

5.4.1   Definition of Recoverable Losses

The concept of damages is not defined explicitly, but recoverable losses are laid down by law. Article 6:95 BW grants a duty to compensate all patrimonial and 'other disadvantage'. Patrimonial damage is further elaborated in Article 6:96 BW

---

[44] See generally Wissink & Van Boom, 'The Netherlands. Damages under Dutch Law', above n 30, pp 143–158. The doctoral thesis by AJV Heeswijck, *Rechtsbescherming van ondernemers in aanbestedingsprocedures,* above 32, covers procurement damages in detail, paying specific attention in particular to the quantification stage.

[45] See AJ Akkermans & EH Pijnacker Hordjik, 'Schadevergoeding en schadeberekening', in WH van Boom et al, *Aanbesteding en aansprakelijkheid* , above n 13, p 19.

[46] Hoge Raad, NJ 1980, 185 (*WHH*) (13 June 1980). The case law in this section is based on Spier et al, above n 25.

[47] This procedure is governed by Arts 612–615b Rv. See, generally HJ Snijders, CJM Klaassen & GJ Meijer, *Nederlands Burgerlijk Procesrecht* (Deventer, Kluwer, 2007).

[48] See articles 612 – 615b Dutch Civil Procedure, Wetboek van Burgerlijke Rechtsvordering.

[49] Hoge Raad, 30 May 1997, NJ 1998, 381 (*Elink Schuurman/Van Gastel qq*).

[50] Hoge Raad, 17 January 1997, NJ 1997, 230 (*Moerman/Bakker*).

to include *damnum emergens* and loss of profit, further reasonable costs in order to limit the damage occurring, in order to establish liability, and to cover the *incasso* proceedings for payment. Article 6:106 BW covers immaterial damage. Damage to the image of the aggrieved tenderer is not usually assumed to constitute part of the compensable losses.[51] Statutory interest is granted according to 6:83 starting from the point of the wrongful act, 6:105 regulates losses which have not yet materialized. Damage is compensated in money, but there is a possibility for *in natura* claims.[52]

It was disputed whether damages are merely of a factual nature or constitute a normative concept. The Dutch Supreme Court has accepted jurisdiction for cassation and determining whether a lower instance had used an incorrect interpretation of the law regarding the concept of damages in the stage of quantification.[53] This would sustain the argument that the concept of damages is normative, as the Dutch Supreme Court does not determine the factual situations giving rise to disputes.

Causality, in the quantification stage of damages, refers to the issue of determining which losses can be compensated according to Article 6:98 BW. The answer to the question has changed over time as varying theories have been advanced. Heads of damages are therefore not subject to a strict *numerus clausus* but to a list which is more or less open and contingent upon the finding of loss.

5.4.1.1   The Positive Interest, or the Lost Profit

If an aggrieved tenderer is able to demonstrate that s/he would have had to receive a contract, lost profits are the standard measure of damages awarded. This 'generous' compensatory measure is coupled with a very high standard of burden of proof: the aggrieved tenderer in principle has to prove that s/he would have obtained the contract.[54] Two cases that successfully established a claim for lost profits are discussed below:

In *Eurosalt/Oldambt*, the municipality had opened a procurement procedure for road salt. Eurosalt was among the bidders, but the municipality was unclear with respect to the award criterion. It stated that the economically most advantageous offer would be awarded the contract, but later on changed this to the lowest price criterion. Both Eurosalt and Beneluxsalt submitted a price of € 52,00 per 1.000 kg, Eurosalt with a grain size of 0–2 mm, Beneluxsalt with a grain size of 0–3 mm. During the interim proceedings it became clear that other factors (such as general

---

[51] Rechtbank Amsterdam, 23 April 2008, ECLI:NL:RBAMS:2008:BE9582.

[52] In the past, this provision has served to sustain that under Dutch law a contract could be declared ineffective on the basis of an 'in-natura damage claim'. In view of Directive 2007/66, we are not going to discuss this argument further.

[53] Spier et al, *Verbintenissen uit de wet en Schadevergoeding,* above n 25, referring to Hoge Raad, 18 April 1986, NJ 1986, 587.

[54] JMJ Van Rijn Van Alkemade, 'Overheidsaansprakelijkheid voor onrechtmatige verdeling van schaarse publieke rechten' (2011) *Overheid en Aansprakelijkheid* 69, p 72.

terms of contract and size of the salt) had influenced the decision to award to the competitor Beneluxsalt. The municipality therefore violated the principle of equality and transparency. However, Beneluxsalt had already delivered the salt to the municipality. The interim judge found that an injunction would not be a suitable solution. Either Beneluxsalt would be disadvantaged if the municipality were ordered by the court to contract with Eurosalt (and the municipality would incur costs as Beneluxsalt would have a damages claim for breach of contract) or the municipality would incur unreasonable costs if it were to be required to buy the salt from both Eurosalt and Beneluxsalt. The interim judge therefore argued that damages should be awarded to Eurosalt on the basis of article 6:96 BW, and that the damages should be for lost profit.[55]

In a procurement procedure for canalization, the contracting authority organized a tender in two phases. After the selection phase, it changed the sub-criteria for the economically most advantageous tenderer in a protocol that was deposited at a notary but not disclosed to the tenderers. Temmink, under use of the weighting of that protocol, came out third and the contract was awarded to KWS. With the weighting that was initially applied in the first stage, Temmink would have ranked higher than KWS. The court found that the contracting authority had breached the public procurement rules as the award criteria needed to be known in advance. This established a wrongful conduct on behalf of the contracting authority. The court proceeded to examine the causality between the loss sustained and the tortious act. In order to establish causality, Temmink had to prove that its tender had been the economically most advantageous one. The scores of Temmink and KWS calculated under the old weighting clearly placed Temmink in a higher position than KWS. The score of other tenders being unknown, it was impossible to conclude that Temmink would have had the highest rank. The contracting authority failed to present arguments to the effect that another tender had submitted a better bid (which it could have done easily according to the court as it disposed of the necessary documents). The silence of the contracting authority led the court to assume that Temmink indeed would have won the contract under the alternative calculation. The court concluded that in principle the claimant was entitled to bid costs as well as the positive contract interest.

The following variables were indicated as relevant in quantifying lost profits: (a) what was the net profit of a contract had it indeed been awarded to the claimant? (b) What was the extent and impact of the shortfall losses on indirect costs? (c) In how far are the indirect costs fixed or variable costs? (d) In how far was the loss limited by substituting contracts?[56] The extent of the lost profits are ascertained according to the case, but can involve expert appointment, average profit margins or reasonable,

---

[55] Rechtbank Noord-Nederland, 7 November 2014, ECLI:NL:RBNNE:2014:5503. Absent the necessary information on the quantification of the damage, the interim judge holds that it does not have the necessary information to determine the amount of damages in the specific proceedings.

[56] Rechtbank Zwolle-Lelystad, 31 January 2007, ECLI:NL:RBZLY:2007:AZ7506, appealed and upheld Gerechtshof Arnhem, 06 April 2010, ECLI:NL:GHARN:2010:BM0044 (*Temmink/ Gemeente Raalte*).

specific profit expectations as expressed, for example, in the bid. In addition, general or overhead costs may be claimed, but facts such as the aggrieved tenderer having used its capacity through alternative contracts may be taken into account.[57] Legal fees are claimable, as long as they are reasonable.[58]

A rather spectacular case of a successful claim for damages in lost profits was recently brought to a sobering end. In first instance, the Dutch land register had been condemned to pay a sum of € 10.000.000 to HLA, an aggrieved bidder, for lost profit *and* consequential damages.[59] Although in this initial judgment the court did base its estimation on calculations involving the likely number of licenses to be sold, the figure of 10 million was an *ex aequo et bono* estimation. In appeal,[60] the court overturned the judgment, holding that HLA was not successful in proving that the contract would have been awarded to it had the land register not acted wrongfully. The court of appeal re-iterated that there is only a duty to pay damages whenever the aggrieved bidder can prove that s/he would have been awarded the contract had the contracting authorities acted according to the procurement rules. In the specific case, the land register had tried to buy a KLIC-viewer. The aggrieved tenderer HLA argued that the fact that it was not invited to the procedure was wrongful, and tried to prove that it would have been awarded the procedure since it already had developed a product ('CableGuard') which complied with the call. The court of appeal however found this to be unsubstantiated as HLA did not provide expert reports or a demonstration of the product in order to support this argument. The case confirms that the burden of proving the hypothetical (namely that an aggrieved bidder would have been the awarded a contract) is onerous indeed.

5.4.1.2 The Negative Interest and Bid Costs

The negative interest, or losses that are more specific, such as bid preparation and bid participation, are generally considered subsidiary claims in case a lost profit claim fails.[61] Some authors presume that aggrieved tenderers can claim bid costs only in cases where no tenderer was successful in claiming for the positive interest and where a reasonable chance is assumed.[62] Others see the burden of proof as lower.[63] The dissonance in doctrine demonstrates that procurement practice and the

---

[57] Hebly & Wilman, 'Damages for Breach of Public Procurement Law. The Dutch Situation', above n 13, p 82.

[58] 6:96 BW.

[59] Rechtbank Zutphen, 28 December 2001, ECLI:NL:RBZUT:2011:BU9991.

[60] Gerechtshof Arnhem-Leeuwarden, 8 July 2014, ECLI:NL:GHARL:2014:5475.

[61] Hebly & Wilman, 'Damages for Breach of Public Procurement Law. The Dutch Situation', above 13, p 83.

[62] Pijnacker Hordijk et al, *Aanbestedingsrecht. Handboek van het Europese en het Nederlandse Aanbestedingsrecht*, above n 3, p 663.

[63] For an overview of opinions, see Van Rijn van Alkemade, 'Overheidsaansprakelijkheid voor onrechtmatige verdeling van schaarse publieke rechten', above n 54, p 73.

courts have not yet found the definite answer to the question on which side the Dutch legal system places the burden of bid preparation in a tender. However, as the law currently stands, it seems that the economic risk of bid costs usually rests with the bidder.[64]

This presumption is broken only under particular circumstances in which during the negotiations the contracting authority has in fact received performances of the other party which it needs to compensate (see case law discussed above[65]). The arguments brought in such cases goes in the direction of unjustified enrichment.

Contracting authorities can include a clause in the procurement documents that excludes compensation for bid preparation costs; the courts have used such clauses to support the finding that a tenderer was not eligible to claim damages.[66] Where the tendering documents explicitly preclude damages claims in relation to the procurement procedure, and there was no wrongful conduct by the contracting authority in the procedure, an action for damages claims fail.[67] It can be concluded that contractual clauses in tender documents are often relevant in judging whether there is a contractual claim for the compensation of bid costs.

5.4.1.3   The Lost Chance

There are several examples of courts using the lost chance in relation to recoverable damage. In *NIC*, the court assessed the chances of both plaintiffs to have been 50 % to receive the award respectively, so that the damages was to be equally distributed among the two (thus equalling 100 % of the total damage).[68] Another case applied the lost chance in the proportional version: a tenderer who belonged to the circle of aggrieved bidders had only a chance of one out of six to be awarded the contract. The damage should be calculated proportionally to that chance. The actual contract value was taken as the basis for the calculation and then multiplied by 1/6 to express the chance.[69] Similarly, an interim judge calculated the profits of the contract as totalling €90.000 over 3 years. Considering that the aggrieved bidder was one out of

---

[64] CEC Jansen, 'Aanbesteding en offertekostenvergoeding', in Bert van Roermund, et al (eds), *Aanbesteding en aansprakelijkheid. Preventie, vergoeding en afwikkeling van schade bij aanbestedingsgeschillen.* (Schoordijk Instituut Centrum voor Aansprakelijkheidsrecht, 2001), p 79 (calling the system whereby bidding costs are not compensated by the contracting authority the 'present system' in the Netherlands).

[65] Gerechtshof' s-Hertogenbosch, 3 November 2009, above n 22.

[66] Rechtbank Overijssel, 6 March 2014, ECLI:NL:RBOVE:2014:1078.

[67] Rechtbank Breda, 21 December 2007, ECLI:NL:RBBRE:2007:BC0940.

[68] Akkermans & Pijnacker Hordijk, 'Schadevergoeding en schadeberekening', above n 44, p 31. The particular constellation of chance and both aggrieved bidders being the plaintiffs in the procedure therefore do not support a proportional attribution of the lost chance.

[69] Rechtbank Utrecht, 4 July 2001, BR 2002/91; and Den Haag, 29 March 2000, *Staat en Nederlands Inkoopcentrum (NIC)* rolnr. 94/3490 (not published), both discussed Pijnacker Hordijk et al, *Aanbestedingsrecht. Handboek,* above n 3, p 661.

the selected three, it concluded that the figure ought to be divided by three (the number of competitors) in order to reflect the value of the lost chance.[70] In another case the court found it likely that in a hypothetical situation the aggrieved bidder would indeed have received the contract; whereas for the follow-up contracts it assessed such chance at only 50 % due to inherent uncertainties. Therefore, for the initial three years the tenderer received 100 % of its lost profit, and for the 2 year follow up 50 % of the lost profits.[71]

The most recent case in which the lost chance doctrine was applied in public procurement is the *Lingotto*[72] case concerning the development of De Hallen carried out by the municipality of Amsterdam. In the documents of the procedure, the municipality had included a criterion that it would not financially contribute to the development scheme. It negotiated with two contractors, Lingotto and TROM. However, the municipality awarded the contract to TROM, promising to buy a parking garage for €5,6 million and a passage for €1,7 million Euro. Lingotto brought the municipality in front of the courts arguing that by agreeing to the purchases, it had substantially changed the terms of the contract to be awarded during the procedure and was therefore in violation of the principles of transparency and equal treatment.

Lingotto further argued that had it known that the municipality was going to purchase the parking garage and the passage, it would have been able to make a more favourable bid than TROM. The court came to the conclusion that it was impossible to determine who would have won the selection procedure. However it held that this did not stand in the way of the fact that the actions of the municipality (district west) deprived Lingotto of the real chance of being awarded the contract. The value of the lost chance, which is determined on one hand by the extent of the chance, and on the other by the financial interest in the potential contract, in principle must be compensated. The municipality argued that Lingotto would not have become a selected bidder. The court disagreed, stating that the speedy development of De Hallen was important, and that therefore the city district had only invited Lingotto and the competitor TROM for the selection procedure. Additionally, all essential points of the contract were agreed upon. Given that only Lingotto and TROM were potential contractors, the court assessed Lingotto's chance at 50 %.

5.4.2   Methods of Quantification

Where the types of losses are determined, the value of the loss must still be quantified. The method of quantification is laid down in 6:97 BW, giving discretion to the judge to quantify the damage in the way most suited to the nature of the loss.

---

[70] Rechtbank Amsterdam, 29 May 2012, ECLI:NL:RBAMS:2012:BX1677.

[71] Rechtbank s' Gravenhage, 28 April 2005, ECLI:NL:GHSGR:2005:AU4277.

[72] *Lingotto*, above n 31.

The damage can be quantified using the abstract or the concrete method for the calculations. While the concrete method takes into account the concrete circumstances of a case, the abstract method relies on a generalized assessment. For cars this is for example an index of the general market value of car models. The abstract method is rarely used – if it is used, it constitutes a minimum threshold, and should a plaintiff expect more damages under the concrete method, s/he is entitled to claim that difference.[73] Generally speaking, public procurement disputes are highly likely to be calculated based on an individual, that is, concrete method of quantification. However, looking at court judgments, in order to calculate the damage that arose and lost profits, courts often make use of standardised or assumed profit margins which are not necessarily closely linked to the market in which an aggrieved bidder operated.

If the extent of the damage is not able to be determined precisely, the judge must make an estimation. The judge then determines the amount of damages *ex aequo et bono*, in which case the rules of burden of proof and evidence do not apply.[74] However, where damage is proven, a claim for compensation of damage cannot be rejected on the grounds of the indeterminability thereof.[75] To some authors, this provision is an expression of the principle of full compensation.[76] Read in this light, the provision grants a wide degree of discretion on one hand, and on the other, leaves the judge with a duty to secure full compensation.[77] The judge does have the option of reducing the amount of damages in order to offset benefits,[78] for own or contributory fault,[79] and mitigation.[80]

5.5 Conclusion

The Dutch system can be characterized as a pragmatic system, less concerned with dogmatic rigidity. Everything – lost profits, bid costs, and compensation for lost chances – is possible, but nothing guaranteed. The point of departure is generous: where a tenderer can squarely prove that s/he would have been the successful

---

[73] Spier et al, *Verbintenissen uit de wet en Schadevergoeding*, above n 25.

[74] AJ Akkermans, *Proportionele aansprakelijkheid bij onzeker causaal verband. Een rechtsvergelijkend onderzoek naar wenselijkheid, grondslagen en afgrenzing van aansprakelijkheid naar rato van veroorzakingswaarschijnlijkheid* (Dissertation, Katholieke Universiteit Brabant, 1997), p 182.

[75] ibid.

[76] AR Bloembergen & SD Lindenbergh, *Schadevergoeding* (Deventer, Kluwer, 2001), p 8.

[77] Spier et al, above n 25.

[78] Art 6:100 BW. A minority view argues that the calculation of costs which are not incurred by the aggrieved bidder due to the non-execution of the contract are to be factored in the quantification on the basis of this article. Most views, for example AJV Heeswijck, above n 32, p 133, oppose such interpretation as non-incurred costs here are not independent benefits, but part of the determination of the extent of the losses.

[79] Arts 6:101 and 6:102 BW.

[80] Art 6:109 BW.

tenderer, lost profits are in order. In principle, full compensation including the lost profits is the regular head of damage. However, the burden of proof is onerous, as the claimant will have to prove that s/he would have been awarded the contract, implying that the aggrieved bidder must have had a valid bid. Where this is not the case, the question is recast as one of a lost business opportunity, and if that fails, the negative interest is discussed. The Netherlands seem particularly averse to granting bid cost claims. The reasoning is based on a strong economic rationale according to which the economic risk of participating in a tender procedure rests with the tenderer. Therefore, bid costs are rarely recovered, unless a claim is based on pre-contractual liability. The lost chance doctrine, then, is used as an instrument of mitigation. Where tenderers are able to demonstrate a privileged position, and more closely define the ring of competitors, the chance can be calculated in simple proportion to the other competitors and provides a basis for damages.

Bibliography

Akkermans, AJ (1997) *Proportionele aansprakelijkheid bij onzeker causaal verband. Een rechts-vergelijkend onderzoek naar wenselijkheid, grondslagen en afgrenzing van aansprakelijkheid naar rato van veroorzakingswaarschijnlijkheid* (Dissertation, Katholieke Universiteit Brabant).

Akkermans, AJ & EH Pijnacker Hordjik, EH (2001) 'Schadevergoeding en schadeberekening', in WH van Boom et al, *Aanbesteding en aansprakelijkheid* (Schoordijk Instituut Centrum voor aansprakelijkheid).

Hebly, JM & Wilman, FG (2011) 'Damages for Breach of Public Procurement Law. The Dutch Situation', in DR Fairgrieve & F Lichère (eds), *Public Procurement Law. Damages as an Effective Remedy* (Oxford, Hart Publishing).

Heeswijck, AJV (2014) *Rechtsbescherming van ondernemers in aanbestedingsprocedures* (Dissertation, University of Groningen).

Jansen, CEC (2001) 'Aanbesteding en offertekostenvergoeding', in Bert van Roermund et al (eds), *Aanbesteding en aansprakelijkheid. Preventie, vergoeding en afwikkeling van schade bij aanbestedingsgeschillen.* (Schoordijk Instituut Centrum voor Aansprakelijkheidsrecht).

Pijnacker Hordijk, EH, Van Boom, WH & Van Nouhuys, JF (2009) *Aanbestedingsrecht. Handboek van het Europese en het Nederlandse Aanbestedingsrecht* (Den Haag, Sdu Uitgevers).

Ruygvoorn, MR (2011) 'Bestaat de "tweede fase" uit Plas/Valburg nog?' 2 *Contracteren*, 39, 40.

Snijders, HJ, Klaassen, CJM & Meijer, GJ (2007) *Nederlands Burgerlijk Procesrecht* (Deventer, Kluwer).

Spier, J, Hartlief, T, Van Maanen, GE & Vriesendorp, RD (2006) *Verbintenissen uit de wet en Schadevergoeding* (Deventer, Kluwer).

van Alkemade, JMJ Van Rijn (2001) 'Overheidsaansprakelijkheid voor onrechtmatige verdeling van schaarse publieke rechten' *Overheid en Aansprakelijkheid* 69.

van Wijngaarden, MA and Chao-Duivis, MAB (2008) *Hoofdstukken Bouwrecht: Aanbestedingsrecht* (Den Haag, Kluwer).

Wissink, MH & Van Boom, WH (1996) 'The Netherlands. Damages under Dutch Law', in U Magnus (ed), *Unification of Tort Law: Damages* (The Hague, Kluwer).

WJ Slagter, WJ (2001) 'Aanbestedingsaansprakelijkheid: grondslagen en knelpunten', in WH van Boom et al (eds), *Aanbesteding en aansprakelijkheid* (Schoordijk Instituut Centrum voor aansprakelijkheid).

Chapter 6
Case Study: The United Kingdom

Abstract This chapter presents public procurement damages claims in the UK, with a particular emphasis on jurisprudential developments. It covers the relevant causes of action, namely breach of statutory duty, implied contract and public misfeasance, and discusses the justiciability of claims. It further examines the quantification aspects of damages claims, notably the recoverable losses (bid costs, lost profits and the compensation for lost chances) and judges' quantification methods.

6.1 Systemic Features of Procurement Claims

The following chapter provides an overview of damages claims in the United Kingdom.[1] This overview primarily covers England, Wales and Northern Ireland, but since the procurement directives are very similarly implemented in Scotland, the divergence between jurisdictions seems by and large negligible. The case law examined highlights the impression that a unitary interpretation is pursued in this specific area of law in relation to damages claims.[2]

---

[1] The main work on UK public procurement is S Arrowsmith, *The Law of Public and Utilities Procurement,* 2nd edition (London, Sweet & Maxwell, 2005); the volume that includes remedies is forthcoming in 2015. Of relevance to practitioners: S Roe & D Harvey, 'Public Procurement 2011', in HJ Preiss (ed), *Getting the Deal Through: Public Procurement 2010* (London, Sweet & Maxwell, 2011). On damages in the UK: D Pachnou, *The Effectiveness of Bidder Remedies for Enforcing the EC Public Procurement Rules: A Case Study of the Public Works Sector in the United Kingdom and Greece* (Dissertation, University of Nottingham, 2003); M Bowsher & P Moser, 'Damages for breach of the EC public procurement rules in the United Kingdom' (2006) *Public Procurement Law Review*, 195; F Banks & M Bowsher, 'Damages Remedy in England & Wales and Northern Ireland', in D Fairgrieve & F Lichère (eds), *Public Procurement Law. Damages as an Effective Remedy* (Oxford, Hart Publishing, 2011); S Arrowsmith, *The Law of Public and Utilities Procurement,* ibid, pp 1379–1385 ; M Trybus, 'An Overview of the United Kingdom Public Procurement Review and Remedies System with an Emphasis on England and Wales', in S Treumer & F Lichère (eds), *Enforcement of the EU public procurement rules* (København, DJØF Publishing, 2011), 227–228 ; C Bovis, *EC public procurement: case law and regulation* (Oxford, Oxford University Press, 2006), 594. To the author's best knowledge there is a dearth of literature dealing specifically with the issue of the quantification and valuation of procurement damages. The findings in this chapter are therefore largely based on own research in the relevant case law databases.

[2] The reader is asked to excuse subsequent imprecisions on the matter.

© Springer International Publishing Switzerland 2016
H. Schebesta, *Damages in EU Public Procurement Law*, Studies in European Economic Law and Regulation 6, DOI 10.1007/978-3-319-23612-4_6

6.1.1 Sources of Law and Implementation of Directive 2007/66

In the UK,[3] the Public Contracts Regulation 2015[4] took effect on 26 February 2015. It implements Directive 2014/24 and re-enacts the relevant provisions of the Remedies Directives as implemented by the UK in the Public Contracts Regulations 2009.[5] Utilities procurement is governed by the Utilities Contracts Regulations 2006 (and subsequent amendments).[6]

Government contracts have historically been mainly unregulated in the UK, subject only to municipal guidelines which, however, would not create rights capable of being invoked in courts. Principles of judicial review were developed as a control mechanism for the exercise of administrative powers. Their application is disputed in public procurement, because judicial review was traditionally required to contain a 'public law element'.[7] Contracts concluded by governments were regarded as private contractual arrangements and consequently in many cases were not open for judicial review as they lacked the required public law element. The Regulations have been held to constitute a 'statutory scheme of relief' and, as in a private law situation, not to benefit from public judicial review.[8] For breaches of general public law duties, a legislative intention to grant a damages remedy will not regularly be implied.[9] In this respect, there was no general damages action for unlawful actions of public bodies. A tort for breach of a statutory duty requires a statutory instrument which confers a right to damages. Misfeasance in public office was the alternative, but the constitutive criteria giving rise to that tort were onerous as they required intentional conduct. Prior to the implementation of the Remedies Directive, section 19 of the Local Government Act 1988 provided the possibility of claiming damages for violations of the public procurement rules for an implied contract and potentially

---

[3] In Scotland, the Public Contracts and (Scotland) Regulations 2006 were consolidated and changed to accommodate the ECJ *Uniplex* ruling through the Public Contracts (Scotland) Regulations 2012 (SSI 2012 No 88) and the Utilities Contracts (Scotland) Regulations 2012 (SSI 2012 No 89).

[4] Public Contracts Regulations 2015 (SI 2015 No 102).

[5] Council Directive of 21 December 1989 on the coordination of the laws, regulations and administrative provisions to the application of review procedures to the award of public supply and public works contracts 89/665/EEC [1989] OJ L395, as amended by Directive 2007/66. The respective implementation measures for Directive 2007/66 were carried out through the Public Contracts (Amendment) Regulations (SI 2009 No 2992), and the Utilities Contracts (Amendment) Regulations (SI 2009 No 3100), followed by amendments undertaken through the Public Procurement (Miscellaneous Amendments) Regulations 2011, which contained minor modifications and brought the time limits for bringing proceedings in line with the CJEU ruling in Case C-406/08 *Uniplex (UK)Ltd v NHS Business Services Authority* [2010] ECR I-00817.

[6] See Utilities Contracts Regulations 2006 and amendments (SI 2006 No 6); and Utilities Contracts (Scotland) Regulations 2012 (SSI 2012 No 89).

[7] For an overview of the public law element variations with regards to procurement cases, see Arrowsmith, *The Law of Public and Utilities Procurement*, above n 1, pp 79–85.

[8] R. (on the application of Cookson & Clegg Ltd) v Ministry of Defence, in Bowsher & Moser, 'Damages for breach of the EC public procurement rules in the UK', above n 1, p 195.

[9] Arrowsmith, *The Law of Public and Utilities Procurement*, above n 1, p 1379.

allowed the recovery of bidding costs for the reason that a fair consideration of one's bid was implicit in a tender offer.[10]

Under the old Public Contracts Regulation, regulation 47C(2) created a statutory duty and stated that compliance with the regulations was *'a duty owed to an economic operator'*. The damages provision, in regulation 47J(2)(c), stated that the court *'may award damages to an economic operator which has suffered loss or damage as a consequence of the breach, regardless of whether the court also acts as described in sub-paragraphs (a) [declaration of ineffectiveness] and (b) [imposition of penalties]'*.[11] Substantively, no major changes were effected by Public Contracts Regulation 2015. Regulation 89 of the latter creates a statutory duty owed to an economic operator from the UK or from another EEA state. Damages may be awarded to an economic operator which has suffered loss or damage as a consequence of the breach where the contract has not been entered into,[12] and where the contract has been entered into regardless of whether ineffectiveness is declared or penalties are imposed.[13]

A particular damages clause is contained in regulation 45I of the Utilities Contracts Regulations 2006, which reflects the divergent approach that is also taken with respect to the damages provision in the Utilities Remedies Directive 92/50:

> (3) Where the Court is satisfied that an economic operator would have had a real chance of being awarded the contract if that chance had not been affected by the breach mentioned in paragraph(1)(a), the economic operator is entitled to damages amounting to its costs in preparing its tender and in participating in the procedure leading to the award of the contract.

The UK thus has no statutory regulation of damages that goes beyond the wording of the Remedies Directives, and the details on damages claims in public procurement are developed by case law.

6.1.2 Jurisdiction

Legal actions for procurement law violations are brought in first instance in front of the High Court of Justice,[14] with the option to appeal to the civil division of the Court of Appeal. After the Constitutional Reform Act 2005, the Supreme Court of

---

[10] This implied contract was examined in *Blackpool and Fylde Aero Club Ltd. v Blackpool B.C.* [1990] All E.R. 237. It also came up again in *Sidey Ltd v Clackmannanshire Council [2011]* ScotCS CSOH 194.

[11] For Scotland, see the identical provision regulation 48(b)(iii) Public Contracts (Scotland) Regulations 2012.

[12] Public Contracts Regulation 2015, reg 97(2)(c).

[13] Public Contracts Regulation 2015, reg 98(2)(c).

[14] Public Contracts Regulation 2015, regulation 91(2). This is usually the Queen's Bench Division, but sometimes its Technology and Construction Court element, wherein construction or engineering matters are dealt with. See Trybus, 'An overview of the United Kingdom Public Procurement Review and Remedies System with an Emphasis on England and Wales', above n 1, p 203.

the UK became the court of last instance.[15] The procedural rules are contained in the Civil Procedure Rules 1998.[16]

6.2 Causes of Action for Damages Claims

The constitutive requirements under English law depend on the action chosen to pursue a claim. *Harmon*[17] is the main authority in relation to a successful claim for damages in the area of public procurement and remains unmatched in its systemic consideration of the various actions for damages claims open to an aggrieved tenderer. It comprises a discussion of three concurrent possible causes of action in English law that allow the bringing of a successful damages claim: (1) breach of statutory duty (UK Public Works Regulations and EU Directives) and the EU Treaties, (2) implied contract, and (3) misfeasance in public office.

The *Harmon* dispute was a very important one in monetary terms, regarding the fenestration of the exterior wall of the UK Parliament in Westminster. The aggrieved bidder alleged several violations by the contracting authority and that the House of Commons had illegally awarded the contract to a competitor. It is clear that the House of Commons in several important respects failed to follow public procurement rules. It advertised the contract under 'overall value for money', without specifying further criteria. Therefore, the lowest price would have to be the decisive factor. The House then accepted a variant of Seele/Alvis, even though this made significant design changes. The House encouraged a 'buy British' policy (unlawfully), applied arbitrary methods to favor the Seele/Alvis tender, and entered into unlawful post-tender negotiations. It then failed to set out the true reasons for its rejection of Harmon's bid in the notification letter to Harmon.

6.2.1 Breach of Statutory Duty

The regular action for claiming damages for violations of the Procurement Regulations is an action for a breach of statutory duty. A statutory duty of compliance with procurement law is established:

---

[15] Or the Court of Session of the Sheriff Court for Scotland. On public contract litigation, see P Craig & M Trybus, 'Angleterre et Pays de Galles/England and Wales', in R Noguellou et al (eds), *Droit comparé des contrats publics* (Bruylant, 2010), p 357.

[16] Civil Procedure Rules 1998 (SI 1998 No. 3132).

[17] *Harmon CFEM Facades (UK) Ltd v The Corporate Officer of the House of Commons* [1999] EWHC Technology 199 (the '*Harmon*' case). See also, S Arrowsmith, 'EC Procurement Rules in the UK Courts: An Analysis of the Harmon case: Part 2' (2000) *Public Procurement Law Review* 135.

Duty owed to economic operators from EEA states

89. – (1) This regulation applies to the obligation on a contracting authority to comply with
–

(a) the provisions of Part 2; and
(b) any enforceable EU obligation in the field of public procurement in respect of a
contract or design contest falling within the scope of Part 2.

(2) That obligation is a duty owed to an economic operator from the United Kingdom or
from another EEA state.[18]

In *Harmon*, breach of statutory duty was the point of departure for the violation
of the Regulations. The House of Commons was held to have breached the Public
Works Contracts Regulations 1991 and obligations under principles of EU law.

6.2.2 Implied Contract

In addition, *Harmon* confirmed the case law that initially developed the doctrine of
implied contract in public procurement damages. In this particular case, the implied
contract doctrine resulted from considerations of fairness and equality in competitive tenders:

25 It may not be difficult to conclude that the first part of the contract contended for by the
petitioners, that is consideration of tenders in accordance with principles of fairness and
equality, was indeed the intention of both parties. That conclusion must, almost inevitably,
flow from my consideration of the public law remedies sought by the petitioners.[19]
…it is now clear in English law that in the public sector where competitive tenders are
sought and responded to, a contract comes into existence whereby the prospective employer
impliedly agrees to consider all tenderers fairly.[20]

The *Harmon* case clearly supported the theoretical possibilities for an implied
contract based on principles of fairness and equality of treatment. The precise conditions giving rise to such a contract remain open. In the 1990 *Blackpool* case, the
court had set a relatively high threshold for implying a contract:

I readily accept that contracts are not to be lightly implied. Having examined what the parties
said and did, the court must be able to conclude with confidence both that the parties intended
to create contractual relations and that the agreement was to the effect contended for.[21]

Based on the *Blackpool* case, *Harmon* repeated that an invitation to tender is not
normally an offer, and for an implied contract to arise, additional criteria must be
met. Several characteristics of the procedure were taken into account: the type of
procedure was considered (it was a restricted procedure), and additionally, the fact

---

[18] Public Contracts Regulation 2015, reg 89.

[19] *Sidey Ltd*, above n 10.

[20] *Harmon CFEM Facades*, above n 17, p 216.

[21] *Blackpool and Fylde*, above n 10, p 1202F–G.

that the procedure of the statutory regime in the Public Works Regulation was not followed (the contracting authorities had discussions with one tender, going beyond mere negotiations or clarification). In the recited case law, implied duties recognized by the court oscillate somewhere between 'considering' all tenders duly received (*Blackpool*), acting 'reasonably' (*Fairclough*) or merely according to views 'honestly held' (*Pratt*).[22] In *Harmon*, the court extended the implied duties to principles of fairness and equality as part of a preliminary contract.[23] The following implied terms were found: (a) submitted alternatives would be considered alongside a compliant, revised tender from that tenderer; (b) any alternative would only be alternative in detail, and not of an entirely changed design; and (c) tenderers who responded would be treated equally and fairly.[24]

Since then, several cases have rejected the argument that an implied contract had arisen. Plaintiffs in *Sidey* argued a breach of an implied contract,[25] but the court found that the notion of being 'economically advantageous' *'lack[ed] the necessary degree of precision to qualify as an implied term'*.[26]

In recent cases, the judges have shown themselves to be reluctant to accept breach of an implied contract, this severely challenges the notion that implied contracts can be applicable in cases governed by the regulations. In *Varney*, the Court held that *'the Regulations create their own regime imposing duties on the Council in relation to any tender submitted. Given that legal regime, it is unnecessary to imply a contract and none will be implied.'*[27] In *JBW Group*, the court held that it would be inconsistent with the purpose of the Directive to imply any such contract.[28] In *Willmott*, the court equally decided that there was *'no room for the implication of any contract'* since the case was governed by the Regulations.[29]

---

[22] See Arrowsmith, *The Law of Public and Utilities Procurement*, above n 1, pp 107–113 and references in fn 22.

[23] Arrowsmith advances an interesting argument as to the unilateral or bilateral nature of the implied contract. If the contract were recognized as a bilateral relationship, certain duties could be incumbent not only on the contracting authority, but also on the tenderers. See ibid.

[24] See answers to Issue 7 in *Harmon Facades,* above n 17 and in particular paras 214–218.

[25] Citing Blackpool and Fylde, above n 10, p1202; Fairclough Building Ltd v Port Talbot Borough Council [1992] 62 BLR 86, p 28; Nolan LJ, p33; Harmon CFEM Facades, above n 17, paras 206, 214 and 216; Pratt Contractors Ltd v Transit New Zealand, paras 44, 47 and 49; J & A Developments Ltd v Edina Manufacturing Ltd, paras 4, 38 and 50. See also, *Sidey Ltd*, above n 10, para 11.

[26] "Economically advantageous' is a term which is highly likely to be dependent upon the subjective stance of the party considering the question. I would find it difficult to see that parties in the position of the petitioners and respondents would agree on such a subjective term without further definition and qualification.' See *Sidey Ltd*, above n 10, para 25.

[27] J Varney & Sons v Hertfordshire CC [2010] EWHC 1404 (QB), paras 233–235.

[28] JBW Group Ltd v Ministry of Justice [2012] EWCA Civ 8, para 59.

[29] Willmott Dixon Partnership Ltd V London Borough of Hammersmith and Defendant Fulham [2014] EWHC 3191 (TCC) (09 October 2014), paras 236 and further.

6.2.3 Misfeasance in Public Office

Misfeasance in public office was an additional possible cause of action recognized in *Harmon* through which an aggrieved tenderer could claim damages. Generally, this tort requires an intentional unlawful act or omission risking injury.[30] Due to the 'bad faith' requirement, this cause of action is regarded as quite onerous, and only rarely delivers any advantages to an aggrieved tenderer.[31]

In *Harmon*[32] the court considered misfeasance, building on the authority of the *Three Rivers*[33] case in order to assess the knowledge that acts were unlawful and knowledge or foresight of the probable injury to the plaintiff. The court concluded that the main person responsible for the new parliamentary building project, Mr. Makepeace, was to be regarded as a public official and continued: 'In my judgment, it is thus clear that Mr. Makepeace had more than merely well founded doubts about the propriety of the process leading to the award of the contract to Seele/Alvis for Option B2 without proper competition'.[34] Although Mr. Makepeace was aware of legal problems, he did not seek legal advice. In that, he was at least to be regarded as reckless.[35] Therefore, misfeasance in public office was an additional head under which the House of Commons was held liable.[36]

6.2.4 The Lost Chance in the UK as a Causality Criterion

Instead of the balance of probabilities, *Harmon* addressed causality through the lost chance theory. The court applied *Allied Maples Group*.[37] For the heads of damages for both lost profits and bid costs, the question boiled down to causality, namely

---

[30] Arrowsmith, *The Law of Public and Utilities Procurement*, above n 1, pp 1379–1380.

[31] Bowsher & Moser, 'Damages for breach of the EC public procurement rules in the UK', above n 1, p 195.

[32] *Harmon Facades*, above n 17, paras 241–256.

[33] *Three Rivers District Council v Bank of England* [1999] EU LR 211. The categories by which to assess knowledge are actual knowledge, willfully shutting one's eyes to the obvious or willfully and recklessly failing to make inquires that an honest and reasonable man would make.

[34] *Harmon Facades*, above n 17, para 256.

[35] The incident also entailed a parliamentary investigation published in the *Report of the Inquiry into Harmon v Corporate Officer of the House of Commons* by Sir Thomas Legg and Mr Peter Bosworth. See www.parliament.uk/documents/foi/foi-2012-Sir-Thomas-Legg-report-March-2000-F12-349.pdf.

[36] Deceit is another possible cause of action, which was considered in *Montpellier Estates Ltd v Leeds City Council* [2013] WL 425703. Again, the burden of proof is so onerous that breaches of the regulations are probably easier to establish. A possible advantage might lie in the much longer time limits.

[37] *Allied Maples Group v Simmons & Simmons* [1995] 3 All ER 907, pp 914–916. In Allied Maples Group, Stuart Smith L.J. had distinguished three scenarios to establish the causal link. The first is the question of causation as a historical fact, or its dependence on future uncertain events.

whether or not Harmon could show that it would have been awarded the contract. The court stated:

> In summary therefore Harmon is entitled to recover its tender costs, taken by themselves, on the grounds that it ought to have been awarded the contract and would then have recovered its costs. If, notwithstanding, H of C had decided to place the contract elsewhere then Harmon would have been deprived of the chance of recovering its costs. I assess that chance as virtually certain – say 90 % – for I do not consider H of C would have been so perverse as not to accept Harmon's tender. It is not therefore truly an expression of a chance for the purposes of "loss of a chance" but more of probability. If H of C had decided to go for some other course such as to award the contract on the basis of a version of Option B2, but after giving the other tenderers the opportunity to tender on the basis of that option or to award it on the basis of a performance specification complying with certain design criteria but with the detailed design being provided by the tenderer, I consider Harmon would have stood as good a chance as any and better than most of being awarded the contract. Unlike the primary scenario (lowest price) there can be no certainty but there is surely a real and substantive chance that Harmon would have been awarded the contract. I therefore assess its chance of doing as 70 %. (I develop my reasons later.) I consider it quite improbable that H of C would run the risks inherent in starting all over again, but would have accepted Harmon's tender which was the lowest. Harmon's capabilities were denigrated solely to advance Seele/Alvis and Option B2.[38]

In *Letting International*, the court held that the claimant has to show that it has suffered 'the loss of a significant chance of obtaining the contract'[39] Since then, causality between breach and loss is regularly addressed through the lost chance theory. The general rule applied in *Mears* was the following:

> The bidder will be able to show that a breach of duty will cause him to suffer loss or damage, or the risk of loss or damage, if he had a chance (which the law recognises sufficiently good to merit consideration) that if the breach had not been committed, the contract would be awarded to it and the breach causes the bidder to lose that chance: Matra Communications SA v Home Office.[40]

However, *Harmon* does not have a large number of successful follow-up cases. The *Mears* case is one of the few cases in which the court entitled the claimant to damages for the lost chance. In the case, the Leeds City Council had run a competitive dialogue procedure for the maintenance of public housing stock. The claimant Mears went through the selection stage, but did not reach the final bid stage. The court found that Leeds had committed several breaches in the procurement procedure, after which the court proceeded to assess the chances for several alleged breaches independently. It found:

> At this stage I consider that there is a real or significant, rather than a fanciful chance that Mears would have been successful given that Mears and the other tenderers were not provided with the weightings to be applied and with knowledge of the correct weightings the

---

The causality of these two ought to be judged according to the balance of probabilities test. In a third category, involving the hypothetical actions of third parties, the plaintiff only needed to succeed in showing that he had a 'substantial chance rather than a speculative one'.

[38] *Harmon Facades*, above n 17, para 266.

[39] *Letting International Ltd v Newham* LBC [2008] WL 2696950, para 141.

[40] *Mears Ltd v Leeds City Council* (No 2) [2011] EWHC 1031 (TCC), para 209.

tenderers would have had the opportunity to concentrate on the answers to the questions which gave the greater share of the marks. Mr. Small's analysis for the questions where Mears complained about the Model Answers shows that Mears would have been able to narrow the gap but not sufficiently to achieve third place, just by taking account of those limited questions. That supports the view that, on the current evidence, there is more than a fanciful chance. Such a finding does not pre-determine what might be the outcome on a full analysis but is sufficient for me to decide that, in principle, Mears is entitled to relief under the Regulations.[41]

Not every breach has the required material effect on the position of a tenderer, and hence not every breach results in the possibility of an action for damages. For example, where a breach was limited and would have made no difference to the outcome of the tendering process, the court rejected the argument that the tenderer had suffered damages as a consequence of that breach.[42] In *Edenred*, the judge considered the position of aggrieved bidder's potential rivals, and concluded that it was 'fanciful to suppose that Edenred would have persuaded HMRC that it was better placed' than competitors.[43] The aggrieved bidder has to prove that it would have suffered any loss as a result of a breach:

on well-established principles that means that Edenred had to satisfy the court that there was a real, as opposed to fanciful, prospect that if it bid for a contract to deliver childcare accounts, it would have been awarded the contract. A real prospect means just that; it does not mean more than 50 %, and previous cases have encompassed awards of damages where the lost chance has been evaluated as low as 17 %.[44]

Therefore, even if there had been a breach, the claim was dismissed as claimant was unable to demonstrate that it suffered any loss.

6.2.5 *Adequacy of Damages in Interlocutory Proceedings*

An important and damages-related line of cases concerns injunctions. In an application for interlocutory injunctions, three tests have to be satisfied. The first is that a serious issue must be tried. Secondly, it must be assessed whether damages are an adequate remedy for the party requesting an injunction and thirdly where the general balance of convenience lies. The basic position in English law is that if damages are an adequate remedy, an application for an interim injunction will normally fail (main authority *American Cyanamid*[45]). Under the adequacy of damages doctrine,

---

[41] ibid, para 214.

[42] *J Varney & Sons Waste Management Ltd v Hertfordshire* CC [2010] WL 2131723.

[43] *Edenred (UK Group) Ltd v Her Majesty's Treasury & Ors* [2015] EWHC 90 (QB). The court continued: 'Edenred bidding for a single provider award by HMRC would not have stood a chance against an independently regulated private sector organization such as a clearing bank' and 'In the alternative scenario where Edenred would be bidding for the provision of support services to NS&I so as to enable NS&I to provide the accounts to HMRC, its chances of successfully outbidding Atos or another BPO are even more remote'. Ibid, para 159.

[44] ibid, p 142.

[45] *American Cyanamid Co v Ethicon Ltd* [1975] AC 396.

several relevant judgments rose. In *Letting International*, the difficulty in assessing the value of a lost chance was one factor that persuaded the court to grant an injunction: '*A loss of an opportunity to take part in a fair tendering process on equal terms with other bidders may be difficult to evaluate in monetary terms but cannot be said to be on no commercial value at all.*'[46] Also in *Morrisons*, the difficulty in assessing damages resulted in inadequacy of a damages remedy: '*in a case where one of the complaints is that of undisclosed criteria, it is very difficult indeed for the court at trial, to assess damages because assessment of what chance has been lost by the claimant, in those circumstances, is virtually impossible.*'[47] Although the respective judgments are not damages claims, the cases show that courts on one hand consider lost chances to hold compensable value, but on the other hand, there is widespread recognition that it is particularly difficult to quantitatively assess chances in a damages action.

6.3 Justiciability of Damages Claims

6.3.1 Informing the Contracting Authority Prior to Damages Claim Is No Longer Necessary

Prior to the Amendment Regulations of 2009 which transposed Directive 2007/66, aggrieved tenderers had to inform the contracting authority – before pursuing litigation – of their intention to bring proceedings under the Regulations, pursuant to old 47(7)(a).[48] The information given had to identify the regulation[49] and the alleged breaches.[50] This requirement has since been dropped. The requirement in

---

[46] *Letting International*, above n 39, para 36.

[47] Morrisons Facilities Services Ltd v Norwich City Council [2010] EWHC 487 (Ch).

[48] The regulation stated:

   (7) Proceedings under this regulation must not be brought unless – (a) the economic operator bringing the proceedings has informed the contracting authority or concessionaire, as the case may be, of the breach or apprehended breach of the duty owed to it in accordance with paragraph (1) or (2) by that contracting authority or concessionaire and of its intention to bring proceedings under this regulation in respect of it; and (b) those proceedings are brought promptly and in any event within 3 months from the date when grounds for the bringing of the proceedings first arose unless the Court considers that there is good reason for extending the period within which proceedings may be brought.

[49] See para 48 of *M Holleran Ltd v Severn Trent Water Ltd* M Holleran Ltd v Severn Trent Water Ltd [2004] EWHC 2508 (Comm), referring to *Luck* v *London Borough Tower Hamlets* [2003] 2 CMLR 12.

[50] For the requirement to have brought a complaint, see *Luck*, ibid (discussing the information requirement which used to be 32(4) of the 1993 Regulations). The Court found that plaintiff had not complied with information duties in para 32: 'In the present case the solicitors' letters identified neither the regulation in question ('this regulation', ie reg 32 of the 1993 Regulations), nor 'the breach or apprehended breach of the duty owed to him. Therefore, subject to the next issue, any

regulation 92(6) now dictates that 'proceedings are to be regarded as started when the claim form is issued.'

6.3.2   De minimis/*Threshold*

For an EU law obligation to arise, either the financial thresholds of the Regulations must be met, or the contract must have a certain cross-border interest.[51] This is of consequence for the remedy of damages to be available. For example the defendants in *Sidey* argued that '[t]he breach of a legitimate expectation did not give rise to a right in damages and gave no more to a right to a declaratory conclusion.'[52] In *Sidey*, the court concluded against a cross-border interest, and based this on the nature and the value of the contract, but also on the professional appreciation of the respondent's procurement officer.[53]

6.3.3   *Standing*

Regulation 91(1) of the Public Contracts Regulations 2015 states that a breach of the duty owed is 'actionable by any economic operator which, in consequence, suffers, or risks suffering, loss or damage'. The court referred to the Advocate General in *Nachrichtenagentur GMBH* C-454/06[54] in a case challenging the London ticketing service, judging that the possibility of harm must be presumed where not manifestly excluded.[55]

---

claim under the Regulations is barred.' The issue of whether the claimant has properly informed the authorities was also dealt with in eg, *Keymed Ltd* v *Forest Healthcare NHS Trust* [1998] EuLR 71, 90–91. The same rule in Utilities Regulation 32(4)(a) was considered in *Holleran Ltd*, above n 49.

[51] The Court applied the CJEU Joined Cases C-147/06 and C-148/06 *SECAP and Santorso* [2008] ECR I-3565 in *Sidey Ltd*, Re Judicial Review [2011] ScotCS CSOH 194, finding that there was no cross border interest.

[52] *Sidey Ltd*, above n 10, para 13.

[53] *Sidey Ltd*, above n 10, para 19: 'It seems to me that such employees familiar both with the nature and scope of the contract in question and with the placing of contracts of this sort in general would be likely to be aware whether or not a contract had the potential to generate any cross border interest.'

[54] C-454/06 *Pressetext Nachrichtenagentur GmbH v Republik Österreich (Bund), APA-OTS Originaltext-Service GmbH and APA Austria Presse Agentur registrierte Genossensschaft mit beschränkter Haftung* [2008] ECLI:EU:C:2008:351.

[55] *Pressetext Nachrichtenagentur GmbH, ibid,* Opinion of the Advocate General, C-454/06, *ECLI:EU:C:2008:167,* especially paras 143 and 148. She pointed out that limited standing for applicants who had an interest in the relevant contract and who could show existing or imminent harm served to exclude applicants with no prospect of success but 'the possibility of harm … must

6.3.4   Time Limits

The 2011 Amendments changed the general time limit within which any court proceedings are to be started. The new time limit is set at 30 days from the date when
the economic operator 'first knew or ought to have known that grounds for starting
the proceedings had arisen'.[56] The courts have discretion to extend this time limit
where they consider that there is a good reason for doing so,[57] but not to more than
3 months after the date when the economic operator had knowledge. The
Amendments take into account the judgment of the CJEU in *Uniplex* which held
certain features of the previously applicable time limits to be incompatible with
EU Law.[58]

The time limits as provided for in the Regulations are now brought into line with
respect to the starting point, which ordinarily requires 'knowledge' of the breach
(i.e. under s. 14A of the Limitation Act 1980). It was further disputed as to which
event 'grounds' refers to, i.e. knowledge of the infringement only or also of the
resulting consequences and losses.[59]

The question remains as to how the shorter statutory time limit should be read in
relation to the longer time periods for both breach of statutory duty and implied
contract – they both have a 6 year prescription period. The courts have been reluctant
to extend the time limits on such grounds. A line of cases had to consider the contractual

---

be presumed where it is not manifestly excluded'. See *Electronic Data Systems Ltd v Transport Trading Ltd* [2008] EWHC 2105 (QB), para 21.

[56] Public Contracts Regulations 2015, regulation 92(2).

[57] The reasons for exercising discretion are 'the length of and reason for any delay; the extent to which the plaintiff is to blame for any delay; the extent to which the defendant may have induced or contributed to the delay; and whether the defendant has been or will be prejudiced by the delay or the grant of an extension'. See *Keymed*, above n 50, p 96B. It was also examined in *Gillen & Anor v Inverclyde Council* [2010] ScotCS CSOH 19. See also, *Dekra Eireann Teoranta v Minister for the Environment and Local Government* [2003] IESC 25 ('In exercising its discretion in such applications the court retains its duty to protect the right of access to the courts. However, there are special weightings which must be given. Thus the requirement under European and Irish law that such applications be brought rapidly is important. So too is the nature of the contract under review. This public contract calls into play the special importance of time and thus the nature of the prejudice to the parties if they are delayed. The court may also consider any prejudice to the public, the common good.')

[58] The 2006 Regulations provided that proceedings must be brought within 3 months, but open the possibility of either shortening or lengthening that time period – where there is good reason to do so, or on the other hand, restricting it in cases where a tenderer may not be evaluated to have acted 'promptly'; enough, ie Regulation 2006 old Article 47(7)(b). Uniplex was applied in the Sita case, above n 10.

[59] An application for damages was time-barred in Sita. See *Sita UK*, ibid, para 30: 'He [counsel of pursuer] says that as a matter of construction that includes not merely the infringement (of which the complainant now has to be aware) but also the fact that loss has been caused.'. The standard was held to be 'knowledge of the facts which apparently clearly indicate, though they need not absolutely prove, an infringement.'

claims due to the divergent time limits of implied contract claims (6 years) as opposed to Regulations claims (now 30 days). In this context, in *Montpellier Estates*,[60] the court held that the implied contract action could not be used to extend the applicable time limits under the Regulations. The court stated in relying on decisions in *JBW Group, Lion Apparel* and *Varney*:

> 465 LCC accepts that a contracting authority may be under an implied obligation to consider tenders in good faith, however Mr. Williams submits that the implication of further obligations are not necessary to give efficacy to the contract, nor could there be a common intention that any implied obligations should extend further than the duties imposed upon the contracting authority by virtue of the EU public procurement regime. In short, he submits, the implied contract adds nothing to the claim.
>
> 466 In JBW Group Ltd v Ministry of Justice [2012] EWCA Civ 8; [2012] 2 CMLR 10, Elias LJ stated:
>
> 58. [The applicant] accepted that if he had succeeded in establishing that there was a service contract, this would add nothing to his case. It would then be unnecessary to imply any contract. Initially he suggested that even then the implied contract argument might entitle him to bring a claim for six years rather than within the much stricter three-month period permitted under the Directive. However, in reply he resiled from that position and conceded that it would be inconsistent with the purpose of the Directive to imply any such contractual right.
>
> 59. That concession was, in my view, rightly made and is consistent with the decisions of two first-instance judges, Morgan J in Lion Apparel Systems Ltd v Firebuy Ltd [2007] EWHC 2179 (Ch) at [212] and Flaux J in J Varney and Sons Waste Management Ltd v Hertfordshire CC [2010] EWHC 1404 (QB) at [232]-[235] citing Monro v Revenue and Customs Commissioners [2008] EWCA Civ 306.
>
> 467 Accordingly, MEL cannot use an implied contract to extend the three-month limitation period in the Regulations. In any event I agree with Mr. Williams that the implied contract claim adds nothing to the claim under the Regulations.

The courts are not inclined to waive the 30 day time limit. Overall, there appears to be a rather large number of damages claims which have been regarded as time-barred or in which an aggrieved tenderer failed to satisfy the old notification requirement.

6.3.5   Access to Documents

Discovery in procurement proceedings was discussed in *Croft House Care*[61] and the judge found that, in principle, tender documents may be confidential, in particular where third parties' tender submissions are concerned. In *Science Research Council v Nassé*,[62] the court held that 'the ultimate test is whether disclosure and inspection

---

[60] See *Montpellier Estates*, above n 36. In an initial application to strike out parts of the claim, the Court had rejected the application holding that *Harmon* was the authority for the potential of an implied contract to arise.

[61] *Croft House Care Ltd & Ors v Durham County Council* [2010] EWHC 909 (TCC).

[62] *Science Research Council v Nassé* [1980] AC 1028.

is necessary for disposing fairly of the proceedings.' The court referred to this test again in para 34 of *Croft House Care*:

> The principle as set out in Science Research Council v Nassé [1980] AC 1028 requires a balancing exercise. Similarly in the Varec case [2008] ECR I-581, para 47 it was said that there had to be balance between the right to confidentiality and the need for the claims to be disposed of fairly. As Coulson J pointed out in Amaryllis v HM Treasury (No 2) [2009] BLR 425, *374 para 52 the ruling in the Varec case is simply a case where, in considering the public interest in open administration of justice and the interest in maintaining commercial confidentiality, the facts of that case led the court to find that the commercial confidentiality of the businesses' secrets outweighed the other interest.

Although the judge considered the CJEU's ruling in the *Varec* case, it distinguished it on the grounds of the different interests at stake. *Varec* balanced the public interest in open administration of justice with commercial confidentiality. In *Croft House Care,* on the other hand, the balancing concerned 'the right of third parties to confidentiality against the necessity for the documents to be provided for the purpose of a fair trial'.[63] Based on the facts, the *Croft House Care* case differed because of the unaccomplished state of the procurement process therein, which would have meant that disclosure would inhibit the possibility of conducting the tendering process again properly.

Elaborate discussions have taken place concerning a so-called confidentiality ring, in particular the practical impossibility of this option in small business circles, where it would be difficult to appoint one director with confidentially oversight who would consequently not be involved in future tenders.

> 66. I have therefore come to the conclusion on the facts of this case that the need for an effective review of the procurement process, including as part of that review, the need in this case under CPR Part 31 for documents to be disclosed to and inspected by the directors and personnel of the Claimants if there is to be a fair hearing, is dominant in the balancing exercise which I have to perform. I do not accept that there is any insurmountable difficulty or impracticality in the Council re-running, if necessary, the procurement process though they will certainly need to review that process in the light of any decision which has then been made by the court and the extent to which information has been provided to and reviewed by some potential tenderers and not others. That however is all part of the necessary decision which the Council would have to make when deciding on the principles and details of any new procurement process.
>
> 67. What is not acceptable is that a party should be precluded from an effective remedy because of concerns that, if the remedy is granted, there may be difficulties in re-running the procurement process. Whilst in some cases it might be necessary and permissible to impose a confidentiality ring, that is not a solution which can apply to the Claimants in the circumstances of this case. Such a process would be unfair to the Claimants who are small family businesses without large and elaborate administrative structures and where the appointment of a person to act within the confidentiality ring is not a practical possibility.[64]

The cases of discovery are too extensive to cover exhaustively. However, the selected samples are a good indication of the kind of balancing the courts undertake

---

[63] *Croft House*, above n 61, para 43.

[64] S Roe & D Harvey, 'Public Procurement 2012', in HJ Priess (ed), *Public Procurement* (London, Law Business Research, 2012).

and the fact that procedural justice values are inherent in the kinds of compromises struck. The nature of the enterprise is one closely related to the facts at issue, and this illustrates the particularization function of procedural law – i.e. the tailoring of applicable laws to the individual circumstances of individual cases.

6.4   Quantification

As noted, *Harmon* remains the principal decision in a successful damages suit. Many damages claims have failed due to time limits[65] or the old notification requirement,[66] while in others, no (sufficient) violation of the procurement rules was determined.[67] In *Mears*, the court found the plaintiff to deserve damages, but did not enter into a discussion of the extent of the latter. Among the already small number of cases it is even rarer for the court to enter into the question of heads of damages. *Aquatron* is such a case; the court awarded lost profits and proceeded to quantify the award.

6.4.1   Available Heads of Damages

The judge in *Harmon* held that it was not necessary to distinguish the bases of the claims (i.e. statutory breach or other obligations) in order to assess the damages.[68]

6.4.1.1   Tender Costs and Lost Profit

If damages are assessed on the basis of tort, then the claimant is to be put in the position that s/he would have been in had the tort not occurred. The question is whether this means that the positive lawful act replaces the wrongful action or not. For tendering procedures, this translates into a drastic change in the hypothetical assessment of the claimant's position: s/he is put in a position as though the tender procedure had never occurred. This would typically mean the possibility of recovering bid costs, but only those. In the alternative scenario, where the position is the lawful continuation of the tender procedure, lost profits would be awarded, but calculated as income through the contract, minus costs. The correct hypothetical

---

[65] See eg, *Sita UK*, above n 58.

[66] See eg, *Gillen & Anor*, above n 57.

[67] See eg, *Brent London Borough Council v Risk Management Partners Ltd* [2009] EWCA 490. In lower instances the damages claim was upheld, but judgment was overturned by the Supreme Court, stating that the contracting authority would be allowed to benefit from the *Teckal* exemption.

[68] See *Harmon Facades*, above n 17, p 302.

comparator is also subject to some disagreement in the UK.[69] In Harmon, the court stated that where compensation is sought by a tenderer for being deprived of an opportunity to be awarded the contract, the approach should be to award damages on a contractual basis rather than a tortious one,[70] except for the lost chance, which would be in tort rather than contract.[71]

In the *Harmon* case, the general issue was whether the plaintiff was entitled to recover tender costs, gross margin, or loss of profit damages.[72] In *Harmon II*, the judge made clear that '[h]ad Harmon been awarded the contract then it would have recovered the costs of tendering from the amounts paid to it under the contract. Accordingly this claim is relevant only if nothing is awarded in respect of loss of gross margin'.[73] The claim for bid costs is therefore subsidiary to claiming the gross margin.

For both tender costs and gross margin the judge held that the aggrieved bidder has to show that it would have been awarded the contract. The question whether the aggrieved bidder would have been awarded the contract differed according to the hypothetical chosen, on the basis of the lowest price (one option), this was regarded by the judge to be virtually certain, while for the other it is still a real and substantive chance (eg. 70 % in this case). The judge further specified that this was not an assessment of the 'strength' of a chance, but an expression of probability. Both are indicators on the probability (not a real chance as the judge explains) that make for sufficient causation and therefore the argument that Harmon would have been awarded the contract.

Consequently, the judge answered the issues whether the breaches caused the plaintiff to sustain a loss in terms of bid costs or gross margin/profit loss in the affirmative.[74]

6.4.1.2   Lost Chance

In *Harmon*, it was made clear that the lost chance damages would be awarded only in case that Harmon should not have been awarded the contract; such damages would be calculated on the basis of tort rather than contract. In the event that damages would be awarded for the lost chance proper, the hypothetical situation is determined not with reference to determining which of the bids that Harmon

---

[69] Arrowsmith interprets the rightful position to be one in which the procedure would have been lawfully conducted. See Arrowsmith, *The Law of Public and Utilities Procurement*, above n 1, p 1381. This is criticizable from a contractual point of view under fn 81, citing Bowsher, arguing that damages ought to be limited to bidding costs, as though the procedure had not occurred. This view is based on the argument that a contracting authority cannot be required (from a private law point of view) to award a contract at all.

[70] *Harmon Facades*, above n 17, p 259.

[71] ibid, answers to issue 19.

[72] ibid, answers to issue 26.

[73] *Harmon CFEM Facades (UK) Ltd v. The Corporate Officer of the House of Commons* [2000] EWHC Technology 84, para 18 [hereinafter '*Harmon II*'].

[74] *Harmon Facades*, above n 17, issue 11.

submitted would have been selected. The hypothetical of the lost chance is therefore more abstract than the calculation of the gross margin.[75] The judge assessed the lost chance as a 35 % probability that the profit would have been earned, taking into account risk and hazards inherent in construction work.[76]

In a later case, *Aquatron*, the court proceeded to award damages for lost profits. The bid submitted by the tenderer was for a 3-year contract for service and repair of breathing apparatus compressors to be tendered in an open procedure. The contract was to be awarded under the 'economically most advantageous' option, which requires the call for tenders to specify the criteria to be used in the evaluation. As the contracting authority used criteria which had not been previously specified, it had breached the Procurement Regulations. After establishing the breaches, the court continued to examine whether 'losses flowed to the pursuers as a result of their exclusion prior to the evaluation stage'.[77] The court proceeded to make a comparative evaluation of the tenders between Aquatron (claimant) and MB Air Systems (the other remaining competitor). The court found that none of the published criteria were pertinent for a contract such as the one at issue – with the exception of the price criterion. Therefore, the price was regarded by the court to be the only decisive criterion for the hypothetical comparative evaluation of tenders. Since Aquatron's bid was lower, the court concluded that it should have been awarded the contract.

Interestingly, the court proceeded to make an *a contrario* argument: 'Even if a much wider number of considerations were permissible, such as quality and technical merit, the pursuers' tender *would still have stood at least an even chance* of acceptance and I would have regarded it as open to the court *to make an award for the loss of such a chance* on the basis that a claim for loss of a chance to obtain a contract is included in averments claiming the full contract value. I would have assessed this loss at half of that contract value.'[78]

Overall, the cases in which lost profits have successfully been awarded remain isolated. However, in several instances the courts have only ruled on the liability of the contracting authority, leaving the assessment of damages to a potential settlement process.

6.4.1.3 Aggravated Damages

In *Harmon*, the aggrieved tenderer claimed damages not only regarding bid costs and lost profit, but also aggravated/exemplary damages. The latter was refused, and the judge did not award aggravated damages because it was 'a bad case but not exceptional (…) and not unconstitutional'.[79] However, in principle, misfeasance actions can give rise to aggravated damages.

---

[75] ibid, issue 20.

[76] ibid, issue 21.

[77] *Aquatron Marine (t/a Quatron Breathing Air Systems) v Stratchyde Fire Board* [2007] ScotCS CSOH 185, para 93.

[78] ibid, para 103.

[79] *Harmon Facades*, above n 17, para 359.

6.4.1.4 Interest Rates in the UK[80]

There is overall uncertainty and broad discretion enjoyed by the courts with regard to interest rates generally, and also to claims in public procurement disputes.

CPR rule 16.4(1)(b) and (2) require the claimant to state that he is seeking interest, on what basis and for what periods, at what rate. In the *Harmon* litigation, for example, the question of the applicability of interest was raised by both parties, although the issue was excluded. The applicants applied for an 8 % statutory margin, while for example in respect of tender costs, the defendant had offered Harmon an interim payment that was based at 2.5 % above the base rate of 1 July 1995.[81]

6.4.1.5 Legal Costs

The successful plaintiff does not always recover all legal costs connected to a procurement action. The cost order can be reduced, as happened in *Mears*:

> … a proportionate costs order was appropriate to reflect the extent to which the successful party had not been selective in the points it had taken and should not recover all of its costs, Multiplex Constructions (UK) Ltd v Cleveland Bridge UK Ltd [2008] EWHC 2280 (TCC), 122 Con. L.R. 88 and BSkyB Ltd v HP Enterprise Services UK Ltd [2010] EWHC 862 (TCC), 131 Con. L.R. 42 applied. A substantial discount of 65 per cent was required to reflect the significant issues on which the local authority had succeeded balanced against the fact that M was the successful party overall.[82]

Therefore the legal costs can take into account the success of plaintiffs in the overall number of claims.

6.4.2 Valuation

In *Harmon*, the judge discussed many damages issues, but main quantification questions were excluded, such as those concerning the costs of the bid preparation, what the gross margin was and which components thereof were recoverable. Was the plaintiff entitled to damages through a gross margin or by reference to the profit that would have been earned if it had carried out the fenestration tender? And, on the basis of the lost chance, if damages were made out to be a proportion of gross margin or lost profit, what proportion ought this to be?[83] In the few cases in which damages have been awarded,[84] there is often no further discussion of the quantification aspect.

---

[80] This issue is also discussed as a case study in the horizontal comparative part, see Chap. 10.

[81] Which was 6.75 %, which with the additional 2.5 % amounts to a 9.25 % rate of interest.

[82] *Mears Ltd v Leeds City Council* (No 2) [2011] EWHC 1031 (TCC); WL 5105153.

[83] These were issues 12, 15 and 21 respectively.

[84] See eg, *Mears Ltd*, above n 82 in which the judge, in the face of insufficiently clear criteria, concluded that the claimant had had a 'real or significant as opposed to a fanciful chance that

6.4.2.1 On Lost Profit

The *Harmon* case had left main quantification issues open. It was followed by the *Harmon II* case, which was the application for an interim payment. Although the ultimate decision on damages would be taken at a later full trial stage, as the judge noted, the parties saw the interim application as a first opportunity to test the quantification value of Harmon's claim. The issue was complex as Harmon had gone into liquidation in the meantime. Clearly, main evidence as concerning the financial value of Harmon's claim was still lacking. The judge, as it concerned an application for an interim payment, based himself on a conservative estimate of the claim base In *Harmon*, the court established a profit margin of between £4.5 and £5.4 million GBP, a base estimation that the court also relied on in *Harmon II* in order to address the question of how much of an interim payment it would be able to grant. Interim payments are made up only to amounts that are securely assumed to be granted in a procedure for the 'precise' calculation of the amount.

For the purpose of assessing the gross margin, the estimated profit by Harmon would have to take account of events which actually occurred when the successful tenderer performed the contract, 'for good or ill'.[85] In any event, Harmon could not recover tendering costs as costs under a gross margin quantification, as such costs would have been incurred even if it had not been awarded the contract. They might, however, be recovered in another way.[86]

The gross margin was assessed at 15 %, which 'one would expect for specialist work of this kind carried out by major contractors where relatively high net profits are to be sought to counter the significant risks encountered during carrying out such work and, of course, the nature of the industry'[87] Further, some of the overhead costs[88] claimed by Harmon would have to be valued against whether Harmon in fact mitigated its losses or whether it could have taken on more work. The duty to mitigate losses was, however, one of the excluded issues. In *Harmon II*[89] the judge again referred to these losses, but unconvinced of the evidence (and given that he was only judging the interim payment) he based his assessment on the most conservative figure arriving at an estimate of £4.5 million GBP. The base of £4.5 million was adjusted by several factors,[90] yielding around £5 million GBP. Taking into account the nature of the interim payment proceedings, he adjusted this figure by 25 %, which the judge assessed to be the maximum adjustment possible in a final judgment.

Mears would have been selected' for the next stage of the tender. However, the amount of damages was not discussed.

[85] *Harmon Facades*, above n 17, para 308.

[86] ibid, issue 12 on the question of the gross margin.

[87] ibid, para 294.

[88] ibid, para 314.

[89] See *Harmon II*, above n 73.

[90] Provisional sums, variations, claims and currency. This sum excluded running costs, overheads and contingencies such as payments to OMC. See *Harmon Facades*, above n 17, para 296.

Thus, had Harmon been awarded the contract, it would not have gone into liquidation, and would have made a profit of £3.7 million.[91]

In another case, *Aquatron*, the losses were calculated on the basis of income generated by the contract, broken up into annual amounts, plus additional income on the basis of extra work. The figures were deduced by costs (i.e. labor costs, adjusted by overheads, multiplied by actual hours of service).

6.4.2.2   The Lost Chance Quantification

It must be pointed out, regarding the percentages of the final damage amount, that the judges' estimate is rather rough. Specifically the reduction in the amount of damages for risk and hazards inherent to a sector by 35 % is a significant part of the ultimate damages award. The lost chance was estimated in *Harmon*:

> 320. On the other hand it remains important to distinguish between the evaluation of the loss of chance of "success" i.e. being awarded the contract, and the probability that the whole of the likely profit might be recovered. In my judgment, Mr. Fernyhough's approach both recognised this distinction and was sensible and practical. He submitted that all that was here required was to make an assessment of the probability of the profit being earned. He suggested that it might be reduced by 50 % to illustrate the risks and hazards inherent in construction work. In my view this is realistic and conservative and I agree with it since it is in my view a reasonable assessment, entirely consistent with experience of the incidence of risk on work of this kind. I therefore answer this issue: 35 %.

The judge ruled that the lost chance was to be established by reference to a proportion of the lost profit or gross margin, in this case 35 %. This assessment was based on rather rough assessments of the kinds of risks inherent to the specific sector. The issue was therefore subject to a significant degree of court discretion. Applied to the base figure of £4.5 million, this yielded an amount of £1.7 million, of which a reasonable proportion was to be accorded in the amount of 75 %; so the final figure was £1.3 million. However the lost chance amount was alternative to the others (bid cost and lost profit).

One rare recent successful case is the Scottish *Aquatron Marine* case In *Aquatron*, the court did not consider the assessment of the lost chance, as it found in a comparative evaluation of the tenders that the plaintiff ought to have been awarded the contract. The court stated that even with greater discretion regarding quality and technical merit, based on a comparative evaluation between its tender and the competitor's tender (a third party was excluded due to insufficient certification), the plaintiff would have stood at least an even chance of acceptance. The judge stated in an *obiter dictum* that he would then have assessed the loss at half the contract value.[92]

---

[91] Of this, the judge estimated Harmon to be able to recover one third (which was granted at 100 %, along with 25 % of the remainder of the balance), resulting in an interim payment of £1,846,466GBP.

[92] *Aquatron Marine*, above n 77, para 103.

The court awarded £122,149.20 GBP in damages for lost profit. This figure was made up of a total loss over the 3 years of £109,555.20, plus interest of £12,594 at 4 % per annum. The estimate is based on the contract works of £222,300, less the cost of those works. The costs were based on the previous contract carried out for the defendant. The annual contract value of £74,100 minus the estimated work costs of £37,581.60 left an annual loss of £36,518.40 GBP.[93]

6.5   Conclusions

In theory, the evaluation of the UK system of damages ought to be quite favorable as, demonstrably, several causes of action can give rise to successful damages claims. It is argued that, in the UK context, one might speak of an 'altered (…) balance of power between tenderers and public sector purchasers'.[94] However, the UK situation is also perplexing, because despite the seemingly very numerous possibilities in terms of causes of action that promise damages to aggrieved tenderers, the number of cases does not correspond. Additionally, despite the Harmon ruling, it appears that in procurement situations an implied contract is almost never assumed. Breach of statutory duty is the main cause of action.

When considering whether or not to grant injunctions, courts have often (not always) held that damages claims are an inadequate remedy. This is an indicator for the difficulty of damages claims in the UK. The present research confirms this impression, as only a few cases of successful damages claims were brought in the last 15 years. The theoretical possibilities of claiming damages do not translate into court action. It is not possible to assess the number of cases which are settled by the mere threat of *Harmon* damages, but with such few follow-up actions, the likely pressure for settlements equally diminishes.

Bibliography

Arrowsmith, S (2000) 'EC Procurement Rules in the UK Courts: An Analysis of the Harmon case: Part 2' *Public Procurement Law Review* 135.

Arrowsmith, S (2005) *The Law of Public and Utilities Procurement,* 2nd edition (London, Sweet & Maxwell)

Banks, F & Bowsher, M (2011) 'Damages Remedy in England & Wales and Northern Ireland', in D Fairgrieve & F Lichère (eds), *Public Procurement Law. Damages as an Effective Remedy* (Oxford, Hart Publishing).

Bovis, C (2006) *EC public procurement: case law and regulation* (Oxford, Oxford University Press).

---

[93] ibid.

[94] Bowsher and Moser, above n 1, p 195.

Bowsher, M & Moser, P (2006) 'Damages for breach of the EC public procurement rules in the United Kingdom' *Public Procurement Law Review* 195.

Craig, P & Trybus, M (2010) 'Angleterre et Pays de Galles/England and Wales', in R Noguellou et al (eds), *Droit comparé des contrats publics* (Bruylant).

Pachnou, D (2003) *The Effectiveness of Bidder Remedies for Enforcing the EC Public Procurement Rules: A Case Study of the Public Works Sector in the United Kingdom and Greece* (Dissertation, University of Nottingham).

Roe, S & Harvey, D (2011) 'Public Procurement 2011', in HJ Priess (ed), *Getting the Deal Through: Public Procurement 2010* (London, Sweet & Maxwell).

Roe, S & Harvey, D (2012) 'Public Procurement 2012', in HJ Priess (ed), *Public Procurement* (London, Law Business Research).

Trybus, M (2011) 'An Overview of the United Kingdom Public Procurement Review and Remedies System with an Emphasis on England and Wales', in S Treumer & F Lichère (eds), *Enforcement of the EU public procurement rules* (København, DJØF Publishing).

Chapter 7
Case Study: Germany

Abstract This chapter presents public procurement damages claims in Germany. It covers the causes of action, in particular the constitutive criteria of the specific statutory legal basis §126 GWB, the doctrine of culpa in contrahendo, and general tort law, their respective constitutive criteria and the justiciability of damages claims. It further examines the quantification of damages claims, notably the recoverable losses (bid costs and lost profits) and quantification methods.

7.1 Systemic Features

7.1.1 Characteristics: The Cascaded System of Sources of Law

Public procurement law in Germany is characterized by a multiplicity of legal sources. This so-called 'cascade system' consists of a threefold relegation of norms: as of 1999,[1] public procurement law was incorporated into German competition law by adding a part four to the German Act against the Restraints of Competition (*Gesetz gegen Wettbewerbsbeschränkungen*, 'GWB'). The provisions therein are supplemented by a lower norm, the Ordinance on the Award of Public Contracts (*Vergabeverordnung*, 'VgV').[2] The Ordinance in turn refers to the *Verdingungsordnungen*, that is, the Procurement Regulations VOB/A, VOL/A, and VOF. This lowest level of the legislative cascade is elaborated with the strong involvement of two private regulatory bodies.[3] The link to the legislative power of

---

[1] Through the legislative act amending the legal basis of public procurement law, *Gesetz zur Änderung der Rechtsgrundlagen für die Vergabe öffentlicher Aufträge* (*Vergaberechtsänderungsgesetz*, 'VgRÄG').

[2] *Verordnung über die Vergabe öffentlicher Aufträge*, issued on the basis of para 97 Abs. 6, §127 GWB.

[3] DVA, Deutscher Vergabe- und Vertragsausschuss für Bauleistungen (DVA) and Deutsche Vergabe- und Vertragsausschuss für Lieferungen und Dienstleistungen (DVAL). They are responsible for ensuring conformity of the procurement regulations with European provisions. While the bodies were formative for the non-Europeanized part of German public procurement law, under the influence of the EU public procurement directives their importance decreases continually. See also M Knauff, 'Das Kaskadensystem im Vergaberecht – ein Regelungsmodell mit Zukunft?' (2010) *NZBau* 657, pp 659 and 661.

© Springer International Publishing Switzerland 2016   117
H. Schebesta, *Damages in EU Public Procurement Law*, Studies in European
Economic Law and Regulation 6, DOI 10.1007/978-3-319-23612-4_7

the State, at least formally, is created through the VgV and §97(6) GWB.[4] By means of the relegation through the VgV, the Procurement Regulations also acquire statutory character. Thereby they are capable of producing external effects, in the sense that they are not merely internal obligations addressed to the administration, but can also be relied on by third parties. The delegation of norms is questioned in relation to the legislative principles of a constitutional state.[5] A reform of this cascaded system has been continuously advocated on grounds of European legality,[6] German constitutionality[7] or efficiency considerations – but so far these calls have gone unheard.

At the same time, the move to incorporate the provisions on procurement into the GWB split German public procurement in two: due to §100 Abs. 1 GWB, in connection with §2 VgV, the GWB public procurement law part is exclusively applicable to contracts falling within the scope of the EU public procurement rules. Judicial protection therefore varies considerably with respect to national as opposed to European public procurement procedures.[8]

7.1.2 Implementation of Directive 2007/66

The changes required due to the amendment of the Remedies Directive by Directive 2007/66 were undertaken together with those required by CJEU judgments. The CJEU had found the German 'budgetary solution' for procurement law, under which aggrieved tenderers could not rely on procurement rights before the courts, to be illegal. Consequently, an important realignment of both primary and

---

[4] M Knauff, 'Das Kaskadensystem im Vergaberecht – ein Regelungsmodell mit Zukunft?' (2010) *NZBau* 657, p 661.

[5] Which require, under the principle of democracy contained in Article 201 GG, a re-traceability to the will of the people. See ibid.

[6] The cascade system relates to the organization of the legal norms at national level, the formal aspects of implementation of which, as the CJEU held, as long as they are effective (principle of effectiveness) and provide enough protection to the individual, are at the discretion of the Member State. Under EU primary law, the compatibility of the cascade principle with the internal market provisions or the principle of transparency could be questioned – for making the exercise of the right to free movement more unattractive, or due to their complex nature for violating the principle of transparency.

[7] German constitutional law provides more highly developed standards regarding the formal quality of legal norms than European law currently does – accordingly, the principle of cascade can be critically examined in relation to the clarity of the legal order, being more developed than the European principle of transparency.

[8] In fact, this dual approach has led to considerable criticism based on a discrimination critique. From the European perspective, it is an interesting example of the implications of the internal situation and reverse discrimination doctrines in EU law. See, for public procurement and the internal discrimination doctrine, the concise essay C Braun & C Hauswaldt, 'Vergaberechtliche Wirkung der Grundfreiheiten und das Ende der Inländerdiskriminierung? Zugleich eine Anmerkung zum EuGH-Urteil Coname' (2006) *EuZW* 176.

secondary law protection took place. The changes were introduced in Germany by means of the *Gesetz zur Modernisierung des Vergaberechts*, which entered into force on 24 April 2009.[9]

7.1.3   Jurisdiction

Special procurement senates are competent for public procurement disputes in general, but damages claims as a post-contractual remedy are adjudicated by the ordinary civil courts according to §13 *Gerichtsverfassungsgesetz* (Courts Constitution Act, GVG), see §104 (3) GWB.

7.2   The Constitutive Criteria for Various Actions

Remedies are categorized in a system of primary and secondary protection. Primary remedies aim to protect or restore initial, original rights – for tenders this means receiving a contract award or restoring the chance to participate fairly in procedures. In Germany, a lot of emphasis is put on primary remedies, while secondary protection takes the form of damages actions. The latter have been described as 'extremely low profiled and lacking in clarity despite its many and quite elaborate regulations'.[10]

The German legal system opens, at least theoretically, a plurality of actions by means of which damages for public procurement breaches can be pursued: the first is a specific statutory legal basis. It transposes the Remedies Directive's damages article in Germany through §126 GWB. A second action is based on the nature of the special and protected relationship between the aggrieved tenderer and the contracting authority by means of the doctrine of *culpa in contrahendo* under §§311(2), 241(2), 280(1) of the Civil Code (*Bürgerliches Gesetzbuch*, 'BGB').[11] Lastly, several practically less relevant causes of action exist, such as the general action for tort, liability of public authorities[12] or Competition law claims.[13]

---

[9] BGBl I, 790. The Bundestag accepted the draft on 19.12.2008 and the Bundesrat agreed on 13.2.2009.

[10] M Burgi, 'A Report about the German Remedies System', in S Treumer & F Lichère (eds), *Enforcement of the EU Public Procurement Rules* (København, Djof Publishing, 2011), p 141 [translation by the author].

[11] §§311(2), 241(2), 280(1) BGB. This is achieved either through a quasi-delictual version, which implies loyalty and information duties having been created in the relationship; or the quasi-contractual version, which takes the parties' statements as offers implying a measure of responsibility for the risk of breakdown of the negotiations.

[12] §823(1) and (2) BGB; §826 BGB; §839 BGB jo 34 GG.

[13] §§33, 20, 19 GWB and possibly §1 UWG (*Gesetz gegen den unlauteren Wettbewerb*, Act Against Unfair Competition).

7.2.1 Damages Claims Based on §126 GWB

§126 GWB is a specific legal base for damages arising out of the violation of public procurement rules.

> *§126 Claim for damages of the expectation damages*
> [sentence 1] *Where the contracting authority violated a provision intended to protect undertakings, and where the undertaking without this violation, in the selection of the tenders, would have had a real chance of having been granted the award, which [the real chance] was, however, adversely affected by that infringement, the undertaking may claim damages for the costs of preparing the bid or for the participation in an award procedure.*
> [sentence 2] *Additional claims to damages remain unaffected.*

The wording of §126 GWB derives from Directive 92/13/EEC (the Utilities Remedies Directive). As observed above, the two remedies directives on claims to damages diverge, as the Utilities Remedies Directive is more precise. Germany has given this article a wider implementation than would have been necessary under the wording of Directive 89/665/EEC. §126 GWB is only applicable to contracts surpassing the EU law-related thresholds and is without pertinence to purely national claims.

7.2.1.1 Constitutive Elements of §126 GWB

§126 GWB constitutes a specific and independent basis for claims of damages.[14] The option to rely on §126 GWB depends on whether or not a contract falls within the scope of part IV of the GWB. The constitutive elements are a) a provision intended to protect undertakings, b) a tenderer that enjoyed a real chance, and, as some authors argue, c) an implicit fault requirement.

7.2.1.2 Provision Intended to Protect Undertakings

§126 GWB requires the violation of a provision 'intended to protect undertakings'. Whether or not legislation is protecting an interest is a question that is very relevant for German doctrine. Over time, the position of aggrieved bidders was considerably strengthened because public procurement legislation increasingly became understood as competition law, and §97 (7) GWB guarantees a subjective right to undertakings for the respect of the public procurement provisions contained therein. Since the renunciation of the 'budgetary solution', §97 (7) GWB reads:

> (7) Undertakings have a right to the contracting authority complying with the provisions on procurement procedures.

The creation of subjective rights must be assumed for all those norms which are determined to protect an interest at the European level. The wording of §126 GWB

---

[14] See OLG Koblenz, 15.01.2007, 5 U 4/06.

raises the question of whether provisions of public procurement law alone give rise
to a damage claim on the basis of this article, or whether other provisions can do so,
too. Given the legislative history,[15] as well as the place of §126 GWB in section IV
on public procurement in the GWB, it is commonly assumed that the violated provision must be part of the public procurement rules. These are part IV (§97 and further) of the *GWB*, the *VgV* (relegation in §§97(6) and §127 GWB) and the
procurement regulations VOB/A, VOL/A und VOF (based on §§97 (6), 127 GWB
and the static relegation under §§4 ff VgV). However, it is commonly assumed that
not all norms in public procurement law are of a protective nature.[16] In order to
determine this criterion, the jurisprudence developed in tort law under §823 (2)
BGB is regarded as pertinent.[17] In addition, most authors rely on the interpretations
that have been made with respect to the primary protection of rights under §107 (2)
nr 1 GWB, as it would constitute an internal incoherency to admit an action for
review under the latter, but subsequently deny secondary protection for the very
same right.[18]

7.2.1.3   Personal Scope

§126 GWB opens a claim to all undertakings that would have had a 'real chance'.[19]
The 'real chance' requirement is the main criterion in determining whether a damages claim under §126 GWB is going to be successful.

The provision thus enlarges the circle of potential claimants from those that
would have been awarded a contract, to those that 'merely' had a chance of being
awardee. However, it has also been interpreted by the courts as containing a 'com-
parability' requirement in the first place, meaning that, for example, *de facto* tenders
without procedure – and hence without comparable bids – cannot fulfil the requirement of a sufficiently closely defined 'chance'. The chance is therefore not entirely
hypothetical, but must have manifested itself. The aggrieved bidder must have had
especially qualified chances of success.[20]

---

[15] From the point of view of an interpretation based on the will of the legislator, quite a story has
been told about the open texture of this article being the result of a drafting mistake; additionally,
the preparatory works express quite divergent opinions on the extent of the subjective right that is
granted in the provision. See, eg P Jebens, 'Schadensersatzansprüche bei Vergabeverstößen'
(1999) *Der Betrieb* 1741, pp 1742–1743.

[16] Weyand, 42.6.2, 'besteht Einigkeit, dass diese Eigenschaft nicht allen Normen des Vergaberechts
zugemessen werden kann, und zwar insbesondere dann nicht, wenn sie haushaltsrechtlichen, ord-
nungsrechtlichen oder gesamtwirtschaftspolitischen Charakter haben.'

[17] C Alexander, 'Vergaberechtlicher Schadensersatz gemäss §126 GWB' (2009) *Wettbewerb in
Recht und Praxis* 28, p 30.

[18] C Alexander, 'GWB §126 Anspruch auf Ersatz des Vertrauensschadens', in H Pünder& M
Schellenberg (eds), *Vergaberecht*, 2nd edition (Baden-Baden, Nomos, 2015), rn 15.

[19] KG 14.8.2003, *NZBau* 2004, 167, 168.

[20] Alexander, 'GWB §126 Anspruch auf Ersatz des Vertrauensschadens', above n 17, rn 24.

7.2.1.4   The Loss of Chance

The concretization of what a chance as a modification of causality entails divides German doctrine: chance could be interpreted as meaning being included in a shortlist (*engere Wahl*), thus forming part of a specific, closely clustered group with the highest chances. According to another view, a chance exists if the contracting authority, within its margin of discretion, *could* have awarded the contract to the bid in question.[21]

The BGH endorsed the latter view in its judgment of 27 November 2007, an important case that provided much needed clarification on several points regarding the claim of damages. The attribute 'real' chance specifies that a bid must have had '*specially qualified prospects of receiving the award*'.[22] A chance in this sense is read as a probability of being granted the award which is higher or qualitatively special. The court reached this conclusion mainly on a historic reasoning, referring back to the legislative amendment in the course of the passing of the *VgRÄG*. Therefore, the real chance has to be interpreted as meaning that, within the margin of its discretion, a contracting authority could have awarded the contract to a tenderer. According to Alexander,[23] the test comprises the following elements: at which stage did a violation occur? Does the possibility to make a hypothetical comparison of the bids exist? Did the aggrieved bidder qualify? Was an award within the margin of discretion of the contracting authority? Following the BGH, the lost chance has to be examined for the concrete case: '*It is a question of the individual case, which can only be answered by taking the award criteria into consideration*'.[24]

The most important instance in which there is no lost chance are cases in which the contracting authority did not award the tendered contract at all. Other examples which preclude a lost chance and hence the recovery of damages include events beyond the contracting authorities' control or a lack of the discretion to award the contract to a tender. There is no lost chance if the award procedure was precluded due to insolvency proceedings, i.e. due to circumstances over which 'the defendant had no influence'. The wording is not clear as to whether or not the requirement is one of causality (i.e. that the 'violation' was due to circumstances beyond the defendant's control).[25] It is more likely that the court will rely on the fact that, due to the insolvency, the contracting authority is not awarding the contract in question at all.

Additionally, where tenderers would demonstrably not have won a contract, they do not qualify for a lost chance. For example, there was no lost chance in a case

---

[21] For authors on the respective positions, see BGH, 27.11.2007, X ZR 18/07=ZfBR 2008, 299, 301.

[22] BGH, 27.11.2007, X ZR 18/07 [translation author].

[23] Alexander, 'GWB § 126 Anspruch auf Ersatz des Vertrauensschadens', above n 17, rn 35.

[24] §25 Nr. 3 Abs. 3 i. V. mit §10a lit. a VOB/A 2006, §11 Nr. 1 Abs. 1 i. V. mit §7 Nr. 2 Abs. 2 lit. i VOB/A-SKR 2006, §25 Nr. 3, §25a Nr. 1, §25b Nr. 1 VOL/A 2006, §11 Nr. 1 VOL/A-SKR 2006, §16 Abs. 2, 3 VOF 2006) and the weighting thereof (Marge, Matrix, Punktsystem, o. Ä.) , see BGH, 27.11.2007, X ZR 18/07.

[25] VK Mecklenburg-Vorpommern, 20.03.2012, 1 VK 1/11.

where a tenderer was ranked second on price, and where the lowest price was presumably the award criterion. The lower court had held that the tenderer had had a chance solely on the basis of having been ranked second. In this case, the contracting authority had no margin of appreciation allowing the award of the contract to the claimant if (as the revising court presumed) the criterion was the lowest price.[26]

7.2.1.5 Fault

It was initially disputed whether §126 GWB implied an unwritten fault requirement. The argument is based on an analogy to the subjective liability requirement under the overarching principles of civil liability. Accordingly, a deviation from the general liability criteria would have to be made explicit by the legislator, as exceptions to this principle under German law are rare.[27] However, the courts sometimes followed this approach without further examining the 'fault' criterion.[28]

Since 2007, the BGH has interpreted §126 GWB as not requiring fault, but it initially based this interpretation on the legislative history of §126 GWB, rather than requirements deriving from European law.[29] That fault cannot be a constitutive criterion, even in cases where it is coupled with a reversal of the burden of proof, was reaffirmed by the CJEU. In *Stadt Graz* in 2010, it held that a fault requirement would contravene Directive 89/665/EC.[30] For EU law claims, the fault criterion is therefore dispensed with. As we will see, however, the question remains open for the German *culpa in contrahendo* doctrine.

7.2.1.6 The Recoverable Loss Under §126 GWB

Under the special legal basis of §126 GWB, the recoverable loss is limited to the negative interest. Further claims based on other legal bases remain possible.

For example, in a tender concerning a flood control installation, the aggrieved bidder placed a bid at 10.733.990 DM and was second ranked after the lowest bid of 9.969.165 DM. The tender had been publicised only nationally, and thereby violated the procurement law. The tender was then withdrawn and procured at European level. The aggrieved bidder claimed bid costs of around 50.000 DM of costs spent in preparing the first national tender and which could not be re-used in the submission

---

[26] OLG Naumburg, 28.10.2010, 1 U 52/10; the judgment was not scrutinized by the revision on this point.

[27] BGH, 27.11.2007, X ZR 18/07. See also for an overview of doctrine.

[28] See for example OLG Schleswig-Holsteinisches, 25.09.2009, 1 U 42/08, para 27.

[29] BGH, 27.11.2007, X ZR 18/07; see also HJ Prieß & FJ Hölzl, 'Drei Worte des EuGH: Schadensersatz ohne Verschulden! – Zur gemeinschaftsrechtskonformen Auslegung des §126S.1 GWB' (2011) 1 *Neue Zeitschrift für Baurecht und Vergaberecht* 21.

[30] Case C-314/09 *Strabag and others* [2010] ECR I-8769.

of the European repeated bid. The court held that a second ranked tenderer had indeed had a 'real chance' and awarded the bid costs.[31]

7.2.2 Non-contractual Obligations: The culpa in contrahendo Under §§280, 311(2), and 241(2) BGB

The second sentence of §126 GWB explicitly regulates the relationship between the different liability bases and states that liability claims based on other provisions are not precluded by the §126 GWB liability. Since §126 GWB grants only the bid preparation costs, it is implied that the provision is relevant only in relation to coexistent bases that would allow the recovery of additional losses. These can be additional losses such as negative interest that is not merely bid preparation, as well as lost profits. The most commonly discussed bases under which a defaulting contracting authority may incur more far-reaching liability is the pre-contractual *culpa in contrahendo,* which permits claims for the negative and the positive interest.

The legal institution of *culpa in contrahendo* can be theoretically justified on account of either contractual or delictual reasoning. Briefly summarized, the quasidelictual version assumes a pre-contractual information duty, which can be breached by one of the parties not correcting the expectations of the other party that the contract will ultimately be concluded, for example, due to a lack of willingness to finally conclude a contract at all. A second variant of the quasi-delictual version constructs a positive duty to the loyal continuation of negotiations. The contractual approach, on the other hand, does not depart from duties in the trust relationship, but from the statements of parties as the point of departure signalling the willingness to contract. Inherent to this conception is an assumption of the risk of the negotiations breaking down. The party statements are therefore conceived as promises. In Germany, this was a judge-made construction which received legislative recognition through the reform of the law of obligations and was codified in the BGB (§§280, 311(2), and 241(2) BGB). The *culpa in contrahendo* leads to the protection of the negotiation relationship that precedes the contract's conclusion.

As public procurement situations involve greatly institutionalized interaction before the contract is concluded, such protection takes great importance. Factually, liability based on the *culpa in contrahendo* is, next to §126 GWB, the most important cause of action. It is significant to the aggrieved tenderer as it may found a claim to the positive interest. The tendency of the courts is increasingly to grant it.[32] However, overall the constitutive criteria are more difficult to satisfy, particularly since an aggrieved bidder must demonstrate that a favorable award decision would have been made.[33] The damages action under *culpa in contrahendo* is relevant for

---

[31] OLG Koblenz, 15.01.2007, 12 U 1016/05.

[32] K Stockmann, '§126 GWB', in U Immenga & EJ Mestmäcker (eds), *Wettbewerbsrecht: GWB,* 5th edition (München, CH Beck, 2014), mn 25.K.

[33] For example recently OLG Koblenz, 06.02.2014, 1 U 906/13.

contracts both above and below the threshold – broadly speaking, the legal doctrine presumes the existence of a prior relationship of trust between an aggrieved tenderer and the contracting authority, or the breach of an implied duty.

7.2.2.1   The Existence of a Protected Relationship

One of the central issues is therefore the determination of the point in time at which a relationship of trust can be said to have formed. This moment varies with the type of procurement procedure followed. However, for all procedures the relationship of trust is found to have been created on the part of the contracting authority when, in whichever formal way, the contracting authority invites expressions of interest. Variations as to when a protected relationship came into existence thus mostly depend on what is required of the behaviour of the tenderer. In an open procedure, it is not necessarily the moment that a bid was submitted; an expression of interest may suffice.[34] For the restricted procedure and the negotiated procedure, the relevant point is determined by the submission of documents by the tenderer. In the purely negotiated procedure, the point in time is again determined by the invitation of the contracting authority.

7.2.2.2   Breach of a Duty

The protected relationship is characterized by several duties, for example the general duty of good faith (*Treu und Glauben*) of §242 BGB. Additional duties of care, clarification, information, and loyalty apply.[35] For the field of public procurement, these are specified (although not exhaustively[36]) in the procurement regulations. The core duty of the contracting authority is to abide by the public procurement rules. For example, according to §25a VOB/A and §25b VOL/A, the contracting authority has a duty to limit itself only to those selection criteria mentioned in the tender notice. Also, a tender can only be withdrawn in accordance with the recognized reasons in §26a VOB/A.

7.2.2.3   Fault Requirement

Apart from §126 GWB with its specific interpretation as not containing a fault criterion, in accordance with the general German principles of liability, fault is a general requirement for the other liability bases. This means intent or negligence according to §276, unless the contracting authority can prove that the breach of duty did not result from its behaviour, and that the damage would have happened even

---

[34] Stockmann, '§126 GWB', above n 32, mn 26 with references to case law.
[35] W Irmer, *Sekundärrechtsschutz und Schadensersatz im Vergaberecht* (Frankfurt, Peter Lang, 2004), p 146.
[36] Stockmann, '§126 GWB', above 32, mn 28.

without a breach of the relevant duty, see §280 BGB.[37] Fault on the part of the contracting authority is easily presumed.[38] However, for example a contracting authority that relied on the not obviously flawed recommendations of a consultant, which later on appeared to be flawed, did not act negligently.[39]

7.2.2.4   The Causal Relationship

Under the *culpa in contrahendo* doctrine, the constitutive criteria regarding causality differ from those of §126 GWB. In order to adequately prove the existence of a causal link between the loss and a violation of the public procurement rules, it is required that the claimant would have been awarded the contract under the regular course of a procurement procedure. This is equally valid for a claim aimed at either the negative or the positive interest if based on *culpa in contrahendo*.[40]

7.2.2.5   Mitigation of Damages

Particularly in a pre-contractual relationship, the actions of aggrieved bidders may impact on the chances of a successful damages claim. Firstly, this concerns whether the aggrieved bidder must necessarily take an action for review or annulment once aware of the faults in a tender procedure; and secondly, how far a failure to challenge a procurement procedure (or indeed the fact that the tenderer brought a challenge) may impact on the chances of success in claiming a damage, as well as on the amount of damages recoverable.[41] Some duties also fall to the aggrieved tenderer wishing to rely on the *culpa in contrahendo*. In what is characterized as a bilateral relationship, the tenderer loses protection under the *culpa in contrahendo* doctrine, for example, if s/he recognizes a breach of the public procurement rules without acting on it – a prohibition against '*dulde und liquidire*' (tolerate then liquidate).[42]

A contracting authority cannot contractually protect itself from secondary damages claims by including a notice in the tender documents that the bidders do not

---

[37] Irmer, *Sekundärrechtsschutz und Schadensersatz im Vergaberecht*, above n 35, p 207; and Stockmann, '§126 GWB', above 32, mn 29.

[38] Irmer, Sekundärrechtsschutz und Schadensersatz im Vergaberecht, above n 35, p 206.

[39] Stockmann, '§126 GWB', above 32, mn 29, quoting BGH vom 20.1.2009, *NZBau* 2009, p 262.

[40] LG Frankfurt/Main, 02.02.2012, 3 O 151/11. In case the claimant's bid did not meet the requirements of the tender specifications either.

[41] 'The omission to launch a feasible and reasonable challenge raises the question of *contributory negligence*. This issue is the subject of animated doctrinal discussion. Some commentators in German legal literature are convinced that contributory fault on the side of the bidder simply affects the quantum of compensation. [reference to Irmer] Others argue that the bidder does (or should) not get any damages at all [reference to Irmer, again].' M Burgi, 'Damages for Breach of Public Procurement Law. German Perspectives', in D Fairgrieve & F Lichère (eds), *Public Procurement Law. Damages as an Effective Remedy* (Oxford, Hart Publishing, 2011), p 26.

[42] BGH 3.6.2004 WuW/E Verg 976. BGH 8.9.1998 WuW/E Verg 129. See in application Decision of VK Mecklenburg-Vorpommern, 20.03.2012, 1 VK 1/11.

enjoy the right of obedience to public procurement rules.[43] However, the contracting authority can rely on the doctrine of 'lawful alternative conduct', according to which, if it can prove that in an alternative and legal course of action an aggrieved party would have sustained the same losses, these are not recoverable.

These general principles of lawful alternative conduct as well as the prohibition of 'tolerating then liquidating' have received a specific interpretation in the field of procurement in the national courts. The reason lies in the special and particularly formally defined legal framework for permissible or required actions that exist. Regarding the tension between a tenderer being aware of the (potential) illegality in a tendering procedure and its participation, the courts have markedly changed course. From the initial (and traditional) prohibition on gaining advantage from facts one knows to be illegal, the courts have recognized the predicament which such a situation represents for tenderers.

7.2.3   Liability Based on Non-contractual Obligations

A further possibility to claim damages is an action in tort under the general provision §823 BGB. This poses a challenge to German doctrine which requires for the law to have a protective character in order to rely on it for tort purposes (*Schutzgesetzcharakter*). By now, it is generally assumed that procurement provisions dispose of the 'protective norm' character, at least to the extent that the national public procurement law is transposing EU law.

Article §823(1) BGB only protects absolute rights, which in the context of public procurement situations would be limited to the protection of business operations. The recourse to this provision is therefore of a mainly theoretical nature.[44] One might, however, conceive of a claim in which a bidder is intentionally and specifically excluded from a bidding procedure to satisfy the §823(1) BGB criteria.[45]

The alternative would be tortuous liability under §823(2) BGB for breaches of statutory norms with protective character. A revival of this action is seen as desirable by some authors.[46] However, the provision also operates under the limitations of the *Schutznormtheorie* – the main counterargument to the pertinence of this provision being that while the provisions within the GWB create subjective rights due to §97(7) GWB, this does not necessarily mean that they are also to be regarded as protective provisions for the purpose of 823(2) BGB.[47] Although some uncertainty and criticism of this view persists, there are several court judgments affirming this view due to the exigencies of EU law at least for claims based on contracts within

---

[43] Y Schnorbus, 'Der Schadensersatzanspruch des Bieters bei der fehlerhaften Vergabe öffentlicher Aufträge' (1999) *BauR*, pp 77 and 81, quoting OLG Schleswig, *ZVgR* 1997, pp 170, 172.

[44] Stockmann, '§126 GWB', above 32, mn 42.

[45] Burgi, 'A Report about the German Remedies System', above n 10, p 29.

[46] Stockmann, '§126 GWB', above 32, mn 45.

[47] Schnorbus, 'Der Schadensersatzanspruch des Bieters bei der fehlerhaften Vergabe öffentlicher Aufträge', above n 43, pp 77 and 85, quoting OLG Düsseldorf, *BauR* 1999, 241, 246.

the scope of application of the European directives.[48] Violations of the procurement regulations could thereby in themselves qualify as torts – provided that they concern public procurement proceedings above the thresholds, again due to the German requirement of a legal instrument being of protective character. Moreover, the violation would have to be based on fault as an additional condition.[49]

This cause of action is significant in particular where violations of public procurement rules occurs at a stage in which the creation of a trust relationship has not yet given rise to a protection under *culpa in contrahendo*. By way of example, these violations could be erroneous calls for tender, violations of publication duties, or errors made in the choice of procurement procedure.[50]

7.2.4   Alternative Causes of Action for Liability

Several other and more specific actions can conceivably ground damages claims: German State liability can arise under either public law, in combination with Article 34 *Grundgesetz* (Basic Law, GG), or under various provisions which hold the individual servant (civil or non-civil servant) liable, or the State as employer vicariously liable. Individual liability of State employees[51] can be incurred in tort for the negligent or wilful breach of an official duty owed to a third party; again the question arises as to whether a law serves the function of protecting a private interest. The official duty (the liability for breach of an official duty) extends to both civil servants under §839 BGB and non-civil servants under §823(1) BGB. The State could be held vicariously liable for its employees for fiscal tasks under §831(1) BGB. An intentional infringement against public policy, such as bribery, corruption or manipulation, might also result in liability under §826 BGB.[52] Additional liability causes, admittedly of minor importance, might be created through §§824, 826 BGB through violation of officious duties, under §839 BGB, Article 34 GG. However, these have regularly been rejected, as the public purchasing process is not recognized as an act of State sovereignty.[53]

Under specific circumstances, claims can be based on the violation of competition law. This cause of action is possible in cases where a contracting authority has

---

[48] OLG Schleswig, 6. 7. 1999, *NZBau* 2000, 100.

[49] S Wilke, Die Bedeutung von Schadensersatz nach Vergaberechtsverößen im Rahmen der Vergabe öffentlicher Liefer- und Bauaufträge (Grin, 2005/2006), p 23.

[50] Stockmann, '§126 GWB', above 32, mn 45.

[51] G Brüggemeier, 'Aansprakelijkheid van Toezichthouders', in CC van Dam (ed), *Aansprakelijkheid van Toezichthouders Met Publieke Taken* (Ministerie van Veiligheid en Justitie, 2006), http://wodc. nl/onderzoeksdatabase/aansprakelijkheid-van-toezichthouders-met-publieke-taken. aspx?cp=44&cs=6802, p 246.

[52] M Burgi, 'Zukunft des Vergaberechts' (2009) *NZBau* 609, p 30.

[53] A Drügemöller, *Vergaberecht und Rechtsschutz. Der inter- und supranationale Rahmen und seine Ausgestaltung in Deutschland* (Berlin, Springer, 1999), p 308.

acted in the capacity as an undertaking, which is any market activity, and it takes a dominating position in his role as the market dominating buyer. Where this is the case, a violation of the prohibition from discrimination under §20 GWB occurs, a provision which is clearly recognized as being a '*Schutzgesetz*' in nature in the sense of §33 (1)s1 GWB. The question of whether discrimination has occurred must be answered in light of the objective justification for differentiated treatment.

7.3 Justiciability

7.3.1 *Statutory Norms with Protective Character*

German doctrine is particularly influenced by the *Schutznorm* doctrine which requires statutory norms to have protective character in order to be invoked. Over the years, the position of undertakings for bringing damages claims for violations of procurement rules has significantly improved. A serious obstacle can be the limitation for bringing claims only where a breach of a subjective right is given. In the case of §126 GWB the issue has been largely resolved. For the general tort provision for statutory breaches of §823(2), it is questionable whether the required protective character is assumed.

7.3.2 *Time Limits*

The regular prescription time for actions arising out of §126 GWB, the culpa in contrahendo and general tort law is 3 years,[54] starting from the point of time that the damaged party had knowledge of both the damage and the identity of the tortfeasor.

7.3.3 *Access to Documents*

Where a tenderer, in the course of review proceedings, has made use of the option to instigate the inspection of files under §111, he can also use the information gained in the exercise of that right in the proceedings for damages claims. Independently of review proceedings, this right of access to information must be rejected for damages claims alone.[55]

---

[54] Under §§195 and 199 BGB.

[55] Schnorbus, 'Der Schadensersatzanspruch des Bieters bei der fehlerhaften Vergabe öffentlicher Aufträge', above n 43, pp 77, 99.

7.4 Quantification

7.4.1 Recoverable Losses

Recoverable losses are determined by the provisions contained in §§249-254 BGB. German liability is governed by the principle of compensation, which entails that only actually realized harms are compensated. The preventive function of liability law is recognized, but not a punitive function of damages claims. The principle of full compensation is based on an all-or-nothing approach. Damages claims are a form of derivative protection of a right, the nature of which is first protected through primary protection and then transformed in material terms, hence secondary protection.

§249(1) BGB reads:

Nature and extent of damages

(1) A person who is liable in damages must restore the position that would exist if the circumstance obliging him to pay damages had not occurred.

The situation is therefore not necessarily judged according to the *Differenzhypothese*, or hypothesis of difference, i.e. the comparison between the state that is and the state which would have existed had the infringement not occurred. The 'position' is not defined as either overall patrimony (and hence interest in the sense of the hypothesis of difference) or a subjective/objective valuation of the loss. Also, the moment in time that the real and potential states of the world would be compared at is indeterminate.[56] Since public procurement concerns pecuniary compensation, these two states have to be expressed and calculated as financial positions.

7.4.1.1 Bid Preparation and Negative Interest

The recoverable loss under §126 GWB is explicitly limited to '*the costs of preparing the bid or for the participation in an award procedure*'. However, the title of that provision is 'negative interest'. In a very literal reading, it is possible to note that the legal concepts of the provision's title (negative interest) and text are not congruent, and that bid preparation and participation costs do not seem to be covered cumulatively. While the title of reads 'negative interest', the coverable damages are limited to costs of *preparing the bid or for the participation in an award procedure*. For example, the profits lost in another transaction (anticipatory profits),[57] which was precluded due to participation in the first (flawed) procurement procedure, would be part of the negative interest, yet are not covered by the wording of §126 GWB.[58] The

---

[56] H Lange, *Schadensersatz* (Tübingen, Mohr, 1979), p 28.

[57] Burgi, 'A Report about the German Remedies System', above n 10, p 33.

[58] T Ackermann, 'Die Haftung des Auftraggebers bei Vergabeverstößen. Ein Beitrag zum Umgang mit den Vorgaben des EG-Rechts für nationales Privatrecht' (2000) 164 *ZHR* 394, p 402.

maximum amount recoverable as negative interest is limited to the amount grantable as positive interest. Items of expenditure covered by the bid preparation costs include, for example, expenses relating to the acquisition of the procurement documentation, costs connected to obtaining required certification and selection requirements, as well as costs of designing the bid, submitting the bid, and participating in the procedure.[59] In both ways, the specific base for awarding damages departs from the generally accepted principles of liability. The losses claimable under the provision is *sui generis*, and differs from the general provision on damages in §249 BGB.[60]

The losses covered in §126 GWB and the *culpa in contrahendo* differ. Legal fees were regarded as not recoverable under §126 where they would have been incurred with or without the tortious conduct of the defendant.[61] Costs incurred when preparing the execution of the tender where not recoverable costs under §126, although the court admitted that they can be claimed under an action for the negative interest for the *culpa in contrahendo*. The court held that costs relating to the execution of the contract can be claimed as reliance damages, where the contract conclusion was obstructed without a sufficient reason.[62]

In a claim under §126 GWB for bid preparation and participation costs, the following losses were covered: labor costs, material costs as well as proportional general costs for the bid and the review proceedings. The compensation was limited only to those bids or variants that had not been rejected by the contracting authority.[63]

7.4.1.2 Positive Interest

§126 GWB is a departure from the general principle of full compensation. Due to its explicit wording, it is commonly accepted that §126 GWB does not grant the possibility to claim positive interest. For the other causes of action, the recoverable losses are determined in accordance with §249 ff BGB, including §252 BGB, which postulates:

> Lost profits
> The damage to be compensated for also comprises the lost profits. Those profits are considered lost that in the normal course of events or in the special circumstances, particularly due to the measures and precautions taken, could probably be expected.

The case law regarding the award of lost profits for aggrieved bidders who are able to prove that they would have obtained contracts (first ranked bidders) has undergone significant changes. Initially, the courts did not grant the positive inter-

---

[59] Irmer, *Sekundärrechtsschutz und Schadensersatz im Vergaberecht*, above n 35, p 268.

[60] HJ Prieß and K Bonitz, 'Das Sonderregime für Schadensersatz bei Vergabefehlern' (2013) *NZBau*, p 477.

[61] LG Magdeburg, 02.06.2010, 36 O 25/10 (007), 36 O 25/10.

[62] OLG Naumburg, 01.08.2013, 2 U 151/12 Hs.

[63] LG Stade 6 civil Senate, 19.12.2003, 6 O 405/02.

est, but limited damages claims to the negative interest. This period was followed by the acknowledgement that sufficient protection of a bidder would also mean granting the positive interest[64] – under the condition that the aggrieved bidder, in the regular course of proceedings, would have obtained the contract.[65] However, more recently, the BGH developed an additional condition to the award of the positive interest: for an aggrieved bidder to be able to claim the positive interest, the actual contract lost must, in 'economically identical form', have been awarded.[66] The rationale is that under considerations of private autonomy, as well as the principles of public procurement, a contracting authority is not bound to award a contract. There is no duty to contract and a procurement procedure can be closed under the conditions detailed in §26 VOB/A. This view has been criticized because it allows contracting authorities to rather easily award a seemingly different contract, while at the same time evading further-reaching damages claims.[67] The tenderer has to prove that without the violation of the public procurement rules, that is, under the regular progression of the tendering process, s/he would have obtained the award.

Implicitly, the legislative *culpa in contrahendo* for public procurement seems to be founded on the quasi-delictual version – i.e. the breach of information and loyalty requirements. This explains why, generally in Germany, the contracting authority cannot be forced into the conclusion of a contract – hence limiting the damages to the negative interest. An illegal cancellation of a call for tenders in violation of §26 VOB/A can result in the granting of a claim of negative interest for all participating tenders.[68] However, this rationale is cancelled in cases where the contracting authority concluded an identical contract with another tenderer. In these cases, it is not considered a forced conclusion of contract, and the courts regularly award the positive interest in damages.[69] The requirement of proof is still ambiguous, namely whether it is on the tenderer to prove it had submitted the best bid or for the contracting authority to prove that another tenderer would have received the award.[70]

In a recent example, the contract concerned the supply of a special form of cement screeds. The aggrieved bidder was ranked fourth, and in the evaluation of the bids, the first ranked bidder had been excluded from the bid so that the contract was awarded to the second bidder. After some time from the award of the contract, the aggrieved bidder gained knowledge of the fact that the cement screeds used by the competitor and contract awardee did not comply with the requirements that had

---

[64] Irmer, *Sekundärrechtsschutz und Schadensersatz im Vergaberecht*, above n 35, p 272, citing several cases between 1988 and 1993, also referring to BGH BauR 1998, 1232, 1237

[65] Confirmed for example in BGH, 3. 4. 2007, X ZR 19/06.

[66] Also confirmed in BGH, 3. 4. 2007, *NZBau* 2007, 523, 524.

[67] Irmer, *Sekundärrechtsschutz und Schadensersatz im Vergaberecht*, above n 35, p 274, who even suggests that a contracting authority might incorporate formal procurement errors in order to provide a loophole for further damages claims.

[68] Stockmann, '§126 GWB', above 32, mn 25; BGH 8.9.1998 WuW/E Verg 121.

[69] Ackermann, 'Die Haftung des Auftraggebers bei Vergabeverstößen. Ein Beitrag zum Umgang mit den Vorgaben des EG-Rechts für nationales Privatrecht', above n 58, p 419.

[70] Stockmann, '§126 GWB', above 32, mn 25; OLG Nürnberg NJW RR 1997, 854.

been set on the tender. Additionally, the third ranked bidder had submitted a bid based on the same and unsuitable cement screeds. The Court concluded that the contracting authority had culpably (in the sense of §276 BGB) neglected to award the contract to the fourth ranked bidder, which as a consequence had a claim for the positive interest.[71]

7.4.2 Valuation of Damages

Under regular circumstances, a claimant bears the burden of allegation (*Darlegungslast*) and the burden of full proof under §286 ZPO for all constitutive criteria of liability.

The amount of compensation in Germany is accorded pursuant to §287 ZPO since the quantification of the amount is insufficiently determined in order to fulfill the degree of proof called for under §286 ZPO.[72] The provision reads:

§287 Investigation and determination of damages; amount of the claim
(1) Should the issue of whether or not damages have occurred, and the amount of the damage or of the equivalent in money to be reimbursed, be in dispute among the parties, the court shall rule on this issue at its discretion and conviction, based on its evaluation of all circumstances. The court may decide at its discretion whether or not – and if so, in which scope – any taking of evidence should be ordered as applied for, or whether or not any experts should be involved to prepare a report. The court may examine the party tendering evidence on the damage or the equivalent in money thereof; the stipulations of section 452 (1), first sentence, subsections (2) to (4) shall apply mutatis mutandis.[73]

According to this provision, the court can proceed to estimate the damage incurred according to §287 GWB.[74] The provision constitutes an exception to the regular §286 ZPO burden imposed, and allows for an estimation of the amount of damages which must satisfy – according to most commentators – a lower level of certainty. The degree of conviction a court must reach is lowered to that of the balance of probabilities. The provision is not a switch in the burden of proof, but it alleviates the amount of evidence or substantiation ('*Darlegungslast*') that is required.[75]

Admittedly, it is difficult to draw specific conclusions on the use of §287 ZPO in damages claims for public procurement violations, precisely because there have been so few successful examples, and fewer still wherein the use of §287 ZPO was elaborated upon.[76] Generally, the provision is particularly relevant for hypothetical

---

[71] OLG Koblenz, 6.2.2014, 1 U 906/13.

[72] In the context of competition law, see JO Rauh, A Zuchandke & S Reddemann, 'Die Ermittlung der Schadenshöhe im Kartelldeliktsrecht' (2012) *Wettbewerb in Recht und Praxis* 173.

[73] Translation taken from www.gesetze-im-internet.de/englisch_zpo/englisch_zpo.html

[74] LG Stade 6 civil Senate, 19.12.2003, 6 O 405/02.

[75] K Bacher, 'BeckOK ZPO §287', in V Vorwerk &C Wolf (edS), *Beck'scher Online-Kommentar ZPO* (Beck, 2012), rn 13–14.

[76] This is different, for example, regarding the quantification of damages for violations of German competition law, whereby the infringer's profits can explicitly influence the determination of damages under §287. See Rauh et al, 'Die Ermittlung der Schadenshöhe im Kartelldeliktsrecht', above n 72, p 173.

causalities.[77] In the few successful cases, the heads of damages that have been awarded were negative interest, positive interest, and reliance damages.

In a judgment awarding damages on grounds of §126 GWB for the negative interest,[78] the quantification was undertaken in accordance with §287(1) ZPO. The claimant had the right to damages for the preparation of the bid and participation in the tender: according to the court this included labor and material costs, together with a proportion of general costs, as well as the cost of processing the tender and the conduct of the bid challenge. Since two side offers and one lot were not eligible (rejected bids), the court estimated the excluded costs to amount to 1/3 of the total losses, which would be reduced to account for the rejected bids.

Regarding specific items, the court discussed the following: the claimant put forward that a 13 % 'sector-surcharge' for some costs was conventional. This was rejected by the court in relation to the general costs, the costs of documentation and the technical expertise in the bid-challenge proceedings. The calculated travel costs were also rejected (the initial claim for €1.20 per km was replaced with a €0.40 per km valuation). As a result, the claimant was successful for €72,704.73.

7.4.2.1 Mitigation and Conduct of the Claimant at the Valuation Stage

A claim can be mitigated by contributory negligence under §287 GWB. In one case, the contracting authority attempted to claim contributory negligence of the aggrieved bidder for bidding in a flawed procedure. The court held that 'a bidder cannot be required to examine the legality of individual tenders. Further, the claimant as tenderer was allowed to trust that the defendant as contracting authority would conform with the legal requirements'.[79] Therefore, the risk of illegality had to be borne by the contracting authority and abusive conduct of the claimant in the sense of §242 BGB was not evidenced.

It is interesting to note that in this last stage, namely in the valuation of damages, arguments of very substantive nature can potentially be re-introduced by a judge, who has great discretion in dealing with the matter according to his or her own convictions. The estimation is firmly understood as procedural law, although the impact on the overall claim can be substantial.

7.5 Conclusions

The German system is characterized by a diversity of causes of actions that are linked to different claimable heads of damages. The statutory procurement damages provision is limited to bid preparation costs. These are awarded where an aggrieved

---

[77] Bacher, 'BeckOK ZPO §287', above n 75, rn 18.

[78] LG Stade 6 civil Senate, 19.12.2003, 6 O 405/02.

[79] LG Stade 6 civil Senate, 19.12.2003, 6 O 405/02.

bidder can demonstrate to have had a real chance of obtaining a contract. The quality of the real chance is still disputed and ranges from aggrieved bidders to have submitted at least a valid bid, to a very stringent assumption that the aggrieved bidder would have had to win the contract. The real chance is not used as a head of damage in the sense of a lost chance, but as an alleviation of the burden of proof with respect to bid preparation costs only.

Lost profits are available under *culpa in contrahendo*, but the bidder must bring the onerous proof of having been awarded the contract without the breach of the contracting authority. In theory, lost profits might also be available under the general tort provision, although court practice does not provide any strong precedents awarding damages under the latter cause of action.

To show that it would indeed have been awarded the contract, an aggrieved bidder must prove that an economically identical contract has been awarded by the contracting authority. One of the main doctrinal obstacle to successful damages claims is the party autonomy of the contracting authority since it is never required to proceed to award a contract at all.

Damages claims for bid preparation costs are relatively effective, but breaches which occur without trust relationship for the purposes of the *culpa in contrahendo* are a gap in the system of secondary protection of rights.

Bibliography

Ackermann, T (2000) 'Die Haftung des Auftraggebers bei Vergabeverstößen. Ein Beitrag zum Umgang mit den Vorgaben des EG-Rechts für nationales Privatrecht' 164 *ZHR* 394.

Alexander, C (2009) 'Vergaberechtlicher Schadensersatz gemäss § 126 GWB' *Wettbewerb in Recht und Praxis* 28.

Alexander, C (2015) 'GWB § 126 Anspruch auf Ersatz des Vertrauensschadens', in H Pünder & M Schellenberg (eds), *Vergaberecht*, 2nd edition (Baden-Baden, Nomos).

Bacher, K (2012) 'BeckOK ZPO §287', in V Vorwerk & C Wolf (eds), *Beck'scher Online-Kommentar ZPO* (Beck).

Braun, C & Hauswaldt, C (2006) 'Vergaberechtliche Wirkung der Grundfreiheiten und das Ende der Inländerdiskriminierung? Zugleich eine Anmerkung zum EuGH-Urteil Coname' *Europäische Zeitschrift für Wirtschaftsrecht*.

Brüggemeier, G (2006) 'Aansprakelijkheid van Toezichthouders', in CC van Dam (ed), *Aansprakelijkheid van Toezichthouders Met Publieke Taken* (Ministerie van Veiligheid en Justitie).

Burgi, M (2009) 'Zukunft des Vergaberechts' *NZBau* 609.

Burgi, M (2011) 'Damages for Breach of Public Procurement Law. German Perspectives', in D Fairgrieve & F Lichère (eds), *Public Procurement Law. Damages as an Effective Remedy* (Oxford, Hart Publishing).

Burgi, M (2011) 'A Report about the German Remedies System', in S Treumer & F Lichère (eds), *Enforcement of the EU Public Procurement Rules* (København, DJØF Publishing).

Drügemöller, A (1999) *Vergaberecht und Rechtsschutz. Der inter- und supranationale Rahmen und seine Ausgestaltung in Deutschland* (Berlin, Springer).

Irmer, W (2004) *Sekundärrechtsschutz und Schadensersatz im Vergaberecht* (Frankfurt, Peter Lang).

Jebens, P (1999) 'Schadensersatzansprüche bei Vergabeverstößen' *Der Betrieb* 1741.

Knauff, M (2010) 'Das Kaskadensystem im Vergaberecht – ein Regelungsmodell mit Zukunft?' *NZBau* 657.

Lange, H (1979) *Schadensersatz* (Tübingen, Mohr, 1979).

Prieß, HJ and Bonitz, K (2013) 'Das Sonderregime für Schadensersatz bei Vergabefehlern' *NZBau*.

Prieß, HJ & Hölzl, FJ (2011) 'Drei Worte des EuGH: Schadensersatz ohne Verschulden! – Zur gemeinschaftsrechtskonformen Auslegung des §126 S.1 GWB' 1 *Neue Zeitschrift für Baurecht und Vergaberecht*.

Rauh, JO, Zuchandke, A & Reddemann, S (2012) 'Die Ermittlung der Schadenshöhe im Kartelldeliktsrecht' *Wettbewerb in Recht und Praxis*.

Schnorbus, Y (1999) 'Der Schadensersatzanspruch des Bieters bei der fehlerhaften Vergabe öffentlicher Aufträge' *BauR*.

Stockmann, K (2014) '§126 GWB', in U Immenga & EJ Mestmäcker (eds), *Wettbewerbsrecht: GWB*, 5th edition (München, CH Beck).

Wilke, S (2005/2006) *Die Bedeutung von Schadensersatz nach Vergaberechtsveröβen im Rahmen der Vergabe öffentlicher Liefer- und Bauaufträge* (Grin).

Chapter 8
Case Study: France

Abstract This chapter presents public procurement damages claims in France. It covers the proceedings through which a damages claim can be brought in France, including their personal scope and time limits. The focus of the chapter is on the discussion of the extra-contractual liability of contracting authorities in public procurement as developed in case law. It further examines the quantification of damages claims, notably the recoverable losses (bid costs and lost profits) and quantification methods.

8.1 Systemic Features

8.1.1 Sources of Law

The legislative implementation measures for Directive 89/665,[1] Directive 92/50[2] and Directive 2007/66[3] in France contained no specific provisions for damages claims. This can be explained by the fact that damages claims for aggrieved tender-

---

[1] Décret n° 2004-732 du 26 juillet 2004 modifiant le décret n° 2004-18 du 6 janvier 2004 pris pour l'application de l'article L.34-3-1 du code du domaine de l'Etat ; Décret n° 92-964 du 07/09/1992 relatif aux recours en matière de passation de certains contrats et marchés de fournitures et de travaux et modifiant le nouveau code de procédure civile et le code des travaux administratifs; Décret no 2009-1086 du 2 septembre 2009 tendant à assurer l'effet utile des directives 89/665/CEE et 92/13/CEE et modifiant certaines dispositions applicables aux marchés publics.

[2] Décret n° 2001-210 du 7 mars 2001 portant code des marchés publics JORF "Lois et Décrets", Code des marchés publics; Décret n° 98-113 du 27/02/1998 relatif aux mesures de publicité et de mise en concurrence applicables à certains contrats de services dans les secteurs de l'eau, de l'énergie, des transports et des communications et portant modification du décret n° 93-990 du 03/08/1993 JO du 28/02/1998; Décret n° 98-112 du 27/02/1998 soumettant la passation de certains contrats de fournitures ou de prestations de services à des règles de publicité et de mise en concurrence et modifiant le décret n° 92-311 du 31/03/1992 JO du 28/02/1998, Décret n° 98-111 du 27/02/1998 modifiant le code des marchés publics en ce qui concerne les règles de mise en concurrence et de publicité des marchés de services JO du 28/02/1998, page 3115 ; Loi n° 97-50 du 22/01/1997 complétant, en ce qui concerne certains contrats de services et de fournitures, la loi n° 91-3 du 03/01/1991 relative à la transparence et à la régularité des procédures de marchés et soumettant la passation de certains contrats à des règles de publicité et de mise en concurrence et la loi n° 92-1282 du 11/12/1992 relative aux procédures de passation de certains contrats dans les secteurs de l'eau, de l'énergie, des transports et des télécommunications JO du 23/01/1997.

[3] Implemented by Loi no 2008-735 du 28 juillet 2008 relative aux contrats de partenariat (1) ; Décret no 2009-1456 du 27 novembre 2009 relatif aux procédures de recours applicables aux

---

© Springer International Publishing Switzerland 2016

H. Schebesta, *Damages in EU Public Procurement Law*, Studies in European Economic Law and Regulation 6, DOI 10.1007/978-3-319-23612-4_8

ers have long been recognized under French administrative law.[4] In addition, French administrative law is traditionally largely judge-made rather than based on explicitly legislative measures. However, the available causes of action were expanded, and have over the last few years received several remarkable extension through case law developments which are also relevant for damages claims brought by aggrieved bidders.

8.1.2   Jurisdiction: Administrative and Civil

French law has developed a strong distinction between administrative and civil law and jurisdictions. This separation also translates to the law of damages and liability of private – as opposed to public – entities.[5] The liability of administrative bodies in principle falls into the separate administrative law track of jurisprudence, rather than a unified one for civil and administrative law liability claims. The general rule is that all contracts applying the *code des marchés publics*[6] (Public Procurement Code, 'CMP') are within administrative jurisdiction. Generally, the administrative court of the place of contract execution is competent.

8.2   Causes of Action

French public procurement law is firmly part of administrative law. The position of aggrieved bidders was precarious, but has changed significantly in the last decade. In principle, various proceedings are open against contracting authorities before the administrative judge: a pre-contractual procedure (*le referé précontractuel*), a contractual procedure (*le réferé contractuel*), the jurisprudentially developed proceedings challenging the validity of public contracts that started with the *recours "Tropic Travaux"* and proceedings for abuse of power (*le recours pour excès de pouvoir*). In order to bring a damages claim, an aggrieved third party bidder has two possibilities, to bring a self-standing damages claim in a full procedure or to bring the damages claim in a procedure challenging the validity of a contract.

---

contrats de la commande publique ; Ordonnance no 2009-515 du 7 mai 2009 relative aux procédures de recours applicables aux contrats de la commande publique.

[4] F Lichère, 'Damages for Violation of the EC Public Procurement Rules in France' (2006) *Public Procurement Law Review* 171 citing the cases CE, 19 February 1930, Société Est et Sud Piketty, lebon p 196 for 'bid cost' and 'lost profit', and CE, 13 May 1970, Sieur Monti c/ Commune de Ranspach, lebon p 322.

[5] J Ghestin & G Viney, *Traité de droit civil / T.II Les obligations 4e Partie Introduction à la responsabilité* (Paris, Librairie Générale de Droit et de Jurisprudence, 1995), 1.

[6] Décret no 2006-975 du 1er août 2006 modifié.

8.2.1 Justiciability

The standing of undertakings not party to a public contract was originally rather limited. In the early 1990s, under the influence of EU law, a pre-contractual summary procedure was created[7] in order to implement the initial Remedies Directive 89/665 and ensure compliance with procurement law before contract signature. Standing extends to those undertakings that have 'an interest to conclude a contract and which interest is susceptible to being infringed'.[8] However, the procedure does not allow for damages claims.[9]

Again in order to implement EU law, the *référé contractuel*, a contractual summary proceeding, was created by the Ordonnance n° 2009-515 of 7 May 2009. This procedure grants the judge powers relating to the modified remedies called for under Directive 2007/66 (such as ineffectiveness). Article L.551-16 of the *Code de justice administrative* explicitly states that damages claims can be brought only as a counter claim in these proceedings.[10]

In an incisive judgment, the *Conseil d'Etat* in *Tropic Travaux* opened a new and specific procedure, which enabled third parties to challenge public contracts. It gave discarded bidders the possibility of bringing challenges to the validity of a contract and damages claims in a full procedure.[11] The time limits, however, are very short – namely two months, beginning two months after the adequate publication of the actual award. Importantly, this procedure was interpreted further with regards to damages claims in *Société Rebillon Schmit Prevot*[12]:

> 2. In order to obtain compensation for rights violated, the ousted contestant has the opportunity to bring before the judge (juge du contrat) a claim for damages, being accessory or complementary to the claims for the termination or cancellation of the contract. He may also bring a separate action in full proceedings, with the exclusive aim of claiming compensation for damage suffered as a result of the illegality of the contract from which he was ousted. In both cases, the presentation of claims for damages by the ousted competitor is not

---

[7] Article L. 551-1 and following of the Administrative Code (*code de justice administrative*, 'CJA'), introduced by Loi n° 92-10 du 4 janvier 1992 and Loi n° 93-1416 du 29 décembre 1993.

[8] CJA, article L. 551-1. Interpreted in the case CE, 3 October 2008, *SMIRGEOMES*, 'manquements qui, eu égard à leur portée et au stade de la procédure auquel ils se rapportent, sont susceptibles de l'avoir lésée ou risquent de la léser, fût-ce de façon indirecte en avantageant une entreprise concurrente'.

[9] N Gabayet in 'Damages for Breach of Public Procurement Law. A French Perspective', in D Fairgrieve and F Lichère (eds) *Public Procurement Law. Damages as an Effective Remedy* (Oxford, Hart Publishing, 2011), p 8.

[10] CJA, article L. 551-16: *À l'exception des demandes reconventionnelles en dommages et intérêts fondées exclusivement sur la demande initiale, aucune demande tendant à l'octroi de dommages et intérêts ne peut être présentée à l'occasion du recours régi par la présente section.*

[11] In CE, 16 July 2007, *Sté Tropic Travaux signalisation,* n° 291545, the court held: 'Tout concurrent évincé de la conclusion d'un contrat administratif est recevable à former devant le juge administratif un recours de pleine juridiction contestant la validité de ce contrat ou de certaines de ses clauses, qui en sont divisibles, assorti, le cas échéant, de demandes indemnitaires'.

[12] CE, 11 May 2011, *Société Rebillon Schmit Prevot*, n° 347002.

subject to the time limit of two months following the completion of the contract disclosures, which is applicable only to claims seeking termination or cancellation.

3. The admissibility of claims for damages, presented as accessory or complementary to an action challenging the validity of the contract, however, is subject, under the terms of general principles, to the intervention of a prior decision by the administration of the nature to bind the dispute, if necessary during the proceedings, except for public works. They also need to be, under the sanction of being inadmissible, motivated and quantified. It is not, in fact, for the judge hearing such an action, to grant the ousted competitor compensation even though the latter did not make any claims in this regard.

The latter case clarified that third party bidders can bring a damages action either as an accessory or complementary claim under a *Tropic Travaux* procedure or as an independent full proceeding. In both cases, the two months period for bringing damages claims would not be applicable. However, a claim presented as accessory or complementary to an action challenging the validity of a contract requires a prior administrative decision. Furthermore, the latter claims to damage have to be motivated and quantified – otherwise risking to be declared inadmissible for these deficiencies alone.

For contracts concluded from 4 April 2014, the *Tropic Travaux* case law was significantly modified by the case *Département de Tarn-et-Garonne*,[13] in which de courts clarified that the third party recourse would be available for all public contracts (not just specific procedures as the terminology 'discarded bidders' had suggested). In terms of standing, the court specified that the interest of the third party had to be sufficiently likely to be harmed, in a direct and certain way. This case law on standing and sufficient interest of third parties vis-à-vis public contracts has undergone drastic modifications through the cited cases and further jurisprudential developments on this point are to be expected.[14]

In the case of competing causes of action, where a regular contract has been concluded between a tenderer and the administration, liability is incurred through the contractual relationship: under the doctrine of 'absorption', all other parallel causes of action are assimilated by the contractual claims.[15] Since aggrieved bidders are not normally regarded to be in a contractual relationship with the contracting authority, and no "implied contract is involved".[16] The cause of action is therefore based on extra-contractual liability, in addition to which a subsidiary cause of action may be possible under unjustified enrichment.[17]

---

[13] CE 4 April 2014, n° 358994, *Dpt Tarn-et-Garonne* : JurisData n° 2014-006635.

[14] E Langelier, 'L'Évolution du Contentieux des Contrats Administratifs: À Quand l'Acte IV?' 47 (2014) *La Semaine Juridique. Administrations et collectivités territoriales*, 2330.

[15] CE 22 December 1922 cited in C Bergeal & F Lenica, *Le Contentieux des Marchés Publics* (Editions du Moniteur, 2010), pp 151 and 181–212.

[16] Lichère, 'Damages for Violation of the EC Public Procurement Rules in France', above n 4, p 172. See also Gabayet, 'Damages for Breach of Public Procurement Law. A French Perspective', above n 9, p 8 ('there is no doctrine of implied contract in French law').

[17] Bergeal & Lenica, *Le Contentieux des Marchés Publics*, above n 15, p 162.

8.2.2 Time Limits

In France, the prescription period for claims against the government, departments, municipalities and public institutions is four years.[18] The time limit starts to run from the first day of January of the year following the claimant's becoming aware of the violation. The relevance of special time limits was discussed above.

8.2.3 The Constitutive Criteria

There is a long-standing tradition in French law to grant damages for the liability of public bodies for illegal actions under a strict liability doctrine (*responsabilité sans faute*) doctrine. The constitutive requirements comprise (i) illegality as fault, (ii) harm (*préjudice*), and (iii) a causal link (*lien de causalité*).

Any illegal act committed by the administration entails fault on behalf of the administration.[19] Unlike EU law, no determination of the seriousness of the breach of law is required.[20] However, the wrongful conduct must have caused harm, and the causality must be established, which normally requires a direct, actual and certain (*direct, actuel et certain*[21]) causal link between fault and harm. The requirement of direct and certain is contrasted with potential (*éventuel*) or hypothetical factors in order to delimit the spheres of recoverable and non-recoverable losses.[22] There is a strong general principle of (full) compensation. The fact that illegality automatically entails fault for the purposes of public procurement violations *de facto* creates a system of 'objective liability', under which any breach of public procurement law results in the satisfaction of this requirement as a constitutive criterion for liability.

Recently, a court decision has explicitly linked "causality" to the lost chance as a causal element. However, in that case the assessment seemed to introduce a new element of causality, which had hitherto been absent – namely the requirement of a causal link between the *specific* violation and the losses sustained: in *Arts&Batiment*,[23] the court of appeal reasoned that there was a lack of causality between the precise violation that had occurred (in this case publicity deficiencies, as well as a lack of weighted criteria) on one hand and the reasons why the tender was eventually

---

[18] This is the so-called *prescription quadriennale* governed by Loi n° 68-1250 du 31 décembre 1968.

[19] CE 26 January 1973, Ville de Paris c/ Sieur Driancourt.

[20] Of course, one may present this conclusion in a different way, saying that illegality by definition entails the specific and sufficient seriousness of the mistake.

[21] Seule constitue une perte de chance réparable, la disparition actuelle et certaine d'une éventualité favourable. Cass. civ. 1 21 novembre 2006.

[22] W Müller-Stoy, *Schadensersatz für verlorene Chancen - Eine rechtsvergleichende Untersuchung* (Albert-Ludwigs-Universität zu Freiburg, 1973), p 6 referring to Mazeaud-Tuno and Tourneau.

[23] CAA Bordeaux, 27 October 2011, *SARL Arts & Batiment*, 10BX00835.

discarded on the other. It remains to be seen how far this reasoning will be further developed and applied by the courts.

Concerning public procurement and damages for aggrieved bidders, a very consistent and solid doctrine has developed in case law. The finding of liability is less preoccupied with the notions of fault, harm and causal links, but instead centres on the question of the likelihood that a tenderer would have been successful in obtaining a contract. At the heart of the issue of establishing the recoverable losses is the doctrine of 'the lost chance', which has been judicially developed in the courts.

8.2.4   The Classification of Chances

In the following, the categories of chances are surveyed. In public procurement cases, a two-step test was established and increasingly rigidified through consistent application by the courts. The first step consists of evaluating whether a tenderer was devoid of any chance of being awarded a contract. Where that question is answered in the negative, the judge proceeds to an evaluation of whether a tenderer had a serious chance. The standard formula on the distinction between 'not being devoid of any chance', and 'serious chance' of being awarded a contract was clarified in an important judgment delivered in 2003:

> … where a contestant for the award of a public contract demands compensation for the damage resulting from its unlawful exclusion from the latter, it is for the court to determine first whether or not the company was not devoid of any chance to win the contract; that, where this is the case, the company is not entitled to compensation; that in the negative, it is entitled in principle to reimbursement of expenses incurred to present its offer; it must then be examined whether the company had serious chances of being awarded the contract; in such cases the company has the right to be compensated for loss of earnings, including necessarily, since they have been integrated into its expenses, the costs for the preparation of its bid which therefore do not need to be the object, unless otherwise provided in the contract, of specific compensation.[24]

The judgment provided for much needed clarification between the different categories of chances, and the steps to be undertaken in order to assess the nature of a chance. It has been consistently affirmed.[25] The courts have stabilized a categorization resting on only two categories: testing (1) whether a tenderer was devoid of any chance, and (2) the evaluation of whether the quality of this chance was of a 'very serious nature'.

Earlier case law seemed to imply that a third category of chances existed, namely a merely 'serious or real' chance as opposed to a 'very serious' chance. Based on the case law rendered in the last ten years, one must consider that the formulation of

---

[24] CE 4 June 2003, N° 249630.

[25] The same formulation has been continuously recalled by the relevant courts. See eg, CAA Lyon, 7 January 2010, *Sarl Chantelauze* n° 08LY00248; TA Cergy-Pontoise, 21 mars 2013, 3e ch., n° 1003154, *Société TRM; or CAA Versailles, 11 September 2014, N° 12VE04165 société Rébillon Schmit Prévot,* to name but a few.

a chance as 'serious' or 'very serious' does not influence the available damages.[26] The first step consists of evaluating whether a chance existed at all; the second step, what the quality of that chance was. The jurisprudence has reached a stable point in which the following types of chances are distinguished in a system of a *numerus clausus* character: Three types of categories of chances thus materialize: no chance (i.e. devoid of a chance); a chance, but one which is not serious; and a serious chance. These are discussed in the following.

8.2.4.1 Was an Aggrieved Bidder Devoid of any Chance?

In the first step of the test, the vagueness of the 'lost chance' leaves room for several parallel inquiries. Behind the finding that a tenderer was devoid of a chance stand two different evaluations: on one hand, 'not devoid' is used to express what in reality is, again, a finding on illegality. This is the case when the court, given the indications of the case file, fails to find that the contracting authority made an '*incorrect material assessment*' or '*a manifest error of appreciation*',[27] for example. Under this approach, the court will review the process by which the contracting authority came to its decision. The nature of this review, however, remains to a certain extent external. The judge reviews the contracting authorities' decision, but does not substitute this with its own assessment in the absence of any illegality and therefore no link to the harm.[28] Only the second form constitutes an assessment of the quality of a tenderer's chance, and whether the nature of a tenderer's implication was sufficient to amount to a chance. Here, a court substitutes its own assessment for that of the contracting authority.

Secondly, an aggrieved bidder is devoid of any chance if a bid was illegal, inappropriate or unacceptable.[29] Examples of disqualifying factors include the fact that a candidate was "not suitable according to its economic and financial standing or professional and technical knowledge or ability",[30] or that a bid did not correspond to a contract notice.[31] Despite a particularly low price, the fact that the qualification criteria were not met deprived a tenderer of a chance.[32]

---

[26] In 2006, Lichère maintained that the consequences of having a 'very serious' as opposed to a 'serious' chance were still disputed, as was the issue of whether the formulations made a difference in the calculation of the amount of the recoverable damages. See Lichère, 'Damages for Violation of the EC Public Procurement Rules in France', above n 4, p 176.

[27] CE, 29 déc. 2006, n° 273783, Sté Bertele SNC.

[28] CAA Paris, 18 September 2007, *SOCIETE ASF.*

[29] *Société TRM*, above n 25.

[30] See Lichère, 'Damages for Violation of the EC Public Procurement Rules in France', above n 4, p 172, citing a case 4 June 1976.

[31] ibid, p 173, citing *Sarfati*, June 30, 1999.

[32] CE 30 June 1999, N° 193925 Lebon 7 / 10 SSR, 'qui n'a pas donné satisfaction au regard des critères de qualité architecturale et d'insertion dans le site, nonobstant son coût particulièrement bas, le requérant était dépourvu de toute chance d'obtenir le contrat de concession si la procédure d'attribution de celle-ci s'était déroulée régulièrement'.

The result of this initial assessment is either that a candidate was entirely devoid of a chance or, on the contrary, that s/he had had a chance. The latter gives rise to the subsequent second step of whether that chance can be classified as serious or not.

8.2.4.2   Not Devoid of a Chance but Not with a Serious Chance

The second class of cases are those in which a court does not find a tenderer to have been devoid of all chances of winning a contract but in which the chance is not ultimately assessed as serious. In other words, the tenderer had a chance, but not a serious one. For this type of chance, bid costs are awarded as the head of damage. In such cases, courts will often simply state that in the particular context the tenderer did not have a right to compensation for lost profits (without explicitly examining the nature of the chance). The fixed linkage between the categories of chances and the recoverable losses then implies that the chance had not been sufficient.

For example, in *Golf de Cognac*, a company participated in two stages of a competitive procedure to win a contract. In the end, the contract was illegally awarded to a competitor that had been eliminated during the first stage. The claimant had been selected as one of five from overall number of 12 competitors. It could therefore not be said to have had no chance of being awarded the contract if the competition had taken place in the regular fashion. Consequently, the aggrieved bidder had a right to compensation for the bidding costs. However, compensation for lost profits in that case was rejected.[33]

8.2.4.3   Serious Chance

Judges often have to make technical assessments in their evaluations of whether chances qualify as serious or not. This is typically done by (1) determining the criteria which would have decided an offer in the concrete case, here the relationship between the lowest price and other criteria is especially relevant; (2) evaluating the contracting authorities' (or relevant selection commission) material assessments of the offers submitted by competing bidders as to their validity most importantly, but also in relation to quality; (3) coming to a conclusion as to the relatively better one; and (4) assessing whether the offer was theoretically acceptable to the contracting authority.[34] Mostly, the parties in court will then rely on expert opinions and technical notices in order to sustain the validity and quality of their bids.[35]

(1) Price versus other criteria. A serious chance can be established where the aggrieved tenderer's bid was the lowest bid, even if the selection was also geared at

---

[33] CE 23 March 1994, *Golf de Cognac*, 1/4 SSR.

[34] On the development of a natural history museum and related technical expertise see, for example, CE, 8 February 2010, *Commune de la Rochelle*.

[35] ibid.

criteria other than price, under the most advantageous/economical offer.[36] One can speak of a 'presumption of a serious chance for the bidder with the lowest offer',[37] although the assumption can be reversed.[38] Reasons for a reversal of a serious chance due to the lowest price include the differential weighting of other criteria.

(2) Validity and objective quality, as well as (3) relative quality of bids. After establishing what criteria the contracting authority would have used to award a contract, the aggrieved tenderer's bid is scrutinized in terms of *validity*. This means scrutiny of a more formal type as to whether in theory, without evaluation, for example, all required documents were contained or, when specific requirements were set, whether these were met. In the second instance, the quality is assessed under the standard of the tender documentation; where any external or expressly stated criteria are used, this amounts to an assessment of the objective quality of a bid. Another type of assessment which is often performed by the courts is one of relative quality. This implies an evaluation of a bid in comparison to bids submitted by other tenderers and involves a hierarchy of tenders.

(4) Theoretical acceptability and possibility of the contracting authority to not award the contract and declare a bid offer to be unfruitful. When classifying the existence and seriousness of a chance, the courts are open to the argument that there was no acceptable bid. Such may be the case where the difference between the price offered in a bid and the contracting authority's realistic estimation of the contract price is so large that there was no acceptable bid. Even if the aggrieved bidder is the only remaining eligible candidate, if the final bid and a realistic estimation are very far apart, in the specific case more than double, a bid may be unacceptable.[39] The judgment follows the free will theory of contracts and opens up a new solid line of defence for contracting authorities, as in many cases it will be impossible to prove that negotiations would have been fruitful.[40]

A good example of how the courts proceed to evaluate an aggrieved bidder's chance of being awarded is the *Commune de la Rochelle* case:

> Taking into account the superiority of the technical value of the offer of Goppion to that of Atelier Blu, the only other company that had submitted a bid, that the … tender regulations provide that the technical criteria is a priority compared to the price, and that it does not appear from the statement that the price proposed by Goppion company, which was 3 %

---

[36] Lichère, 'Damages for Violation of the EC Public Procurement Rules in France', above n 4, p 174.

[37] ibid, p 174, citing Administrative Court of Appeal of Nancy, 31 May 2001, *Société RTP*; Administrative Court of Appeal of Lyon, 8 November 2001, *SARL Pugny BTP*; Administrative Court of Appeal of Douai, 21 May 2002, *Société Jean Behotas*; Administrative Court of Appeal of Bordeaux, 10 February 2005, *SA Urbaco*.

[38] Lichère, 'Damages for Violation of the EC Public Procurement Rules in France', above n 4, p 174.

[39] CAA Paris, 8 March 2011, *SOCIETE ETABLISSEMENTS CARRE*.

[40] Under German law, this line of argumentation is perfectly common and acceptable, but the case law has already developed further, the rebuttal being that the will to contract is proven if the contract has actually been awarded or if an economically identical one has been retendered. To the author's best knowledge, these considerations are not yet common in French litigation.

lower than the estimate of the contracting authority, would have prevented that its can be accepted, the Goppion company is correct in arguing that it lost a serious chance to carry out the lot 1 of the restructuring the natural History Museum of La Rochelle[41];

In assessing the aggrieved bidder's chance, the court took into account the quality of the offer, in particular compared to the other bids, the number of competing submissions and the price of the bid in comparison to the estimates of the contracting authority. It concluded that Goppion indeed had a serious chance and hence should be awarded lost profits.

8.3 Quantification of Damages

8.3.1 Recoverable Losses

As in many legal orders, the point of departure of damages claims is that of full compensation. Although there are clearly some important nuances in relation to the exhaustive nature of compensation, it is nevertheless regarded as one of the founding principles of liability and the law of damages.

8.3.1.1 The Lost Chance

Most of the damages case law in France focuses on the notion of a chance, namely whether and what kind of a chance an aggrieved bidder had in order to determine which losses are recoverable. However, this is not the lost chance doctrine in its strong version, which postulates that the lost chance is autonomously recoverable as a head of damage. In other areas, French courts have held that the lost chance must be measured independently:

> Compensation for the damage consisting in the loss of a chance is to be measured based on the value of the lost chance and cannot be equal to the benefit that would accrued if the chance had been realised.[42]

The area of public procurement, however, clearly defies this approach to the lost chance. Damages are not to be only partially compensated for, and the principle of proportional liability is not (officially) accepted in public procurement cases. The court recognized that the aggrieved bidder with a serious chance of having been awarded a contract has *"a right to reimbursement of the entire lost profit he would have received by becoming the successful tenderer."*[43]

---

[41] *Commune de la Rochelle,* above n 34.

[42] Cass. Com 7 Janvier 2004, n° 01-17.426, 'La réparation du préjudice consistant dans la perte d'une chance doit être mesurée à la valeur de la chance perdue et ne peut être égale à l'avantage qu'aurait procuré cette chance si elle s'était réalisée'.

[43] CE, 27 January 2006, *Commune d'Amiens.*

Under this approach, the lost chance constitutes an alleviation of the burden of proof to claim specific heads of damages. Different classes of chances result in a different extent of losses to be claimable: a chance, but one that was not serious results in the compensation of bid costs, while a serious chance results in the compensation of lost profits. This fixed link between specific classes of chances and heads of damages introduces an element of proportionality. One may hence speak of a 'categorized proportional liability'. *De facto*, a categorized proportional liability effectively mediates between the two different loss of chance theories by combining a limited proportionality in strict categories with differing burdens of proof for different heads of damages.

8.3.1.2 Bid Costs and Lost Profit

The finding that an aggrieved tenderer was not devoid of all chances to win a contract results in a right to claim the costs of the bidding procedure, but not the lost profits.[44] Further reaching losses in the form of lost profits can be claimed if an aggrieved tenderer had a serious chance.[45] This had already been established in a 1980 case and has since been consistently reconfirmed:

> Given that it results from the hearing that the illegal decision [by the contracting authority] was of a nature to result in the liability of the Seclin hospital centre because it deprived the undertakings Aubrun of a serious chance to win the award of the contract; therefore, the undertakings Aubrun have the right to compensation in the amount of the lost profits as a result of that decision.[46]

Although a tender was sometimes said to have 'only' had a serious chance, the consequences in terms of heads of damages did not differ from those of a very serious chance – in both cases, lost profits can be claimed.

In *Groupement entreprises solidaires ETPO Guadeloupe, Sté Biwater et Sté Aqua TP*, the procurement commission of Lamentin had decided to award a contract for the extension of a waste water treatment plant to the ETPO group. The contracting authority went back on this decision and requested the procurement commission to conduct a new evaluation of the bids, following which the contract was awarded to the group Sogea-Dodin. The court held that under such circumstances it could be hardly disputed that the group had a serious chance of keeping the contract in question.[47]

Regarding the relationship between damages for lost profit and bidding costs, it is unsettled whether it is possible to claim both heads of damages in parallel. The courts have regularly decided that bidding costs are 'necessarily included' in lost profits, unless otherwise stated in the tender notice.[48] There is no accumulation of

---

[44] CE, 23 March 1994, *Golf de Cognac*.

[45] *Commune de la Rochelle*, above n 34.

[46] CE, 28 March 1980, *Centre Hospitalier de Seclin*, 1/4 SSR, 11292.

[47] CE 4 June 2003, N° 249630, *Groupement entreprises solidaires ETPO Guadeloupe, Sté Biwater et Sté Aqua TP*.

[48] ibid.

the two types of loss, unless stipulations to another effect have been made, for example, through a notice from the contracting authority stating that it would reimburse tenderers for a part of their investment in the bid submission. To illustrate, in the 2003 *ETPO* judgment, the *Conseil d'Etat* held:

> Considering, however, that expenses incurred by the group for the preparation of its bid, in the absence of contractual provisions according to which they are for at the expense of the contracting authority, are among those that are normally incumbent upon [a bidder] to obtain the contract and which are reflected in the remuneration for the realization of the latter; thus the Groupement entreprises solidaires ETPO Guadeloupe, Sté Biwater et Sté Aqua TP is not entitled to ask for their compensation.[49]

Although the aggrieved bidders had the right to be compensated for the loss of benefits it expected from the contract execution, the bid preparation costs for submitting the offer would not be compensated, if no explicit deviating provisions had been made to the contrary. Bid costs formed part of a normal business risk assumed when partaking in a procedure.

8.3.2   The Burden of Proof

As Lichère notes, establishing whether an aggrieved bidder was 'not devoid of any chance of obtaining a contract' shifts the burden of proof in favour of the allegedly aggrieved bidder. First, the lack of a chance must be established; this is a negative wording, the presumption implicitly being that a chance existed. Secondly, it appears that the conviction (as distinct from the evidence) of a judge is sufficient to fulfil the first step of scrutiny.[50]

However, the right to receive compensation for bid costs can be forfeited where an aggrieved bidder does not explicitly claim them, or where they are not sustained through evidence:

> Whereas, however, the applicant, who has never sought reimbursement of preparation costs of the tender, and … despite the contention that the estimate of this head of damage was flawed, has not produced any evidence to assess the extent and amount of his right to compensation as such, must be deemed to have waived compensation expenses it incurred in presenting its offer.[51]

In finding that an aggrieved bidder had a serious chance, the court tends to look at the evidence objectively. In some cases it appears as though the aggrieved bidder must provide evidence for the contention that s/he would have been awarded a contract. The formulations vary slightly, and other times the courts deploy a negative formulation which effectively shifts the burden of proving that an aggrieved bidder did not have a serious chance towards the contracting authority. In one case, for

---

[49] ibid.

[50] Lichère, 'Damages for Violation of the EC Public Procurement Rules in France', above n 4, p 173.

[51] *SOCIETE ETABLISSEMENTS CARRE*, above n 39.

example, the court stated: 'it does not appear that the price would have prevented that its [the aggrieved bidder's] offer can be accepted.'[52] The aggrieved bidder did not have to prove that its price was so low that its offer would certainly have been accepted but only that it was within a price range that made it *acceptable*.

In the future, the motivation of courts with respect to how a chance is assessed will likely become more detailed. In a recent judgment, the *Conseil d'Etat* squashed a judgment of the lower court which had held that an aggrieved bidder had no serious chance for insufficient motivation thereof and stated:

> By merely observing … that the ousted candidate had no serious chance of being awarded the contract without exposing factual considerations to motivate this assessment while the ousted undertaking argued that it had such a chance because, first, its bid price was lower than that resulting from the awarded bid; second, that only two companies had expressed interest in the contract, third, that the technical value of the offer could not be compared to that of the successful tenderer's, the court insufficiently motivated its decision with regard to the arguments before it and has not put the court (juge de cassation) in a position to exercise its control.[53]

The *Sté Pradeau et Morin* case therefore creates a stronger duty on behalf of the courts to motivate the categorization of the respective chances an aggrieved bidder possesses.

8.3.3 Valuation Methods

In France, the number of procurement damages cases dealing with valuation methods are relatively manifold. The quantification of damages is based on a twofold reasoning: the estimation of turnover, and the profit rate applicable.[54] While the usual profits can be taken into account,[55] the lost profit is calculated on the basis of the net profits which would have accrued to a tenderer in the specific market, rather than at the rate of gross profit of overall activities.[56] In this recent ruling, the *Conseil d'Etat* dealt with the question of how lost profits ought to be calculated. This is remarkable, as quantification methods of damages are usually regarded to belong to the discretion of the judge, and are rarely scrutinized by higher courts. The court held that the lower court (the CAA Lyon) had erred in assessing the lost profits on the basis of a gross margin and not on the basis of net profits which would have accrued to the aggrieved bidder if it had obtained the lots in question.[57]

---

[52] *Commune de la Rochelle*, above n 34.

[53] CE, 27 oct. 2010, n° 318023, *Sté Pradeau et Morin*.

[54] Lichère, 'Damages for Violation of the EC Public Procurement Rules in France', above n 4, p 177.

[55] ibid.

[56] CE, 11 février 2011, *communauté de communes du pays d'Arlanc*.

[57] ibid.

Damages for overheads are usually not granted.[58] At the same time, the fact that an aggrieved bidder was able to secure subsequent independent contracts, which effectively charge his or her capacity, does not invalidate his compensation claim for a lost contract – a tenderer can thus 'effectively [be] paid twice'.[59]

The existence of an extreme level of competition lowers the level of damages.[60] In the estimation of the applicable profit rates, arguments relating to the relevant market are accepted, for example, referring to the market for glass showcases, which has a 15 % profit margin, rather than to the general glass market, which has an estimated 4.23 % share.[61] Relatively generous percentages have been accepted in recent cases (ranging from 1.25 %, up to 5 %, 11.63 % and 34 %).[62] The profit margins observed do not exhibit normal or standardized rates, but rather they are characterized by an increasingly specialized, case by case assessment. This corresponds to a trend moving away from abstract towards concrete quantification of damages.

In *Societe Eurovia*, the court granted damages for lost profit, including (in absence of stipulations to the contrary in the tender contract) bid preparation costs, but excluding the company's general/fixed costs. Lost profit was determined, not by the *brut* marginal percentage, but based on the net benefit that would have been obtained. The net margin was assessed at 'habitually 10 %'. The offer of the company was taken as the base value, amounting to €2,123,899, therefore the loss was fixed at €59,000.[63]

Once liability for lost profits is established, the damages may cover liability for both material and immaterial damages. In claims for immaterial damages, such as business reputation, the characteristics of the market can be taken into account – for example a high level of competition precluding recovering a loss of commercial reputation. In *Centre Hospitalier de Seclin*, it was not established that the illegal exclusion from the procurement procedure resulted in a damage to the business reputation of the aggrieved bidders to the detriment of their activities in the upcoming years, given that the severity of the competition for the contract award limited the benefits which could normally have been expected from the execution of the contract.[64]

---

[58] Lichère, 'Damages for Violation of the EC Public Procurement Rules in France', above n 4, p 178.

[59] ibid, p 177; *Commune d'Amiens*, above n 43.

[60] Lichère, 'Damages for Violation of the EC Public Procurement Rules in France', above n 4, p 177.

[61] *Communauté de communes du pays d'Arlanc*, above n 56.

[62] Lichère, 'Damages for Violation of the EC Public Procurement Rules in France', above n 4, p 177.

[63] CAA Nancy, 9 February 2012, *Societe Eurovia*.

[64] CE, 28 March 1980, *Centre Hospitalier de Seclin*.

8.3.3.1   The Applicable Interest Rates

The interest rate applicable is the legal rate, and starts to run on the date of receipt of the date for the first preliminary application for damages.[65] Applying Article 1154 of the Civil Code, compound interest (i.e. interest accrual on interest) can be granted where this has been judicially applied for or by special agreement and when due for over a year.

8.4   Conclusion

The French system is marked by the administrative law approach to public procurement. Under French law, the conditions giving rise to liability are (i) fault, which however is established by illegality alone; (ii) harm; and (iii) causality, that is, a direct link between fault and harm. France demonstrates a firm approach in case law to the question of bid costs and lost profits. The determination of whether and which damages are awarded happens through a two step evaluation of the chances that an aggrieved tenderer had of actually obtaining a contract. This two step process involves, first of all, establishing whether an aggrieved bidder was deprived of all chances of being awarded a contract – usually where he would not have qualified at all for being awarded a contract. Secondly, the chance is qualitatively evaluated in relation to whether it was serious or not, which is assessed based on the circumstances of the case and the objective hypothetical prognosis of the individual scenario; an assessment which the judge is required to motivate.

An aggrieved tenderer without any chance will receive no compensation; where s/he can prove to not having been devoid of the chance to obtain a contract, the bid costs are rather easily granted by French courts in the face of the illegality committed by the public authority alone. A serious chance usually leads to the award of lost profits. This special solution of France mediating the lost chance can be described as one of 'categorized proportional liability'. It is noteworthy that the French system does not have a role for pre-contractual liability.

As to the types of losses that are claimable – while the judge has a large margin of discretion, the Conseil d'Etat has recently pronounced judgments providing guidance on the quantification of damages in public procurement. The margin of maneuver for judges narrowed, based on a two step calculation of first, the estimation of turnover, and second, the applicable profit rate.

Court actions are relatively numerous, which results in a sophisticated approach also to the quantification of damages. Jurisprudence of higher courts is not limited to the constitutive criteria of procurement damages, but includes issues as 'technical' as the burden of proof in procurement cases and the valuation method for the calculation of lost profits.

---

[65] *Communauté de communes du pays d'Arlanc*, above n 56.

Bibliography

Bergeal, C & Lenica, F (2010) *Le contentieux des marchés publics* (Editions du Moniteur).

Gabayet, N (2011) 'Damages for Breach of Public Procurement Law. A French Perspective', in D Fairgrieve and F Lichère (eds) (2011) *Public Procurement Law. Damages as an Effective Remedy* (Oxford, Hart Publishing).

Ghestin, J & Viney, G (1995) *Traité de droit civil / T.II Les obligations 4e Partie Introduction à la responsabilité* (Paris, Libraire Générale de Droit et de Jurisprudence).

Langelier, E (2014) 'L'Évolution du Contentieux des Contrats Administratifs : À Quand l'Acte IV ?' *47 La Semaine Juridique. Administrations et collectivités territoriales* 2330.

Lichère, F (2006) 'Damages for Violation of the EC Public Procurement Rules in France' *Public Procurement Law Review* 171.

Part III
Transversal Discussion of Damages

One of the prime findings of the country studies is that damages claims are not a concept capable of unitary definition. Instead, several 'issues' define the overall availability of damages at the same time. In the following, we unbundle the different sites of damages claims topically grouped together in three chapters. Chapter 9 covers systemic, institutional and constitutive criteria; Chap. 10 focuses on the quantification aspects of damages; while Chap. 11 discusses the lost chance in its multifaceted versions, addressing at times causality, burden of proof and claimable losses.

In the following part, the issues were restricted in following a problemistic approach, guiding the inquiry to instances where internal uncertainty prevailed, differences between jurisdictions were pronounced, or tensions with EU law were foreseeable. Also examined is the extent to which EU law has developed requirements on the relevant items in order to indicate the degree to which specific sub-issues are determined at EU level, or open to national discretion.

The purpose of the following horizontal issue-based analysis is also a conceptual endeavor. It aims to provide an abstract and *a priori* understanding of the elements which frame damages. The abstraction is carried out by the use of case studies, overviews of EU requirements, and theory. In several instances, the results of the comparative law overview are given by presenting one national jurisdiction in greater detail. These case studies are used variably, as examples or illustrations, or in order to enhance general statements through specificity. The section is written with the European point of view in mind. Sometimes a mere statement of the law for all jurisdictions was rationalized, if the detailed discussion of one legal system was suitable in order to discover the underlying qualitative issues of a given rule from the point of view of EU law. It is often the case that a particular rule has given rise to contention in one particular legal order but has gone relatively undisputed in other jurisdictions (as is the case for the award of interest). Lastly, and where possible, legal solutions have been combined with a theoretical perspective to enable a deeper understanding and to provide a reference point to allow the classification of differences.

Chapter 9
Issue Based Analysis of Public Procurement Damages

Abstract This chapter identifies and discusses systemic, institutional and constitutive factors that affect damages claims at the national level. In particular it considers the national policy making sphere, the institutional framework, the determination of the applicable law, various causes of action and the justiciability of public procurement norms (material conditions, standing, and prescription).

9.1 National Public Procurement Policy Space

EU policy making takes place in a multi-level policy making framework in which European procurement policy coexists with the national legal policy sphere. Common EU policy is complemented by how the policy area (public procurement) and precise issue (damages) are perceived in the given national policy contexts.

9.1.1 Public Agenda

Enforcement of and compliance with EU public procurement rules is significantly influenced by the national context. The public procurement rules are framed by national policy measures which may generally raise awareness of procurement duties, publicly monitor compliance or impose reporting and auditing of procurement activities.

To take a prominent example, Dutch procurement policy was incisively marked by a public procurement construction sector scandal (see box below). The discovery of systemic fraud in the sector prompted a national outcry and put compliance with public procurement rules in the spotlight. Empirical compliance studies were commissioned by the government. These included a study on judicial protection in public procurement bringing forward a rather devastating assessment of the availability of damages claims in the Netherlands.[1]

---

[1] JM Hebly, ET de Boer & FG Wilman, *Rechtsbescherming bij aanbesteding* (Paris, Uitgeverij Paris, 2007).

© Springer International Publishing Switzerland 2016
H. Schebesta, *Damages in EU Public Procurement Law*, Studies in European Economic Law and Regulation 6, DOI 10.1007/978-3-319-23612-4_9

Policy Context of Legal Relevance: The Dutch Construction Sector Scandal

In 2001, the popular Dutch TV Show Zembla screened a documentary entitled 'cheating with millions'.[2] The emission uncovered systemic corruption, shadow accounting, tax evasion and fraud, and of course persistent and systemic violations of public procurement and competition law rules. The public was enraged. The government quickly responded by setting up a parliamentary commission, the 'Enquete Bouwnijverheid', to examine the scandal. The final report was very critical of the sector and identified major anomalies in procurement proceedings. In response to the findings, the defense minister Korthals resigned. The report also proposed several measures for the future. Additional compliance studies were drawn up on a biannual basis in the '*Nalevingsreport*' for 2002–2010.[3] In addition, under the initiative '*Rechtmatigheid Gemeenten*', several categories of contracting authorities have to file annual accountants' declarations assessing the legality of accounts, among others with public procurement rules.

---

[2] Zembla, 'Sjoemelen met miljoenen' (9 November 2001), zembla.vara.nl/seizoenen/2001.

[3] Significant BV, *Nalevingsmeting Europees aanbesteden* for various years, www.rijksoverheid.nl.

Clearly, the fact that public procurement started to be higher on the public agenda influenced the policy making process to a significant degree. Compliance studies were conducted for the first time and provided an estimate of the extent to which contracting authorities across the Netherlands followed public procurement rules. In addition, several legislative initiatives were taken which related to the reporting and auditing duties of public authorities. Such general policy measures can act as an additional deterrent, and encourage compliance. External influences, such as negative reports of auditors, have been demonstrated to be a highly effective stimulus to induce compliance of contracting authorities with public procurement legislation.[4] Several years after the introduction of such Dutch framing measures, overall compliance with EU procurement legislation had significantly improved.[5]

9.1.2   Structural Implementation

Another important aspect of national policy making is the way in which a Member State chooses to implement EU law. The procurement directive is a good illustration of the different ways in which the legal interface between national and transposable EU law can be designed. One of the key findings in the jurisdictions covered

---

[4] Significant BV, *Nalevingsmeting Europees aanbesteden 2010* (2012), www.rijksoverheid.nl.

[5] Significant BV, *Nalevingsmeting Europees aanbesteden 2008* (2010), www.rijksoverheid.nl.

concerned the divergent implementations for damages actions: the 'structural cou-
pling', i.e. the way to assure transposition of EU rules into the domestic systems,
exhibited strong variations. Germany passed a specific provision to deal with public
procurement damages. The Netherlands, on the other hand, 'implemented' through
non-implementation – the general tort law scheme which covers Member State liability also governs public procurement damages claims. In France, the situation at
face value is similar, namely the resort to a general liability scheme without express
implementation efforts. However, public procurement specific case law has been
developed in great detail by the judiciary. This judge-made law, then, is more comparable to the common law approach. In the UK, the English Procurement
Regulations contain an explicit damages provision. As the latter does not go beyond
the wording of the EU Remedies Directive, the details of damages actions are
authoritatively stated in case law, notably the *Harmon* case.

There are EU requirements on Member States' implementation of EU law.
Specifically, implementing provisions must guarantee the ascertainability of rights
granted and requirements of legal certainty must be met: they must be of '*unquestionable binding force, or with the specificity, precision and clarity required in order
to satisfy the requirement of legal certainty*'.[6] It is doubtful in how far some of the
'implicit' implementations of public procurement damages indeed constitute specific, precise and clear obligations. Particularly enforcement measures are often
developed in case law as the country studies have shown. Such case law does not
always succeed in creating a solid damages doctrine, making it less predictable and
subject to further judicial interpretations.

At the same time, the quality of the implementing measures is linked to the quality of the primary obligation at EU level. There is an enormous discrepancy between
the highly detailed nature of substantive EU public procurement law, leaving almost
no margin of discretion in terms of implementing substantive rules; the detailed
overall remedies regime that necessitated legislative action in all Member States to
comply; and the merely vague damages obligation, the precise content of which
remains rather unclear.

The ineffectiveness of procurement damages at national level is therefore not only
the result of unclear national obligations, but also of the opaque nature of the EU obligation to provide damages. This uncertainty is aggravated because the vague requirement of damages is part of an otherwise highly regulated field of law. It seems to cause
Member States to feel a certain 'irresponsibility' towards the obligation of damages. In
other areas of law, the legislature or the courts would turn to national general principles
to determine and potentially raise the adequate level of judicial protection. The fact
that Member States formally comply with a vague damages EU law requirement
obstructs the development of further reaching secondary protection. Formal compliance with implementation duties weakens the motivation to find an adequate level of
protection of aggrieved bidders at national level through additional measures.

Hence, the vagueness of the damages provision at EU level leads to an equally
vague implementation at Member State level. Implementations of the damages

---

[6] Case C-354/98 *Commission v France* [1999] ECR I-04927, operative part.

article vary between specific legislative implementation, case law developed procurement liability actions and applicability of general tort law clauses. The EU legislator should consider clarifying the meaning of the lost chance in the Utilities Remedies Directive and as a minimum align the Public Sector and the Utilities Directives by including the lost chance provision for both regimes. Since public procurement remedies are highly regulated at EU level, it is unlikely that Member States are going to pass further reaching damages legislation in the area on their own initiative. National regulation of damages claims in public procurement is contingent on the specific EU obligation. These are compelling circumstances calling for clarification and legislative action at EU level.

9.2   Institutional Framework

Damages claims in public procurement are also influenced by the institutional structures in which claims are handled. The forums which are designed vary between the Member States. Broadly speaking, one can distinguish between arbitration as an extra-judicial forum, special review bodies which are characterized by a special degree of technical expertise in the field of procurement, and the general administrative and civil courts. The Member States' public procurement remedies systems exhibit crucial differences in their institutional structure and the nature of the claim can determine the institution that is competent.[7]

Two particular issues can be identified with respect to the institutional framework, namely arbitration and the type of procedure (full or summary) in which procurement damages claims are brought.

There are specific EU law requirements on review bodies. In the Remedies Directive, the requirements on the non-judicial bodies reviewing contracting authorities' decisions are the following:

> Article 2(9): Where bodies responsible for review procedures are not judicial in character, written reasons for their decisions shall always be given. Furthermore, in such a case, provision must be made to guarantee procedures whereby any allegedly illegal measure taken by the review body or any alleged defect in the exercise of the powers conferred on it can be the subject of judicial review or review by another body which is a court or tribunal within the meaning of Article 234 [now Article 267 TFEU] of the Treaty and independent of both the contracting authority and the review body.
>
> The members of such an independent body shall be appointed and leave office under the same conditions as members of the judiciary as regards the authority responsible for their appointment, their period of office, and their removal. At least the President of this independent body shall have the same legal and professional qualifications as members of the judiciary. The independent body shall take its decisions following a procedure in which both sides are heard, and these decisions shall, by means determined by each Member State, be legally binding.

---

[7] See also the overview provided in SIGMA, *Central Public Procurement Structures and Capacity in Member States of the European Union*, Sigma Paper No 40 (OECD 2007), pp 18–20.

As to the legality of those independent bodies under the Directive, Article 2(9) sets requirements for non-judicial bodies regarding: the qualification of their members; the possibility of appeal to a court or tribunal with a prospect of making a preliminary reference to the CJEU; the procedural guarantee such as that both sides must be heard; rendering a decision that is legally binding; and a decision that is based on written reasons. These are quite far-reaching stipulations on the composition of procurement bodies, and quite deeply define the nature of the judicial organization of the Member States for the purposes of public procurement.

9.2.1 Arbitration as Extra-Judicial Proceedings

Arbitration is a generally critical issue from the point of view of EU law. The independence of tribunals, bias towards specific interest groups and the role of arbitration in enforcing the 'proper' application of EU law has been repeatedly criticized. The questionable nature of arbitration within the EU legal order is aggravated by the explicit and stricter requirements set in the Remedies Directive.

Specifically, the potential for appeal to a judicial organ within the meaning of Article 267 TFEU and the specific details on the composition of such a body are requirements which arbitration tribunals may come short of fulfilling. Arbitration tribunals themselves do not usually qualify as courts or tribunals entitled to make preliminary references under Article 267 TFEU. At the same time, the nature of arbitration brings with it the fact that arbitration tribunals never operate in pure isolation from the judiciary, but as a pre-stage. Regular public courts can always be a fall-back jurisdiction in the form of award annulment or enforcement proceedings. However, their scrutiny of cases is limited to public policy and hence theirs is a lower standard of review on substance.

The independence and composition of arbitration tribunals can also be a critical issue. Regarding the qualification of members of arbitration tribunals, it is often asserted that arbitration provides better technical expertise, which in a specialized field such as procurement is highly valuable in order to adjudicate on the merits of a case. That being said, arbitration panels risk being insufficiently independent. Precisely due to their technical specialization, the circles between claimants and arbitration panelists may be biased in favour of interest groups. For example, in the case of the Dutch arbitration tribunal for the construction sector, the nomination of the members has been accused of bias.[8] The Netherlands is a jurisdiction which made a lot of use of arbitration in cases of procurement disputes. In the box below, the Dutch experience is illustrated in greater detail in order to understand the possible pitfalls of arbitration.

---

[8] See also kamerstuk 28244 nr 11, p 68.

Arbitration Tribunals in the Netherlands
In the Netherlands, arbitration used to be common in the field of public procurement, as the legal system had highly institutionalized the use of arbitration tribunals. This was due to the fact that several regulations such as the UAR-EG 1991 or the UAR 1986 (now UAR 2001) contained arbitration clauses, through which disputes were submitted to the *Raad van Arbitrage voor de Bouwnijverheid* ('RvA'). After the corruption scandal in the construction sector, the RvA was identified as one of the systemic weaknesses in Dutch judicial protection by a government report, due to which the regulations were amended so that arbitration was no longer agreed upon by default clauses. Due to the automatic arbitration in the construction sector through the RvA, arbitration in the Netherlands was an important dispute settlement mechanism. Although the importance of arbitration has declined significantly because the public procurement regulations for construction no longer provide for arbitration by default, there are still a large number of disputes submitted to the RvA. This has been one of the key issues in the implementation process for Directive 2007/66, with the Wira explicitly addressing the matter.[9]

The RvA, composition and characterization as independent body

The RvA was created in 1907 by the *Koninklijk Instituut van Ingenieurs* (KIVI), the *Koninklijke Maatschappij tot bevordering der Bouwkunst, Bond van Nederlandse Architekten* (BNA) and the *Vereniging Algemeen Verbond Bouwbedrijf* (AVBB). Changing the statutes of the RvA requires the approval of the Minister for Traffic, Public Works and Water Management, as provided by the Statutes themselves. The body is made up of the president, up to 100 members nominated by KIVI, BNA and AVBB, and up to 30 extraordinary members nominated by the governing board of the RvA itself. All members must be approved by Minister for Traffic, Public Works and Water Management. The RvA is not a court or tribunal which is entitled to make a preliminary reference under Article 267 TFEU,[10] but an independent body.[11]

---

[9] Not only was criticism on arbitration voiced from a national perspective, especially in relation to the construction sector scandal, but the conformity with European law also became increasingly questioned. Kamerstuk 2005/2006 30 502, nr 4, pp 4–5.

[10] Characteristics taken into account in order to judge whether a body qualifies as a part of the judiciary are the legal basis of the organ, its permanent character, the bindingness of its jurisdiction, the principle of being heard, the independence of the organ and so on.

[11] This is also the conclusion reached in the 'Enquete Bouwvernijheid' report, see kamerstuk 28244 nr 11, p 66.

(continued)

Interests represented in arbitration panels

Since the major groups of interest representation for tenderers are responsible for the nominations, one might regard the RvA[12] as a one-sided organ in which contracting authorities are not represented.[13] In a dispute against one of those tender groups, an arbitration panel could be called to make an award against an organization by which it was nominated. For contracting authorities or enterprises not part of the organizations, there might be the impression of bias.

Appealing arbitration awards

Taking the Dutch legal order as an illustration: in order to enforce an arbitration award, leave to execute needs to be granted by the judiciary, that is the president of the court (Article 1062 Code of Civil Procedure, *Wetboek van Burgerlijke Rechtsvordering*, 'Rv'). Apart from several formal grounds, permission to execute an arbitration award can be denied in cases where the arbitration award is against the *ordre public* or *contra bones mores* (Article 1063 Rv). In addition, a request for annulment of an arbitration award can be filed (Article 1064 Rv), again to be granted next to formal reasons on the grounds of being against the *ordre public* or *contra bones mores* (Article 1065 Rv). These reasons must be interpreted in conformity with the Directives,[14] hence one way of arguing that Article 1064 Rv constitutes an effective appeal is by defending the position that a breach of the European public procurement rules always counts as a reason for public policy and in every case therefore results in an inquiry into the award on the merits. Granted that when assessing the validity of a legal act the Dutch Supreme Court in *Uneto/deVliert*[15] held that a breach of public procurement rules is not necessarily to be regarded as a violation of public policy, this argumentation does not hold in Dutch praxis.[16]

---

[12] Kamerstuk 30501 Nr. 3 p 26.

[13] In the context of the Dutch construction scandal, the RvA was named as one of the structural characteristics which was responsible for the limited sanction of irregularities, see the 'Enquete Bouwnijverheid', above n 11, nrs 5–6, p 57 stating that, contrary to regular arbitration, the RvA has no representative of contracting authorities, kamerstuk 28 244, above n 11, nr. 24 p 13, proposing a reformulation of the role of the RvA.

[14] For this comment see Nota naar aanleiding van het verslag kamerstuk 32027 C, p 2.

[15] HR 22 January 1999, NJ 2000,305 (*Uneto/De Vliert*).

[16] Article 4.26 of the *Aanbestedingswet 2012* provides that, in case of arbitration, the annulment procedure for arbitration awards under Article 1064 Rv must be made available.

9.2.1.1   The EU Perspective

From the perspective of EU law, the issue of arbitration raises an institutional problem concerning access to justice, by which disputes relating to EU rights become
distanced from the reach of the legal process under which a preliminary reference
can be made to the CJEU. The judicial link to an EU law interpretative authority
breaks. This raises challenges as to whether these bodies are required to apply EU
law, and if they are doing so, whether a uniform interpretation is guaranteed.

Arbitration clauses in public procurement are unilaterally imposed, rather than
freely agreed upon. The procurement process relies on the uniformity of the conditions in an offer of tender – which the tenderer has to accept by filing a bid. These
kinds of clauses can generally not be seen as an exercise of a tenderer's party autonomy to renounce his or her rights. A different case is the scenario where *ex-post*,
that is after a dispute has arisen, the parties – tender and contracting authority –
agree on arbitration.

The public procurement directives specifically address the composition of the
forum dealing with disputes and put forward the possibility in a framework of a
forum that can make preliminary references. This is a choice which demonstrates
the public nature of the procurement rules. Arbitration is essentially private dispute
settlement, from which mandatory rules are excluded. By requiring at least the possibility of appeal, the institutional connection to EU law is always guaranteed.
Public procurement law, due to its explicit requirements, constitutes a *lex specialis*
to the general EU law approach on arbitration.

The above example serves as a specific illustration of the generally uneasy relationship between arbitration and EU law. Arbitration awards are not generally subject to full review by the courts, but judges are often granted marginal powers of
review to annul an award if it is contrary to public policy. The question is then
whether breaches of EU law qualify as being contrary to public policy.[17] Under this
point of view, the breach of a public procurement directive, as a rule ranking as
public policy, would justify the review of a case on public policy grounds.[18] In the

---

[17] The above example serves as a specific illustration of the generally uneasy relationship between
arbitration and EU law. The issue most clearly arose in Eco Swiss in Competition law, from where
it spilled into Consumer law, an area in which numerous references to the topic illustrate the legal
uncertainty surrounding arbitration. See C-126/97 *Eco Swiss* [1999] ECR I-3055.

[18] This is the reasoning endorsed, in eg kamerstuk 28 244, nr. 11, above n 11, p 31. This requires a
chain of argumentation: First, a reading of *Eco Swiss* to the effect that an arbitration award in violation of ex-Article 81 EC must be annulled. Secondly, the reasoning to be applied to the public
procurement directives, as implying that a breach of the public procurement directives constitutes
(like a breach of ex-Article 81 EC) a breach of public order. For secondary legislation, the case law
has developed this position in *Asturcom* to the effect that under the principle of equivalence, a
provision in consumer law had to be treated as such a fundamental provision that it would count in
the equivalence test as a provision of public policy. There, the ECJ held '*[a]ccordingly, in view of
the nature and importance of the public interest underlying the protection which Directive 93/13*

Dutch context, this argument is used in order to defend the position that the arbitration system includes a mechanism of appeal to a body entitled to make a preliminary reference, thus satisfying the conditions of the Remedies Directive.[19] It is questionable whether this argument can be accepted because procurement would not usually classify as public policy.[20] For arbitration bodies to comply with the Remedies Directives, in particular to enable access to a body which is entitled to make a preliminary reference, arbitration awards should systematically be made open to full review.

9.2.2 Summary Proceedings Versus Procedures on Merit

In several jurisdictions, the kinds of proceedings available for public procurement disputes vary. Summary procedures are common, and these usually exhibit only limited testing of the merits. Due to the need for swift and rapid mechanisms in public procurement, for general litigation these short litigation procedures are preferable to the claimants. In terms of procedural justice, they strike a different balance between the costs of cases, for example in terms of time and money, and the value that is attributed to the accuracy of the outcome itself. This is reflected in the fact that less importance is given to procedural steps such as the evaluation of evidence and that more discretion is allowed to the judge and his or her estimate. The box below contains the example of the Netherlands, which illustrates in greater detail how the rules for the two types of procedure typically differ from each other.

---

confers on consumers, Article 6 of the directive must be regarded as a provision of equal standing to national rules which rank, within the domestic legal system, as rules of public policy' (para 52). Whether or not the public procurement rules can be considered as equally fundamental for the European legal order as consumer law would have to be judicially determined.

[19] Hordijck et al also argue that one 'can' defend the position that the annulment of an arbitration award (such as the Dutch ex Article 1064 Rv) counts as a review along the Directives. See EH Pijnacker Hordijk, WH van Boom & JF van Nouhuys, *Aanbestedingsrecht. Handboek van het Europese en het Nederlandse Aanbestedingsrecht* (Den Haag, Sdu Uitgevers, 2009) They refer, for example, to the general fact that arbitration proceedings are clearly not excluded, and are even implicitly endorsed through the provision on independent bodies, under the Directive. They are certainly right on the argument that if one were to require full scrutiny by a civil judge, arbitration loses its advantages of being less time and cost intensive.

[20] Critical views are also expressed in kamerstuk 28244, above n 11, nr 11 p 68.

Procedural Differences Between Summary and Regular Proceedings

The *kort geding*[21] is a summary procedure, which allows adjudication by an interim judge under Article 254(1) Rv for all urgent matters, which – taking into consideration the interests of parties – require immediate interim relief to grant these.

Compared to regular procedures, its procedural rules are much more flexible: for example, legal representation is not binding, the pleadings are generally not exchanged in writing, time periods for submission of documents are different and the legal rules of evidence are not applicable, which leaves the evaluation of evidence at the discretion of the interim judge.[22] Usually, a case is decided after one hearing only. Also, the legal exigencies in relation to the judgment's motivations are lower. It must be based on a balancing of parties' interest when granting interim measures,[23] a task that is to be undertaken by the judge *ex-officio*.[24] This does not translate into a duty to evaluate the parties' chances of success in a regular procedure. On the other hand, the interim judge remains – of course – limited by general principles of procedure, such as the prohibition of arbitrariness. An interim procedure does not have *erga omnes* effect but remains limited to the parties of the procedure without third party effect and without definitely establishing legal relationships (Article 257 Rv). Overall, the interim judge has a considerably greater margin of discretion in the interim injunction procedure. The procedure is informal and rapid. Although the regular procedure is the standard procedure in civil litigation generally, public procurement disputes are mostly resolved by means of interim procedures. Such public procurement disputes typically have the following aims: to stop an ongoing procurement procedure, to re-procure, to allow the claimant party to the inscription process, a prohibition of awarding a contract, the duty to reopen the tender procedures anew with a view to preventing the conclusion of a contract and the potential performance thereof.[25]

The *bodemprocedure*, on the other hand, being the regular court procedure in the Netherlands, is subject to the general body of civil procedural law. It is more formal and is subject to greater scrutiny, for example, in the hearing of experts. The regular procedure takes substantially more time, which also renders it more costly. Yet the regular procedure is the procedure which is mainly

---

[21] The *kort geding* summary procedure is regulated by Arts 254 – 260 Rv. See also W Hugenholtz & WH Heemskerk, *Hoofdlijnen van Nederlands Burgerlijk Procesrecht* (Den Haag, Elsevier, 2006). References to case law in this section derive from their account.

[22] HR 31 January 1975, NJ 1976, 146.

[23] See Art 257 Rv.

[24] HR 2 February 1968, NJ 1968, 62.

[25] By way of example, see kamerstuk 2008/2009 32 027, Nr 3, 3. See also Hebly, de Boer & Wilman, *Rechtsbescherming bij aanbesteding*, above n 1.

(continued)

used in public procurement for damage claims, as the time factor does not weigh so heavily, but substantive scrutiny is necessary.[26]

Differently from Dutch administrative law, the interim procedure is not contingent upon the existence of a regular court procedure – there is no requirement of connectivity. Even though also the effect of the regular procedure is limited as between the parties, it can be used to establish definite legal relationships and render declaratory rulings. It is therefore up to an aggrieved tenderer to decide which track s/he wishes to take, although the interim judge retains the possibility of holding that a dispute is not suitable for settlement through an interim procedure.[27]

---

[26] ibid, p 51.
[27] See Art 256, 257 Rv.

The choice between the two kinds of procedures greatly impacts upon procurement litigation. The capacity of the summary judges to pass judgment in a technical area such as public procurement is questioned, these concerns may relate both to resource constraints and to expertise. The desire for efficient and rapid procedures on one hand (procedural economy) has to be weighed against concerns relating to the quality of litigation.

From the EU point of view, so far the question of summary judgments has not come under the full scrutiny of the CJEU. The issue was raised incidentally in *Combinatie Spijker*,[28] but the Court did not pick up on this specific point. However, these procedures on the merits are much longer in terms of duration, and ultimately, more weighty in terms of costs. The degree of accurate application of law is compromised to some extent through the rationalizations of process economy. The question is, at what stage does the degree of just approximating 'the truth' (ie the correct application of EU law) become insufficient to satisfy the effectiveness postulate of EU law?

The relevance for damages claims varies from other actions, as damages are often separable from summary proceedings and can be claimed in a different procedure that will go into the merits. In France, the tenderer has a choice between summary and full procedures; the UK is at the interim stage only preoccupied with the question whether damages prima facie would constitute an adequate remedy. In Germany the damages procedure is a full procedure, and also in the Netherlands this is normally the case, as judges have shown themselves reluctant make findings on damages in summary proceedings. In the case of damages, the arguments for rapidity are much less pressing than in case of injunctions. Further, in order to show damage, the parties must be given rather ample opportunities to present evidence. Full procedures are thus more suitable for damages actions, in particular given the important amounts of money that are involved.

---

[28] Case C-568/08 *Combinatie Spijker Infrabouw* [2010] ECR I-12655.

9.3   The Applicable Law

Public procurement disputes are often perceived as exclusively national disputes. However, they can include important cross-border connecting factors, so that issues of international private law remain relevant. Before entering into the conditions for damages and the consequences thereof within one legal system, a precursory question concerns the applicable law. The applicable law depends on which type of action a claim is classified as, since the cause of action is the primary connecting factor in determining the applicable law.

9.3.1   *Applicability of the Rome II Regulation*

The Rome II Regulation[29] governs the conflict of laws concerning the law applicable to non-contractual obligations.

A specific exclusion on the applicability of the Rome II Regulation is provided for in Article 1(1) 'to the liability of the State for acts and omissions in the exercise of State authority (*acta iure imperii*)'. An argument to the effect that government procurement acts constitute the exercise of State authority could be made. However, by their very nature, government purchases seem to qualify by definition as commercial matters, and hence as *acta iure gestionis*. In EU law, the CJEU has interpreted acts of official authority narrowly. Although highly specific public procurement transactions such as defense spending might be characterized by State authority, regular purchases would be classified as *acta iure gestionis* – resulting in the applicability of the Regulation.

Public procurement law could be characterized as being overriding mandatory provisions, which always result in the exclusive application of national law. Such a view had been endorsed by German courts, for example, relying on the old Article 34 EGBGB (now repealed).[30] This allowed recourse to German public procurement law in instances where German law 'imperatively' governed a situational context[31]; although the public contract itself could have been governed by foreign law.[32] This view commits to a separability between public procurement law and the law of the contract. Article 34 EGBGB (repealed) is now expressed in Article 9 of the Rome I Regulation for contractual obligations, and Article 16 of Rome II for non-contractual

---

[29] Regulation (EC) No 864/2007 of the European Parliament and of the Council of 11 July 2007 on the law applicable to non-contractual obligations [hereinafter 'Rome II'].

[30] Art 34 Einführungsgesetz zum Bürgerlichen Gesetzbuche (EGBGB): 'Dieser Unterabschnitt berührt nicht die Anwendung der Bestimmungen des deutschen Rechts, die ohne Rücksicht auf das auf den Vertrag anzuwendende Recht den Sachverhalt zwingend regeln'.

[31] GS Hök, 'Zum Vergabeverfahren im Lichte des Internationalen Privatrechts' (2010) *ZfBR* 440, p 442; OLG Düsseldorf 14.05.2008 – Verg 27/08, VergabeR 2008, 661, 663.

[32] ibid. This might result in a splitting of the law applicable to a procurement situation – however, it seems that within our treatment of cases of damages claims that aspect can be neglected.

obligations – the mandatory provisions exceptions. In order for these exceptions to apply, one would have to conceive of the whole body of public procurement law as constituting mandatory provisions. They are defined as:

> provisions the respect for which is regarded as crucial by a country for safeguarding its public interests, such as its political, social or economic organisation, to such an extent that they are applicable to any situation falling within their scope, irrespective of the law otherwise applicable to the contract under this Regulation.[33]

Damages claims that form part of a country's general liability scheme, for example under contract or tort, can hardly qualify as mandatory provisions. It might be possible to distinguish between the public procurement specific statutory damages basis contained in the German §126 GWB and other causes of actions. However, this argument is not convincing as it would always rely on a qualification of all procurement law as meeting the condition that it is crucial in the safeguarding of the country's public interest.

Within the system of the Rome II Regulation, damages may fall within the public policy exception of Article 26 where they are perceived as excessive. If the damages regime of another country is perceived to be excessive, the legal damages regime of the forum should be applicable. At the same time, in intra-EU cases, punitive damages for public procurement violations could only be awarded very rarely (for example, on the basis of abuse of power in the UK), so that this provision in the context of procurement claims is less relevant.[34]

Probably the most serious challenge to the applicability of the Rome II Regulation to damages claims for breaches of public procurement law in some jurisdictions lies in the limitation of the scope to civil and commercial matters, and thus the exclusion of administrative measures under Article 1(1). This provision might be specifically relevant in countries with an administrative law tradition in the area of public procurement such as France. For civil law-regulated damages claims, however, this reasoning is not pertinent. However, EU public procurement does not constitute a purely budgetary – and hence internally, administratively shaped – field of law, but to a large extent is seen to belong to competition law in a broad sense.[35] Arguably therefore, public procurement law, at least for those contracts above the thresholds of the EU Directives, lack administrative character for all EU Member States.

---

[33] Article 9(1) Regulation (EC) No 593/2008 of the European Parliament and of the Council of 17 June 2008 on the law applicable to contractual obligations [hereinafter 'Rome I'].

[34] R 32 of the Rome II Regulation states: *'Considerations of public interest justify giving the courts of the Member States the possibility, in exceptional circumstances, of applying exceptions based on public policy and overriding mandatory provisions. In particular, the application of a provision of the law designated by this Regulation which would have the effect of causing noncompensatory exemplary or punitive damages of an excessive nature to be awarded may, depending on the circumstances of the case and the legal order of the Member State of the court seised, be regarded as being contrary to the public policy (ordre public) of the forum.'* See Rome II, above n 29.

[35] AS Graells, *Public Procurement and the EU Competition Rules* (Oxford, Hart Publishing, 2011).

9.3.2   Application of the Rome II Regulation

The non-contractual obligations are governed by Article 4(1) which as a basic rule, designates as applicable law that of the country *'in which the damages occurs'*. Before the general rule is applicable, however, it has to be considered whether a special provision might preclude the application of Article 4(1). In several countries, this might vary with different causes of actions.

Accepting a dimension of Competition law would lead to the additional applicability of Article 6(3)(a): *'The law applicable to a non-contractual obligation arising out of a restriction of competition shall be the law of the country where the market is, or is likely to be, affected.'* For example in Germany, damages actions under §126 GWB are part of competition law legislation. Public procurement damages could arguably be qualified as guaranteeing competition between tenders, an interpretation strongly supported by the move from budgetary to competition legal instrument; the applicable law could therefore be determined under Article 6.[36]

Actions based on the *culpa in contrahendo* doctrine on the other hand are governed by the provisions of Article 12,[37] which designates the law of the contract as the applicable law:

> The law applicable to a non-contractual obligation arising out of dealings prior to the conclusion of a contract, regardless of whether the contract was actually concluded or not, shall be the law that applies to the contract or that would have been applicable to it had it been entered into.

One can turn this reasoning around and ask what seems to be a 'fitting' solution for the connecting factor. The general rule of Article 4 leaves too many potentially applicable laws, especially considering that multiple bidders having sustained damage would lead to one situation being governed by different laws. In view of party autonomy, there is an argument to be made in respect of the choice of the parties, or the inclusion of a choice of law contained in the invitation for tender. As a matter of simplicity, the law of the contracting authority's seat could be made applicable to the determination of damages. By their very nature, public purchases are connected to the legal order of one country; the factual circumstances in any public procurement situation are such that recourse to the law of the contracting authority usually constitutes the closest connection. A connecting factor based on the seat of the contracting authority seems a just solution. Such an interpretation could be construed on the basis of Article 4(3):

> Where it is clear from all the circumstances of the case that the tort/delict is manifestly more closely connected with a country other than that indicated in paragraphs 1 or 2, the law of that other country shall apply. A manifestly closer connection with another country might be based in particular on a preexisting relationship between the parties, such as a contract, that is closely connected with the tort/delict in question.

---

[36] Hök, 'Zum Vergabeverfahren im Lichte des Internationalen Privatrechts', above n 31, pp 440–448.

[37] GS Hök, 'Neues europäisches Internationales Baurecht' (2008) *ZfBR* 741, p 747.

It has been demonstrated that the international private law qualification of pro-curement damages actions may lead to different results in different countries, based on the qualification of an act as administrative or for reasons of the nature of the underlying causes of action at issue. None of the options above discussed are con-clusive, and it will ultimately be up to the judgment of the CJEU in this matter.

9.4   Causes of Action

As argued above, the qualification as tortious or contractual and pluralities of causes of action can make a difference with regard to the law applicable under private inter-national law. The EU procurement directives do not prescribe the cause of action which the national law must provide for – by their nature, directives impose only an obligation of result.

The public procurement damages regime differs greatly between the selected countries. In Germany, a specific statutory provision for liability of public procure-ment damages co-exists with other causes of action. This is different in both the Netherlands and France, which largely govern public procurement damages liability by means of tort law. The Netherlands deploys a provision on the constitutive criteria of torts, whereas the quantification is governed by a single article for both contractual and tortuous liability. France also relies on tort law in order to govern liability claims, but it has consequently been developed through the courts. It was observed that the case law on liability has been developed in a divergent manner for different areas of law. The English common law system, on the other hand, has a broad statutory dam-ages provision in the Procurement Regulations, but relies heavily on the *Harmon* case, the main precedent and accepted authority for damages claims, which gave flesh to the general damages provision of the Regulations and beyond. At the same time, the comparison of liability of damages in public procurement confirms that each legal system has developed strong strands of case law that are public procurement specific, and molds pre-existing general principles to the specific needs of the sector.

The German system has introduced a statutory liability regime (special in terms of the constitutive criteria), yet which only leads to bid costs as heads of damages. Further reaching damages such as lost profit can only be achieved through another cause of action, most prominently through pre-contractual liability.

The French system, on the other hand, delegates claims for damages to the gen-eral principles of Tort law which, being extraordinarily broad, have been developed in case law. In addition to this, there is a schism between the tort case law regarding administrative and civil jurisdictions – these came to the fore for example in public procurement, which is an area in which French case law has developed particular conditions and interpretations. The French claims of damages discussion is largely determined by assessing the chances a tenderer had to be awarded the contract. Two types of chances exist; one that was a chance, resulting in bid costs and a serious chance, resulting in lost profits.

In the Netherlands, in the absence of a specific public procurement provisions, the general system of tort law has to come to terms with the specific issues of public procurement. It visibly struggles to do so. National judges have referred cases to the CJEU for guidance, and the results reached in case law regarding the application of the general tort law regime and the pre-contractual liability doctrine are not always congruent. So far, the adjudication of disputes appears to be an individual, case-by-case assessments leaving a wide margin of discretion to the judge. The result is legal uncertainty, as also observed strongly in doctrine, and in practice translates into a reluctance to litigate in order to claim damages against unlawfully acting authorities.

In the UK, the *Harmon* case as the authoritative source of law on the issue discussed four possible causes of action for the claimant. These were breach of EU law, statutory breach, implied contract, and public misfeasance. Regarding the statutory breach, however, the court found: *'As a matter of general approach I consider that where compensation is sought by a tenderer for being deprived of an opportunity to be awarded the contract, the approach should be to award damages on a "contractual" basis rather than on a "tortious" basis, although the remedy is a statutory remedy and usually the assessment of damages for breach of statutory duty is akin to those for a comparable tort.'*[38] While for the heads of damages, the difference is probably without distinction (if one accepts that the contractual 'positive interest' is used), the difference in claims is not devoid of practical significance. In particular, characterization as tort or contract can impact on limitation periods, and perhaps on 'the appropriateness of applying the 'loss of a chance test".[39]

9.4.1 Member State Liability as a Cause of Action

In some jurisdictions, however, the damages article is implemented (sometimes partially) by means of Member State liability as a cause of action. For example, the Netherlands uses an identical cause of action for public procurement and Member State/*Francovich* liability. In other jurisdictions, the available causes of actions are multifaceted and do not correspond. France in this respect formally governs both forms of damages through the same provision in the code civil, yet under different conditions as fleshed out in case law. Germany has explicitly distinct causes of actions, and national State liability is the cause of action through which Member State liability manifests in the national court.[40] In England on the other hand, *Francovich* liability is a self-standing, autonomous cause of action.

While viewed from the EU perspective, Member State liability is developed as though it were a self-standing remedy, this is not the sole view in the national

---

[38] *Harmon CFEM Façades (UK) Ltd v Corporate Officer of the House of Commons* (1999) 67 Con LR 1 at 196, para 259.

[39] M Bowsher & P Moser, 'Damages for Breach of the EC Public Procurement Rules in the United Kingdom' (2006) *Public Procurement Law Review* 195, p 203.

[40] In Germany, the literature holds different views on the relationship of *Francovich* liability and the German State liability regime of §839 BGB combined with Article 34 Basic Law. A pragmatic solution combines both aspects, providing for damages via the German liability course of action, which – if necessary – may be reinterpreted through the EU law-derived constitutive criteria as trumping national, more restrictive, ones. In order to claim damages in public procurement, the national State liability provision is generally not viewed as a pertinent or effective cause of action.

jurisdictions: some authors defend the view that national law alone is pertinent and that *Francovich* liability materializes only through a recognized national course of action, while others maintain that *Francovich* liability is self-standing. Inversely, an implementation of the damages provision by Member States through just a reference to Member State liability might not constitute a sufficient implementation measure either.[41] In a case against Germany, the CJEU rejected the German government's argument that the direct effect of directives constituted a sufficient implementation action:

> This minimum guarantee, arising from the binding nature of the obligation imposed on the Member States by the effect of the directives under the third paragraph of Article 189, cannot justify a Member State's absolving itself from taking in due time implementing measures sufficient to meet the purpose of each directive.[42]

By analogy, a reference to Member State liability as implementation of a damages article simply may not be sufficient.[43] A Member State liability reading of the Remedies Directives' damages article as advocated in *Combinatie Spijkerbouw*[44] is problematic when viewed through the national lens of the available causes of action. Thinking about Member State liability in terms of causes of action is misleading, because it follows an *ibi remedium, ubi ius* approach that prescribes a result. Member State liability is compensation limited to pecuniary damages and has constitutive conditions which can be more onerous to meet than some of the national damages provisions. The problematic nature of the conflation between damages in procurement law and Member State liability damages was discussed in Chap. 4 and can be confirmed from the national perspective.

9.4.2 Relevance of Having Different Causes of Action

The number of causes of actions which are generally regarded as useful for a tender varies considerably between countries. The main difference is between tort based approaches and systems which (in addition) recognize pre-contractual causes of actions (all surveyed jurisdictions with the exception of France). A claim being based in tort or contract carries great weight, with regards to the claimable heads of damages and the way losses are quantified (discussed in Chap. 10).

From a legal process point of view, the notion of a damages claim appears more and more disintegrated, consisting of many different causes of actions which present the aggrieved tenderer with various constitutive requirements and possible heads of damages. Overall, these findings challenge the unitary way in which the CJEU

---

[41] V Eiró & E Mealha, 'Damages under Public Procurement: The Portuguese Case', in D Fairgrieve & F Lichère (eds), *Public Procurement Law: Damages as an Effective Remedy* (Oxford, Hart Publishing, 2011).

[42] Case C-433/93 *Commission v Germany* [1995] ECR I-2303, para 24.

[43] Eiró & Mealha, 'Damages under Public Procurement', above n 41.

[44] Judgment in *Combinatie Spijker Infrabouw-De Jonge Konstruktie and Others*, C-568/08, ECLI:EU:C:2010:751.

seems to deal with what it terms 'damages claims' at the national level. What appears as '*the* national damages claim' from an EU perspective is in reality often a multiplicity of causes of action.

9.5   Justiciability: Terms of Material (Normtype), Personal (Standing) and Temporal (Prescription) Scope

The laws implementing EU public procurement create different effects in terms of the invocability that damages claims enjoy. Legal norms can limit the ways in which they can be relied on in courts by individuals. For example, public procurement administrative regulations that were strictly internal laws in Germany precluded the creation of rights that could be relied on in courts. Similarly, several doctrines restrict the capacity to invoke a norm to those provisions intended to confer subjective rights. A variation on such a limitation is found in standing rules which require a person to enjoy a protected interest to be relied upon. Furthermore, invocability may be limited in time through prescription periods which bar an action from being brought in the courts. Material justiciability, subjective rights requirements, requirements of protected interests and time limits are all rules which in one way or another contain a formal limitation of the scope of a given rule, which is why they are here grouped together under the heading of 'justiciability'.

9.5.1   Invocability

In countries in which public procurement was conceived of as administrative law, the position of the tenderer has typically undergone some strengthening over time, owing to the EU derived reconceptualization of the purpose of public procurement regulation. Government purchasing was perceived as merely enabling the internal working of the administration in the proverbial 'pencil purchase'.[45] As internal regulations, procurement norms lacked external effect, leaving tenderers in a vulnerable position. Individuals were unable to rely on these norms in the courts as they were non-justiciable norms. The underlying public procurement rationale, therefore, was highly crucial for the position of the tenderer. For example in Germany, public procurement underwent a shift from budgetary to competition law under the influence of EU law. The organization of the sources of law and the fact that aggrieved tenderers lacked subjective rights became subject to Union law through the Directives. In addition, a challenge was targeted at the German legal system in the form of a Commission action for infringement of the EC Treaty in which the CJEU ended up condemning the German 'administrative solution' to public procurement law.[46] This judgment (discussed in greater detail in the box below) was decisive in enabling damages claims for aggrieved tenderers in the first place.

---

[45] M Burgi, 'Zukunft des Vergaberechts' (2009) *NZBau* 609, p 612.
[46] *Commission v Germany*, above n 42.

Case Study: German Law Under European Influence

The Commission[47] alleged that Germany had failed to adopt the necessary measures to comply with the provisions of the old substantive Public works and public supply Directives.[48] The temporal aspect of this judgment is relevant; at the European level the facts were situated in time before Directive 89/665 was applicable, and at the national level, Germany had not yet implemented the changes through the 'budgetary solution'.

The Commission put forward the following arguments: (i) the procurement regulations VOL/A and VOB/A were to be regarded as purely private bodies of rules and therefore not binding on contract awarding authorities; (ii) the pure requirement pursuant to internal administrative circulars did not create any right for individuals to rely on those rules[49]; and (iii) purely administrative practices that could be altered on a whim were inadequate.[50] The position of the Commission was that a correct transposition required individuals to be able to ascertain the full extent of their rights, as the Public works and Public supplies directives were designed to make individual suppliers and undertakers rely on those rights as against public awarding authorities. This was precluded by the formal way in which Germany had chosen to transpose the provisions of the public procurement directives, namely through the internal administrative circulars, which lacked external effect upon which aggrieved tenderers could rely. Additionally, the Commission relied on C-361/88 *Commission v Germany,*[51] in which the CJEU had, similarly, dealt with a general administrative circular (in that case 'Technical instructions concerning air

---

[47] Following the usual infringement procedure, involving a formal letter from the Commission on 27 February 1992 and reasoned opinions given on 3 December 1992, on 3 November 1993 the Commission sought a declaration that the Federal Republic of Germany had failed to fulfill its obligations under the Treaty.

[48] Directive 89/440/EEC of 18 July 1989 amending Directive 71/305/EEC concerning coordination of procedures for the award of public works contracts and with Council Directive 88/295/EEC of 22 March 1988 amending Directive 77/62/EEC relating to the coordination of procedures on the award of public supply contracts and repealing certain provisions of Directive 80/767/EEC.

[49] *Commission v Germany,* above n 42, Opinion of Advocate General Elmer (11 May 1995), para 4.

[50] Commission v Germany, above n 42, para 5.

[51] Case C-361/88 *Commission v Germany* concerned Germany's implementation of Directive 80/779 on Air pollution and fixing of limit values applicable to concentrations of sulphur dioxide. Regarding the mandatory nature of the administrative circular, the ECJ

(continued)

purity') and condemned the lack of binding character thereof vis-à-vis third parties.

Germany did not deny the lack of individual rights of tenderers under the administrative circular solution, but advanced that (i) it was only with the adoption of Directive 89/665 that rules were established regarding breaches of Directives 88/295 and 89/440. (ii) Germany tried to rely on the direct effect of the Directives as opening a way for individuals to rely on the Directives against public authorities having infringed those rules.[52]

The CJEU agreed with the arguments put forward by the Commission regarding the non-mandatory nature of the legal rules in question. Although it stressed the possibility that '*a general legal context may, depending on the content of the directive, [would] be adequate*' for transposing directives, but that this is only so where '*the full application of the directive [has taken place] in a sufficiently clear and precise manner so that, where the directive is intended to create rights for individuals, the persons concerned can ascertain the full extent of their rights and, where appropriate, rely on them before the national courts*'.[53] In addition, the Court clearly rejected both of Germany's pleas. The first by relying on the first and second recital of Directive 89/665 which state that the introduction of the directive has only the purpose of reinforcing existing arrangements for ensuring '*effective application of Community directives*'. It is, however, without bearing on the obligation to transpose the Public works and public supplies Directives themselves.[54] The Court equally rejected the direct effect argument:

---

found the existence of an administrative circular to constitute an absence of a general mandatory rule: '*It must be stated that, in the particular case of the technical circular "air", the Federal Republic of Germany has not pointed to any national judicial decision explicitly recognizing that that circular, apart from being binding on the administration, has direct effect vis-à-vis third parties. It cannot be claimed, therefore, that individuals are in a position to know with certainty the full extent of their rights in order to rely on them, where appropriate, before the national courts or that those whose activities are liable to give rise to nuisances are adequately informed of the extent of their obligations. 21 It follows from the foregoing considerations that it is not established that Article 2(1) of the directive has been implemented with unquestionable binding force, or with the specificity, precision and clarity required by the case-law of the Court in order to satisfy the requirement of legal certainty.*' See C-361/88 *Commission of the European Communities v Federal Republic of Germany* [1988] ECR I-2567.

[52] *Commission v Germany*, above n 42, para 21.

[53] ibid, para 18.

[54] ibid, para 23.

(continued)

whereas the Court has in specific circumstances (…) recognized the right of persons affected thereby to rely in law on a directive as against a defaulting Member State. This minimum guarantee, arising from the binding nature of the obligation imposed on the Member States by the effect of the directives under the third paragraph of Article 189, cannot justify a Member State's absolving itself from taking in due time implementing measures sufficient to meet the purpose of each directive (see in particular, the judgment in Case 102/79 Commission v Belgium [1980] ECR 1473, para 12).[55]

In the meantime, what happened was a rather technical legal reshuffling of public procurement regulation. The German legislator tried to implement the European Directives by changing the *Haushaltsgrundsätzegesetz* (HGrG, Framework Law on the Budget).[56] Thereby, on the basis of §57 HGrG, the *Vergabeverordnung* (VgV, Ordinance on the Award of Public Contracts) of 1994 was issued, as well as the *Nachprüfungsverordnung* (NpV, Ordinance on the Review Procedures for the Award of Public Contracts). In 1997, final changes required for Procurement regulation for the award of independent contractor services (VOF) and an amendment to VOL/A were effected. The sector specific provisions were taken out of the Procurement Regulations, into the *Sektorenverordnung*. This 'budgetary solution' was explicitly not geared towards the creation of subjective rights, however, the Procurement Regulations for Public Works (VOB/A) and Public Supplies and Services (VOL/A) which had been deemed to be only of internal administrative effect, were finally given statutory character for contracts above the European thresholds.

Yet again, the CJEU held this system to be in breach of the public procurement directives. Only under the influence of European regulation through the public procurement directives did subjective rights for tenderers become recognized. This resulted in a third and last reorganization of public procurement law, which became part of Competition law, the 'Competition law solution'. Finally, for contracts falling within the scope of the European public procurement directives, the 'budgetary solution' was abandoned with a comprehensive revision and the incorporation of the material law into part 4 of the German Act against the Restraints of Competition, the *Neufassung des Gesetzes gegen Wettbewerbsbeschränkungen (GWB)* of 29.05.1998, §97 GWB and following.

---

[55] ibid, para 24.

[56] 26 November 1993 (BGBl. I S. 1928) das Haushaltsgrundsätzegesetz, HGrG, Statute on the Principles on the Spending of Public Funds.

9.5.1.1　The Schutznormtheorie and Theories of Protected Interest

The legal construction that norms only offer legal protection if they are protecting specifiable interests is important in the German legal system, and referred to as the *Schutznormtheorie*.[57] It is widely recognized that the doctrine is problematic in relation to EU law. This has led to calls for modification of several variants, and even abolition thereof, but a reconciled understanding is still lacking. The discussion of the subjective right and the Schutznorm are highly controversial in Germany; in France it is mirrored in a weaker version, the protected interest theory. Also in the Netherlands, general tort law provisions require a condition of 'relativity' (6:163 BW). Relativity tests the objective and purpose of a statutory norm regarding both the protected person/entity and protected losses. The UK focuses more on the interest in relation to protected losses.

Following one view, it would be for the *national legal order* to determine whether subjective rights can be claimed. To take the national interpretation of the protective scope of European norms would result in diverging interpretations and seems to violate the European legislator's intention to create uniform rules. Many authors argue that the *Schutznormtheorie* is not pertinent for claims deriving from EU procurement law.[58] A moderate view requires an invocable provision to at least be intended to protect the interests of undertakings in competition. This version still requires the specific protective purpose of a provision, but the purpose is more widely phrased and will, in the case of public procurement, be met in most instances. Another view suggests a differentiation on the basis of the direct applicability of a directive.[59] A variation of protected interest is based on conditions for individual concern comparable to those elaborated under 263 TFEU. The CJEU has easily assumed a legally protected interest, based on various different protected requirements – thus not following any version of a protected interest theory strictly, yet always requiring (weaker) legal protection of some sort, making a complete abandoning of the protected interest theory impossible.[60] However, as the requirement concerns the interpretation of EU law, it is to be determined at EU level.

9.5.2　Time Limits

A further limitation of damages claims comes in the temporal form of prescription periods, that is, the amount of time after which a claim 'expires'. The time period can be calculated in various ways, for example, it can start to run from either the

---

[57] In order to indicate the fact that the legal instrument is at the heart of this definitional matter, the term 'theory of protective provision' seems more accurate.

[58] See K Péguret, *Schadensersatzansprüche übergangener Bieter im Vergaberecht* (Jenaer Wissenschaftliche Verlagsgesellschaft, 2010), p 74.

[59] ibid, p 78.

[60] ibid, p 81.

commission of the illegal act or after the claimant has acquired knowledge thereof. The durations of prescription periods are most often laid down in legislative instruments, while the application in concrete cases may require an assessment of, for example, when exactly the claimant became aware of his or her claim; this is mainly developed by the courts. In some instances, derogations from statutory limits can be undertaken by contract, in the case of public procurement in tender notices or the applicability of standardized tender conditions. However, even these will usually be subject to possible scrutiny by the courts regarding their fairness.

In France, the prescription period is governed by the *prescription quadriennale*, under the law of 31 December 1968. The time limit starts to run from the first day of January following the claimant's becoming aware of the violation and is four years. In Germany, the applicable regular prescription period is 3 years, according to §195 BGB. Following §199 BGB it starts to run at the end of the year in which the claim arose, or in which the claimant ought to have had knowledge of those circumstances. In the Netherlands, the standard applicable period for damages claims is laid down in Article 3:310 BW and the regular period is 5 years. The period starts to run on the day following the claimant's learning of the damages and the person to be held liable. However, it seems possible to contractually agree on shorter time periods (often around 90 days) as is the case, for example, in the standard tendering regulations.[61] In England, the prescription period has been subject to litigation in front of the CJEU, and consequently the rules have been changed to 30 days.

9.5.2.1 EU Law Requirements

Time limits have been the subject of much critical scrutiny by the CJEU, as they are so closely connected to the enjoyment of a right, and are usually qualified as material in nature rather than procedural. Specifically, the CJEU has held that time limits in the field of public procurement can only start to run 'from the date of the infringement of those rules or from the date on which the claimant knew, or ought to have known, of that infringement.'[62] EU law in public procurement precludes the time period for prescription from running from the date of infringement, but requires the claimant's knowledge of a violation. The Court further held that the fact that a tenderer has been rejected is not sufficient in order to presume that he had knowledge of, or sufficient information to establish, the illegality.

> It is only once a concerned candidate or tenderer has been informed of the reasons for its elimination from the public procurement procedure that it may come to an informed view as to whether there has been an infringement of the applicable provisions and as to the appropriateness of bringing proceedings.[63]

---

[61] JM Hebly & FG Wilman, 'Damages for Breach of Public Procurement Law. The Dutch Situation', in D Fairgrieve & F Lichère (eds), *Public Procurement Law. Damages as an Effective Remedy* (Oxford, Hart Publishing, 2011), p 85.

[62] Case C-406/08 *Uniplex (UK)* [2010] ECR I-00817, para 35.

[63] ibid, para 31.

While the CJEU scrutinized the conditions for the starting of the time period, it did not consider the question of whether three months is a sufficient time period in absolute terms. The English rule used to be that proceedings must '*be brought promptly and in any event within three months from the date when grounds for the bringing of the proceedings first arose, unless the Court considers that there is good reason for extending the period*'. The CJEU further explained that Member States have an obligation to establish a system of limitation periods that is sufficiently precise, clear and foreseeable to enable individuals to ascertain their rights and obligations.[64]

The case turned on the discretion of the judge and the resulting legal uncertainty, which in this case failed the effectiveness principle:

> Directive 89/665 precludes a national provision, such as that at issue in the main proceedings, which allows a national court to dismiss, as being out of time, proceedings seeking to have an infringement of the public procurement rules established or to obtain damages for the infringement of those rules on the basis of the criterion, appraised in a discretionary manner, that such proceedings must be brought promptly.[65]

However, although the Court has not delimited the time limits more closely, it has drawn attention to the fact that due to the rapidity sought for purposes of the Remedies Directive, time limits could be relatively short, as long as they were reasonable.[66]

The growing amount of case law on time limits is another indication that there is a law of damages in creation and, in institutional terms, the interpretation at the discretion of the judge shifts the burden of implementation of EU law to the legislatures. Especially in the field of civil procedure, where the judge enjoys a wider margin of discretionary responsibility, one can expect a shift towards legislative codification, as exemplified by the *Uniplex* case in the UK.

9.6 Fault Requirements

9.6.1 EU Case Law

Fault is one of the constitutive criteria in which the CJEU has not been reluctant to intervene and held that the Remedies Directives damages provision is a strict no-fault requirement and diverging regimes would be in violation of EU law.

---

[64] ibid, para 39.

[65] ibid, para 43.

[66] Case C-314/09 *Strabag and others* [2010] ECR I-8769, para 37. Among others referring to Case C-470/99 *Universale-Bau and Others* [2002] ECR I-11617, paras 74 to 78 and *Uniplex*, above n 62, para 38 as authority.

9.6.1.1   The Portuguese Case Line on the Fault Requirement

The Commission opened proceedings against Member States for failures of implementation, wherein the CJEU scrutinized whether national laws constituted sufficient or valid implementation of the Remedies Directive. One case law thread[67] which generated little resonance or discussion at EU level[68] in the field of public procurement was the Commission's infringement procedure against Portugal. The infringement targeted a national law making the award of damages to persons harmed by a breach of Community law relating to public contracts, or the national laws implementing it, conditional on proof of fault or fraud.[69] In its observations, the Commission underlined that such proof is tremendously difficult to provide, given the fact that the individual responsible for the faulty or fraudulent act is extremely difficult to discern. The requirement of proof therefore did not satisfy the effective and rapid review mechanisms called for in the directive. Portugal most interestingly put forward that the liability scheme as imposed by the directive is not objective. Secondly, it referred to the fact that proof of serious fault or intention is required only in the internal liability between the individual responsible and agent or their joint liability. Lastly, it put forward that administrative practice differs from the rules. Without entering into a discussion on the intricacies of the Portuguese national law, the CJEU found it to be in violation of Article 1(1) and 2(1)c in so far as proof is required for the 'faute ou d'un dol commis par les agents d'une entité administrative déterminée'.[70] This part of the judgment specifically links the burden of proof with being against an individual (agent). For the remainder, the formulation on proof is more sweeping: any need to prove fault breaches the respective Article of the public procurement Remedies Directive. The latter formulation disregards the identity of the tortfeasor. Several remarks can be made on the judgment: primarily, the judgment concerns the question of the burden of proof. Nevertheless, one may imply fault and intention are not valid criteria at all in a claim for damages based on the public procurement rules. However, the way in which the notion of fault is to be interpreted is open, most importantly in relation to whether it includes notions of negligence or not, as in some Member States this still seems to be a substantive condition for a successful claim for damages.[71]

---

[67] See also Chap. 4 fn 9 for details on the 'Portuguese saga'.

[68] Two annotations are listed on the ECJs website, only one -an admittedly brief case note- in English: M Dischendorfer, 'The Conditions Member States May Impose for the Award of Damages under the Public Remedies Directive: Case C-275/03 Commission v Portugal' (2005) *Public Procurement Law Review* 19.

[69] Case C-275/03 *Commission v Portugal* [2004] (unpublished).

[70] ibid, paras 31, 32 (judgment only available in French).

[71] It seems that several Member States made, or possibly still make, claims for damages subject to a condition of negligence. See D Pachnou, *The Effectiveness of Bidder Remedies for Enforcing the EC Public Procurement Rules: a Case Study of the Public Works Sector in the United Kingdom and Greece* (Dissertation, University of Nottingham, 2003), s 2.8.2.

9.6.1.2   The Strabag Case

Strabag addressed the doubts that remained due to the oscillating formulations in the Portuguese judgments. Were all fault requirements prohibited or only in instances where the burden of proof was imposed on the tenderer? The Court replied:

> In that regard, it should first be noted that the wording of Article 1(1), Article 2(1), (5) and (6), and the sixth recital in the preamble to Directive 89/665 in no way indicates that the infringement of the public procurement legislation liable to give rise to a right to damages in favour of the person harmed should have specific features, such as being connected to fault – proved or presumed – on the part of the contracting authority, or not being covered by any ground for exemption from liability.
>
> That assessment is supported by the general context and aim of the judicial remedy of damages, as provided for in Directive 89/665.[72]

If further held that a fault requirement would contravene Directive 89/665/EC:

> must be interpreted as precluding national legislation which makes the right to damages for an infringement of public procurement law by a contracting authority conditional on that infringement being culpable, including where the application of that legislation rests on a presumption that the contracting authority is at fault and on the fact that the latter cannot rely on a lack of individual abilities, hence on the defence that it cannot be held accountable for the alleged infringement.[73]

For EU law claims, the fault criterion is therefore dispensed with. The justification for the no-fault requirement is drawn largely from the specifics of the case, although it is quite clear that the finding of the ruling will be of general application. The discussion does not focus on the question of whether materially, a fault criterion as a constitutive criterion for damages claims would be warranted. The reasoning depends, on one hand, on the rapidity and length of proceedings that *proving* culpability would require. Also, a reversal of the burden of proof through a presumption of fault on behalf of the contracting authority is not permitted. The CJEU cited the possibility that through the application of a specific rule, namely under the doctrine of the 'excusable error', the Austrian contracting authority would have an escape clause in order to rebut culpability.

While the CJEU is clear in the prohibition of fault, it is less clear as to *why* this is the case. It is inherently true that a fault criterion would preclude the liability of contracting authorities in certain cases. None of this reasoning addresses the underlying question of whether or not a fault criterion in damages claims is perhaps justifiable under specific factual situations. As others have pointed out, these limitations from a policy aspect might serve a legitimate purpose.[74] The resulting liability might be disproportionate, the prime example being a simple error of law.

---

[72] *Strabag*, above n 66, paras 35–36.

[73] ibid.

[74] C Alexander, 'Vergaberechtlicher Schadensersatz gemäss §126 GWB' (2009) *Wettbewerb in Recht und Praxis* 28, p 36.

9.6.2   Fault at National Level

In principle, fault requirements are therefore not permissible for damages claims at the national level. While this issue is settled, it is open as to how far no-fault requirements are valid for all parallel causes of action. In Germany, for example, there is more than one action for damages. And while it is now accepted that for the specific statutory causes of action, the fault criterion is not permissible, the question remains open for the *culpa in contrahendo* doctrine. According to common opinion it is still based on fault. For the purposes of EU law, is it sufficient if one of the causes of action available to an aggrieved tenderer is open, without a fault requirement? In particular, in Germany the no-fault cause of action is limited to claims for bid costs – lost profits are available only under the pre-contractual liability doctrine (which includes a fault criterion). Again, the 'holistic' view of damages claims taken by the CJEU is translated back into the national legal systems with difficulty, due to the frayed nature of damages claims at that level.

9.7   Conclusion

Damages claims are structurally defined by systemic, institutional and constitutive factors. At systemic level, they are embedded in the national policy environment. A strong national enabling environment is key to achieve compliance with EU public procurement legislation. Despite a 'unitary' policy-making body at EU level, the national level disposes of its very own policy sphere, which is often driven by independent factors. The damages legal process is further channeled through different institutions (extra-judicial, administrative or civil, with or without procurement expertise). The chapter discussed how these peripheral systemic and institutional rules frame damages claims.

One of the core findings is that the way in which Member States have implemented the damages obligation varies significantly. Structurally, some Member States have chosen an explicit implementation, while in most Member States general doctrines are used and adapted to the concerns of the public procurement area. This results in a variety of available causes of actions including general tort-based claims, statutory breaches, pre-contractual liability and implied contract as the most pertinent, next to more peripheral actions such as public misfeasance. These different type of claims correspond to different constitutive criteria for their success and are conditioned by often divergent substantive factors, such as standing, time limits and fault requirements.

These findings challenge the unitary notion of damages as a remedy; the holistic understanding of 'the' damages claim must be reconceptualised as a bundle of rules. While the frayed nature of damages claims is apparent at the constitutive level of damages, it is paired and amplified, on the constitutive side of quantification, with varying heads of damages and types of losses that may be claimed.

Bibliography

Alexander, C (2009) 'Vergaberechtlicher Schadensersatz gemäss §126 GWB', *Wettbewerb in Recht und Praxis* 28, 36

Bowsher, M & Moser, P (2006) 'Damages for Breach of the EC Public Procurement Rules in the United Kingdom' *Public Procurement Law Review* 195, 203.

Burgi, M (2009) 'Zukunft des Vergaberechts' *NZBau* 609, 612.

Dischendorfer, M (2005) 'The Conditions Member States May Impose for the Award of Damages under the Public Remedies Directive: Case C-275/03 Commission v Portugal', *Public Procurement Law Review* 19.

Eiró, V & Mealha, E (2011) 'Damages under Public Procurement: The Portuguese Case', in D Fairgrieve & F Lichère (eds), *Public Procurement Law: Damages as an Effective Remedy* (Oxford, Hart Publishing).

Graells, AS (2011) *Public Procurement and the EU Competition Rules* (Oxford, Hart Publishing).

Hebly, JM, de Boer, ET & Wilman, FG (2007) *Rechtsbescherming bij aanbesteding* (Paris, Uitgeverij Paris).

Hebly, JM & Wilman, FG (2011) 'Damages for Breach of Public Procurement Law. The Dutch Situation', in D Fairgrieve & F Lichère (eds), *Public Procurement Law. Damages as an Effective Remedy* (Oxford, Hart Publishing).

Hök, GS (2008) 'Neues europäisches Internationales Baurecht' *ZfBR* 741, 747.

Hök, GS (2010) 'Zum Vergabeverfahren im Lichte des Internationalen Privatrechts' *ZfBR* 440, 442.

Hugenholtz, W & Heemskerk, WH (2006) *Hoofdlijnen van Nederlands Burgerlijk Procesrecht* (Den Haag, Elsevier).

Pachnou, D (2003) *The Effectiveness of Bidder Remedies for Enforcing the EC Public Procurement Rules: a Case Study of the Public Works Sector in the United Kingdom and Greece* (Dissertation, University of Nottingham).

Péguret, K (2010) *Schadensersatzansprüche übergangener Bieter im Vergaberecht* (Jenaer Wissenschaftliche Verlagsgesellschaft).

Pijnacker Hordijk, EH, van der Bend, GW & Van Nouhuys, JF (2009) *Aanbestedingsrecht. Handboek van het Europese en het Nederlandse Aanbestedingsrecht* (Den Haag, Sdu Uitgevers).

SIGMA (2007) *Central Public Procurement Structures and Capacity in Member States of the European Union*, Sigma Paper No 40 (OECD).

Chapter 10
Quantification of Claimable Losses

Abstract This chapter deals with the quantification of claimable losses in public procurement damages actions. It discusses the theoretical divergence in the identification of losses, and how the latter impacts on what is meant by actual damage, covering the most pertinent heads of damages in public procurement, namely bid costs, lost profits and interest. Further, the relevance of the burden of proof and evidentiary rules, as well as institutional and structural rules in relation to judges' discretion are treated. The chapter closes with a consideration of valuation methods.

10.1 Quantification of Damages

The quantification of damages is the last step in the transformation of legal norms into real outcomes in a legal procedure. It can significantly impact upon the monetary amount, and therefore the ultimate outcome of a case. Taking into account the importance of the quantum of a damages award as to the overall result of a legal case, the study of quantification rules has been neglected in comparison with the constitutive criteria. The following discussion of the heads of damages and valuation methods provides aims at transcending the isolated national understandings of the country studies (Part II) by providing a conceptual and functional analysis as a backdrop against which the individual jurisdiction's rules can be contextualized and better understood.

10.1.1 Theoretical Perspectives

The kinds of losses which are to be quantified depend on the underlying understanding of what counts as legally recognized damage. In particular, one can distinguish *between a natural and a normative understanding of damage*. A natural definition of harm refers to the non-legal understanding of damage as any detriment caused. It may thus seem too broad. Normative damage, in contrast, requires some kind of a legal recognition of the interest that the *laedens* (the person harmed) holds in

© Springer International Publishing Switzerland 2016
H. Schebesta, *Damages in EU Public Procurement Law*, Studies in European
Economic Law and Regulation 6, DOI 10.1007/978-3-319-23612-4_10

relation to the initial state of affairs. The term 'normative damage' thus implies the fact that a loss is legally protected. For example emotional pain and suffering are certainly natural forms of harm, but the extent to which legal recognition is granted to such harm in legal systems differs. This is the distinction that can be expressed in French between '*dommage*' and '*préjudice*'[1]; damage/harm and loss, *damnum* and *injuria*.[2]

In the definition of the losses which can be subject to a damages claim, quantification relies on different types of comparisons in order to assess the extent of a given loss. One may commonly distinguish between an *objective* and a *subjective assessment* of losses incurred. In a subjective assessment, one takes account of the specific losses that a certain wrongful act inflicts on a particular victim. The concrete method takes into account and bases the damage on all individual circumstances of the case. This is the regular method for calculation of damage. The objective method departs from more abstract, i.e. general and universal criteria by comparing the damage that all *laedens* would have sustained in a similar position. Under the objective conception of damage, losses are independent of the victim and of the victim's particular situation. The setting of criteria for quantification by the legislature constitutes a move towards more abstract quantification of damages.

Under the *Differenzhypothese*,[3] two states of patrimonies are compared under a 'hypothesis of difference'. This is the comparison between the state which is and the state which would have existed had an injurious act not taken place (hypothetical state). Mommsen called this the 'interest'.

> da das Interesse die Differenz zwischen dem wirklichen Betrage eines Vermögens und demjenigen Betrage desselben ist, wie er ohne die Dazwischenkunft des beschädigenden Ereignisses gewesen wäre, so kann das Interesse nur aus solchen Gegenständen bestehen, welche zu Vermögensobjecten sich eignen.[4]

The difference hypothesis refers to the overall comparison of patrimonies before and after a detrimental event. Apart from the hypothetical operation, a slight difference emerges if the method of quantification relies on the overall patrimony as opposed to individual items of loss. This is different to a subjective-objective approach because the point of reference is not the individual value of lost items. There are several theories which lie between overall patrimony and specific individual damages. An *abstract normative approach* to damages has been accepted by several courts and entails that, next to the thesis of difference comparison of overall patrimonies, the protective scope of legal norms is taken into consideration and the recoverable losses are replaced or adjusted accordingly. For example, from the point of view of insurance, only a particular part of the overall patrimony is compared,

---

[1] M Sousse, *La Notion de Réparation de Dommages en Droit Administratif Français* (Libraire Générale de Droit et de Jurisprudence Librairie, 1994).

[2] Throughout the thesis, the terms damage and loss have been used interchangeably since it is not committed to the understanding thereof in a particular legal system.

[3] Developed by F Mommsen, *Zur Lehre vom dem Interesse* (Braunschweig, Schwetschke, 1855).

[4] ibid, p 11.

namely that part which is specifically protected by the legal norm guaranteeing the interest. This is less than the overall patrimony, yet neither is it an individualized account of protected losses.[5]

Compensation is a relational concept that compares two states of the world, an imaginary and a real one. The hypothetical nature of the comparison fundamentally differs between actions for liability under non-performance of contract and torts. Let us imagine that a course of events unfolds, marked by a tortuous act. From this string of events, the real scenario leads from the tortuous act to the world we live in. But which state of the world should be the comparator? To assess the hypothetical comparator state, it is possible to merely eliminate the tortuous wrongful act, or else to replace it with the rightful one in order to project the hypothetical image of the world.[6]

Under breach of contract, the present situation is compared with a perfect world in which the contract was faithfully executed. The head of damage arising therefrom is called the positive (contractual) interest. By contrast, in the case of defective legal acts underlying a contract, the hypothetical situation, the perfect world, is precisely one in which the contract was not executed. This is then termed negative (contractual) interest. Because they refer to mutually exclusive either/or comparisons, they cannot be simultaneously claimed.[7]

Positive and negative forms of contractual interest are therefore not congruent with those of lost profits and costs sustained. Lost profits and costs do not refer to the comparator situation, but the heads of damages, which can be both claimed in a single comparison. Lost profits (*lucrum cessans*) are the gains not realized due to an incident; actual or positive costs (*damnum emergens*) either mean a decrease in assets or an increase in liabilities. In public procurement, the distinction is highly pertinent. Given that some of the selected jurisdictions conceive of procurement damages in tort, and others resort to (pre-)contractual considerations, the causes of action are factors that can potentially influence the available compensation. Generally, under a tort-based approach to wrongful conduct bid costs are not claimable as they would have been made even without the tort, while under a contractual approach bid costs will be claimable.

---

[5] H Möller, *Summen- und Einzelschaden. Beiträge zur Erneuerung der Schadenslehr vom Wirtschaftsrecht aus* (Berlin, de Gruyter, 1937).

[6] T Honoré, *Responsibility and Fault* (Oxford, Hart Publishing, 1999). The opinion of Honoré of replacing an act with rightful conduct rather than the mere elimination thereof is especially pertinent in the context of this thesis in which we are dealing with breaches of statutory duties. This means that the content of the rightful act can at times be positively asserted through the content of the statutes. This implies that in certain cases the 'rightful *act*' we can project to the future is none other than not acting, which is then identical to the mere elimination of the tortuous act from the hypothetical course of events. It seems the most difficult state posed for the replacement approach is one in which the rightful act is indeterminate yet not an omission, or where there are alternative rightful acts.

[7] J Spier, T Hartlief, GE Van Maanen & RD Vriesendorp, *Verbintenissen uit de wet en Schadevergoeding* (Dveneter, Kluwer, 2006); MH Wissink & WH Van Boom, 'The Netherlands. Damages under Dutch Law', in U Magnus (ed), *Unification of Tort Law: Damages* (The Hague, Kluwer, 1996), p 146.

Simply put, establishing losses requires a comparison. Different kinds of comparisons use quite different units of comparison, for example overall patrimony, as opposed to individual loss items. Also, the hypothetical situation can be one in which the wrongful act is eliminated, or replaced with the rightful act. Again, terminology sometimes obscures the finer distinctions between these operations.

10.2 Heads of Damages: Bid Preparation, Lost Profit and Interest Rates

The CJEU judgments in *Courage*[8] and *Manfredi*[9] can be read, in simple terms, to require that for violations of EU law, *damnum emergens, lucrum cessans*, and interest must all be claimable. The CJEU uses the terminology of actual loss in an identical sense to *damnum emergens*, and loss of profit in an identical sense to *lucrum cessans*. A brief survey of each of these heads of damages for the field of public procurement demonstrates how the concepts translate into quite diverse content on theoretical and national levels.

All jurisdictions claim to adhere to the general principle of full compensation.[10] Yet systems vary in whether and to what extent they regard losses as either normative or factual concepts. Under a normative system, losses are enumerated in *numerus clausus* type closed categories of those losses that are regarded as legally relevant. Where losses are more of a factual question, the recognition of losses requires the demonstration that losses were incurred through sufficient evidence and in combination with the necessary connection to the injurious act.

10.2.1 Preparation of Bid Costs

The costs of preparation of a bid in their broadest definition are costs relating to the preparation of a tender. Examples of preparation of bid cost items are costs relating to: the obtaining of tender documents; obtaining the required certificates and documentation; analysis of the tender; the development of bid solution and possibly models; price calculations and possibly variants; negotiations, both pre- and post-tender.[11] In public procurement, the preparation of bid costs can add up to

---

[8] Case C-453/99 *Courage v Crehan* [2001] ECR I-6297.

[9] See, eg for Joined Cases C-295/04 to C-298/04 *Manfredi and others* [2006] ECR I-06619, para 94.

[10] JT Oskierski, *Schadensersatz im Europäischen Recht: Eine vergleichende Untersuchung des Acquis Communautaire und der EMRK* (Baden-Baden, Nomos, 2010).

[11] See CEC Jansen, 'Aanbesteding en offertekostenvergoeding', in B van Roermund et al (eds), *Aanbesteding en aansprakelijkheid. Preventie, vergoeding en afwikkeling van schade bij aanbestedingsgeschillen* (Schoordijk Instituut Centrum voor Aansprakelijkheidsrecht, 2001), p 71.

substantial amounts of money. To illustrate, Versatel allegedly invested €1.5 million in the preparation of a bid for UMTS technology.[12]

Beyond this simple formulation, there are varying definitions of this type of loss. Preparation of bid costs are *costs which a tenderer incurs* when placing a bid. Defined in the negative, they are those *costs which would not have existed*, had a tender not participated in the public procurement procedure. It is clear that the kind of costs incurred varies with the type of procedure chosen by the contracting authority, as well as the type of contract proposed.

Conceptual distinctions can also be based on the *purpose of the costs* (preparation costs versus contract performance costs) or the question of *enrichment*. One may then distinguish between the pure *costs of the preparation* of the bidding procedure and acquisition of the tender and, on the other hand, those *costs which relate directly to the performance of the contract* itself. An example of pure acquisition costs are costs for filing the documentation required in the bidding procedure. On the other hand, in an architectural design contest, the costs for designing a model are directly linked and form part of the performance of a contract. The concepts are not identical to the splitting of bids based on *who is enriched* from the incurred costs – that is, whether costs incurred by the tenderer in the preparation stage confer an advantage on the contracting authority. The distinction is similar in that a cost conferring an advantage onto the contracting authority will normally also fit into the category of cost meant for performance of the bid itself. However this will not always be the case *vice versa*, since costs can be incurred with the object of performing, which the contracting authority does not benefit from later on.[13]

In practice, there is therefore a difference between the terms 'bid preparation', 'costs of participation' and 'negative interest'. For example in Germany, the court found a discrepancy between the losses covered in §126 GWB and under the contractual *culpa in contrahendo*. While §126 GWB allows for bid preparation costs and costs of participation, the *culpa in contrahendo* doctrine covers losses on the basis of negative and positive interest, but these are dependent on a stricter causality. The stricter *culpa in contrahendo* excluded legal fees for consultancy on the tender submission, as they would have been incurred with or without the tortious conduct. Under §126 GWB, by contrast, these legal fees may arguably be claimed.[14] On the other hand, recoverable bid costs were also read more narrowly in the context of §126 GWB as covering only bid preparation. Further reaching costs relating to the execution of the contract were claimable on the basis of the *culpa in contrahendo*. In the Netherlands, a similar approach is taken under the pre-contractual approach,

---

[12] van Rijn van Alkmade JMJ, 'Overheidsaansprakelijkheid voor onrechtmatige verdeling van schaarse publieke rechten' (2001) *Overheid en Aansprakelijkheid* 69, fn 36.

[13] To illustrate, take the example of a design study, which is a cost incurred in relation to the performance. A contracting authority might award the contract to another tender, yet still rely in parts on the design study, in which case it has received an advantage. If it does not, the two categories would not overlap.

[14] LG Magdeburg, 02.06.2010, 36 O 25/10 (007), 36 O 25/10.

under which costs relating to the execution of a contract (rather than merely the preparation of the bid submission) can be recovered. Bid costs which are not pure submission costs, but costs made in relation to the execution of the work are recoverable under pre-contractual causes of action.

10.2.1.1 Economic as Opposed to Legal Reasoning on Preparation of Bids

Essentially, the answer to the question of whether or not to award damages for the preparation of bids depends on the question as to who is held liable for incurring those costs in the first place. The issue is one of initial cost allocation on either the contracting authority or tenderer. However, if the contracting authority is liable, in the end the public pays.[15] In the alternative, namely the tenderer being liable for the costs, the tenderer is forced to include the costs within his or her general costs. Effectively such costs are transferred to the contract price, or must be covered by the profits of ulterior contracts. Two positions may be held in that regard, either that the costs are at the economic risk of a tenderer or that the costs need to be covered by whoever causes them. Additionally, contracting authorities sometimes include an allocation of costs clause in tender invitations, stating that preparation costs will or will not be reimbursed. In any event, the economic reality is that considerable bidding costs may be involved in a tender.

The general considerations on the allocation of the burden of costs for the preparation of bids are the basis for any debate on the inclusion of bid preparation as a head of damages. Two scenarios in between can be imagined: in one, a legal system, or a particular clause in the tender documents holds the contracting authority (economically) responsible for the preparation of a bid. In the other scenario, a tenderer is expected to cover the preparation costs, in the event of a successful bid, from the proceeds of that bid. In the first scenario, the contracting authority would be expected to cover the preparation costs. In this case, those general (economic) considerations would be enough to ground a claim. In a system whereby the initial allocation of costs does not rest with the public authority, in order to make the case for preparation bid reimbursements, additional arguments need to be advanced (which tend to be of a legal nature).

From a welfare economics point of view, the costs of unsuccessful bids must be counted as part of the total transaction cost of a public procurement procedure.[16] Accordingly, under an incentive theory, the most efficient cost allocation can be achieved by assigning costs to whoever is most suitable to control the costs. Jansen notes the distinction between the economic and the legal approach to preparation of

---

[15] Jansen, 'Aanbesteding en offertekostenvergoeding', above n 11, p 75ff (being in favor of introducing compensation for the preparation of bids in public procurement procedures in general, rather than examining the question as one arising out of a breach of statute of a contracting authority).

[16] ibid, p 77.

bids. Whereas the economic efficient transaction approach departs from a macro level efficiency debate, the legal argumentation focuses on the micro level as between parties. In his words, 'the fact that Party A incurs costs which benefit Party B is reason enough for a lawyer to go and look for a legal basis upon which Party B has a duty to compensate in relation to A.'[17] Whereas one view (economic) tends to consider the overall welfare, the other (legal) point of view departs from the party relationship.[18]

Accepting the logic that the contracting authority precluded a tenderer from having a fair chance of winning the procurement procedure, one must theoretically also accept that this holds true for all those that submitted a bid. Assume that contracting authority A invited bids, but was already determined to award to B. All other tenders (Cn) have been precluded from successfully participating. Based on this reason alone, A would be liable for all costs in Cn's preparations for bids. In order to limit the effect of the duty to pay damages for the preparation of bids, another element of liability would have to be included again, such as (the most basic one) the eligibility of the bids, or alternatively, the likelihood of succeeding in the absence of other factors. For example, Jansen takes the view that costs should be compensated only where three conditions are met: (a) the price of the bid must have been valid, (b) the bid must have been serious, that is it must have been adequate, and (c) the costs must have been incurred in good faith.[19] The concerns addressed through the conditions also remain validly addressed in relation to bid preparation as a head of damage.

One could make a better case for bid preparation damages as a residuary head of damage in relation to situations in which the claim of lost profits is precluded. This could arise out of the difficulty of proving the causality or difficulty in proving the loss itself. In both these cases, the preparation of a bid could serve as a minimum threshold for damages.[20]

For bid costs, one of the main issues concerns the items of loss which are legally covered by the notion. As such, bid costs do not necessarily correspond to *damnum emergens*. In addition, to claim bid costs and lost profits in parallel, or *damnum emergens* and *lucrum cessans*, must result in an appropriate method of evaluation in order to avoid double counting. There are valid arguments for either solution, but the underlying concerns ought to be addressed by any court.

---

[17] ibid, p 82 [translation by the author].

[18] At the end of the day, both disciplines have the capacity to adopt more nuanced points of view. Law, for example, takes 'welfare' into account by means of public policy arguments. In the end, the disagreements are about assumptions pertaining to recognized interests in either economic models or doctrines of law and hence are identical for both law and economics.

[19] ibid, p 87. He assumes a duty to compensate for the following items: deciding whether or not to tender, development of bid solution, price calculations. However, the other costs he rejects on rather factual grounds, for example, due to the fact that obtaining documents or pre-qualification do not usually create costs for an undertaking.

[20] The residual nature of the bid profits can be explained by several rationales, namely double counting, in the case that an aggrieved tenderer claims both bid costs and lost profits. Then, lost

10.2.1.2   The Relationship Between Lost Profit and Bid Preparation

The initial starting point for a legal system on the allocation of costs for bid preparations also influences a head of damage for the preparation of bids in relation to other
heads of damages, in particular in claiming lost profits. Specifically when it comes
to party agreements concerning cost allocation, whether a claim for bid preparation
is based in obligation or tort makes a difference.

One issue regarding the parallel claim of lost profits and bid preparation is that
of double counting. Depending on to whom a legal system initially allocates costs,
bid preparations are economic risks which ought to be borne by the bidder and
hence discounted from the expected profits. In order to avoid double counting,
either the two heads of damages are not available in parallel, or the quantification
method used for this evaluation must account for this cost allocation.[21]

A more fundamental difficulty arises regarding the chosen hypotheticals. It is the
difference mostly reflected through tort or contract as the cause of action. From a
contractual point of view, compensation implies that the plaintiff is put in a position
either as though the contract had never been performed (negative interest), or as
though the contract had been performed (positive interest). The hypothetical in this
case is exclusive, and based on this reasoning, the parallelism of both heads of damages is logically flawed.

10.2.1.3   Overview

In France, the category of 'not devoid of a chance' and 'chance' result in the recov-
erability of bid costs and lost profits respectively under one common cause of action.

In the Netherlands, the two main causes are tort law and pre-contractual liability.
Under tort law, proof that tenderer would have been awarded a contract results in
lost profits. Bid costs are generally not awarded alone under the full compensation
principle (all-or-nothing). This approach has been mitigated by the chance that tenderer would have been awarded a contract resulting in the award of damages corresponding to a lost chance (commonly the lost profit divided by remaining
contestants). Additionally, the existence of a pre-contractual relationship may be
sufficient to make termination without restitution of some costs unlawful ('stage 2'
of negotiations). In that case, bid costs are covered, in particular bid costs which
were made for the execution of the contract.

---

profits can lead to overcompensation, for example, due to the lengthy nature of the contract or the
high level of risk inherent to actually carrying out the work. In addition, there may only be weak
evidence in order to assess the extent of damages.

[21] See the recognition of this problem in the divergent practice of investment arbitration tribunals.
For example, J Gotanda, 'Recovering Lost Profits in International Disputes' (2005) 2 *Transnational
Dispute Management*, quotes the following arbitral award: '[The plaintiff should be] put … in the
same pecuniary position as they would have been in if the contract had been performed. But the
repayment of the expenses incurred in concluding the contract would tend to put them in the

In Germany, a real chance under §126 GWB leads to the compensation of bid preparation costs. Under the pre-contractual *culpa in contrahendo* doctrine, further reaching bid costs may be covered (e.g. including bid preparation and execution). Proof that a contract would have been awarded to a tenderer will result in lost profits.

In the UK, the main causes are statutory breach and implied contract. Lost profits are available. Bid costs are necessarily included in lost profits, but it is questionable whether they can be claimed alone. The lost chance is theoretically a head of damage, based on an 'abstract' calculation of chance of making profits, minus risks inherent in the sector.

An analysis of these overall highly diverging systems shows that different causes of action can nevertheless lead to similar results. For example the German and French solutions, although formally on the basis of different causes of actions, are similar. Both grant bid costs for a 'real chance'. Lost profits are available for a serious chance in France and arguably more than a serious chance in Germany, namely the necessity to demonstrate to have been awarded the contract in the counterfactual scenario.

Although, clearly, a tort-based approach (the Netherlands and the UK) is at the detriment of the availability of bid costs in principle, those countries that follow the approach have accepted the lost chance as a head of damage in order to mitigate the dichotomy of the all-or-nothing approach.

The results show that the lost chance plays a crucial role in all surveyed jurisdictions, and serves to mitigate the available heads of damages. The lost chance is further discussed in the following chapter.

10.2.2 Lost Profits

10.2.2.1 Availability of Heads of Damages

Lost profits are theoretically available across the jurisdictions, yet are rarely successfully claimed. In the Netherlands, they are available, but subject to a high burden of proof, in that the aggrieved bidder has to prove that he would have been awarded a contract. In the UK, in *Harmon*, the claimant was awarded lost profits, but 15 years later, successful follow-up cases are very rare. In France, subject to the tender having had a serious chance, lost profits are available and are regularly awarded. In Germany, lost profits are available under *culpa in contrahenda*, but the statutory article of §126 GWB is limited to claiming bid costs. Overall, while lost profits are available in all

---

position they would be in if the contract had never been concluded (negative damages).... Undoubtedly, the plaintiff was justified in hoping to recover the expenses of making the contract out of the profit which they were expecting. But this is an element included in the compensation for loss of profit. Adding positive and negative damages together is a contradiction, and cannot be allowed. Sapphire Int'l Petroleums Ltd. v. Nat'l Iranian Oil Co., Arbitral Award (Mar. 15, 1963), reprinted in 35 I.L.R. 136, 186–87 (1967).'

jurisdictions, the rate of incidence of successful awards varies greatly. In Germany and the UK only a very small number of cases are known, as is the case in the Netherlands. Only in France do courts regularly award lost profits. In addition, the Netherlands and France are reluctant to award lost profit and bid costs at the same time, while in the UK it is ambiguous whether bid costs can be regularly claimed.[22]

10.2.2.2   Appreciation

We have seen in the country studies that the extent to which lost profit claims are available varies significantly between the countries surveyed. In the United States, lost profits are generally not awarded at all in public procurement proceedings.[23] The reason for this doctrine lies in the fact that the respondent is the State, and any damages cashed out are ultimately paid for by the taxpayer. Damage claims are therefore limited due to the mainly public nature of the defendants. The question of awarding (or not) lost profit damages in public procurement proceedings then becomes a question of State immunity. However, the doctrine as expressed in the United States is hardly ever put forward in EU countries. The non-availability of lost profits in the EU is not motivated by the identity of the State. Drawing on the experience of investment arbitration, which is also directed against States, this rationale is also not accepted in other fields of law and overall lost profits are regularly awarded. The reason is simple; if damages are compensation damages, then the award must approach the natural pecuniary damage to some degree.

For the judicial development of the damages doctrine, the principle of full compensation would provide the starting point. The availability of specific heads would then be assessed according to the actual situation. Mainly, the breach itself impacts on which hypothetical scenario is chosen for the comparison, and whether this results in lost profit and preparation bids being claimable at the same time. Based on these choices, the evaluation method used to decide lost profit surfaces as the main determinant of the extent of lost profits.

---

[22] M Trybus, 'An Overview of the United Kingdom Public Proucrement Review and Remedies System with an Emphasis on England and Wales', in S Treumer & F Lichère (eds), *Enforcement of the EU public procurement rules* (København, DJØF Publishing, 2011), p 229; and S Arrowsmith, *The Law of Public and Utilities Procurement* (London, Sweet & Maxwell, 2005), p 1381 (arguing for a tort approach under which the tender is put in a position as though the tort had not occurred, which in many cases will preclude bid cost claims as such costs would have been made anyways).

[23] D Gordon & M Golden, 'Money Damages in the Context of Bid Protests in the United States', in D Fairgrieve & F Lichère (eds), *Public Procurement Law: Damages as an Effective Remedy* (London, Hart Publishing, 2011).

10.2.3   Interest Rates

The award of interest at the national level is often marked by the broad discretion enjoyed by the courts with regards to the applicable interest rates. The most salient issues arising usually concern which cases courts award interest in, what the applicable rate and method (simple or compound interest) are, and what time period is covered. The box below provides the example of England in greater detail in order to illustrate that, even at the national level and therefore from an internal point of view, the question of damages tends to be foreseen with important question marks. The judges' practice of awarding interest was noted to be highly variable, and in some instances the high percentage of interest awarded almost seemed to amount to a punitive element.

The Issue of Interest Awards in England

The Law Commission in England in 2004 published a study on the availability of interest.[24] Overall, it found a wide disparity in the calculation of interest and the methodologies used, in addition to which interest rates should be clarified as containing no punishing element as regards the defendant.

Historically, interest was only rarely awarded by the courts at common law. Later on, interest became recoverable through the statutory provision thereof in the Law Reform (Miscellaneous Provisions) Act 1934. Doctrine only later developed in such a way that interest came to be seen as special damages as opposed to general damages. In cases of claims based in equity and admiralty courts, interest was also available.

Details on the award of interest are set out in section 35A of the Supreme Court Act 1981, and section 69 of the County Courts Act 1984. There is wide discretion left to the courts as to how interest rates are set. However, statutory interest is simple and not compound (ie 'interest on interest'). Again, in equity

---

[24] *As a result of these developments, pre-judgment interest may now be awarded in one of seven ways: (1) under a contract or trade usage (when it may be simple or compound according to the agreement or usage); (2) as special damages (simple or compound); (3) under the equitable or Admiralty jurisdictions (simple or compound); (4) where proceedings have been commenced, under section 35A of the Supreme Court Act 1981 or its county court equivalent (which is limited to simple interest only); (5) as of right under certain other statutes (simple only); (6) by arbitrators, exercising their discretion under the Arbitration Act 1996 (which may be simple or compound); or (7) after trial, where the defendant has been held liable for more than a refused claimant's offer, under Part 36 of the Civil Procedure Rules (simple only).* Law Commission, *Pre-Judgment Interest on Debts and Damages,* LAW COM no 287, lawcommission.justice.gov.uk/publications/prejudgement-interests-on-debts-and-damages.htm, p 10. The following paragraphs are based on the Law Commission's report.

(continued)

and admiralty courts, the position on compound interest differed. The 1996 Arbitration Act on the other hand provides the powers to award compound and simple interest to arbitration tribunals.

What is the applicable rate and method of interest computation?

Section 17 of the Judgments Act 1838 currently provides for an 8 % rate, which could, depending on the current base rates, be considerably higher than usual rates. (The recent base rates of interest have been at around 0.5 %, making the applicable statutory interest rate a good 7.5 % above the base rate.) Deviation from this statutory rate can be made in a commercial transaction, for which it has been acknowledged that 'interest should reflect the commercial value of money'.[25] With variations over time, established rates usually seem to be somewhere between 1 % and 4 % above the base rate.[26] *McGregor on Damages* notes fluctuations over time, but estimates a current norm of around 1 % above bank rate, adjustable to the actual borrowing situation of the defendant.[27] The Law Commission study recommended a standard (though variable) interest rate of the base rate plus 1 %.

Taking these changes into account, it remains true that simple interest prevails in common law. Compound interest is still not regularly awarded, and only in cases where this reflects trade practice and custom, as well as in equity and the admiralty courts. However, the prevailing position may change with increased recognition of the fact that simple interest does not fully compensate an injured party.[28]

What time period is covered?

It is acknowledged as the general rule that loss will start to run from the time of accrual of the loss. However, it has been stated that 'there is certainly no rule that interest will invariably run from the date of loss.'[29] In addition, undue delay in bringing the lawsuit may result in deprivation of (parts of) the interest.

---

[25] DA Thomas & H McGregor, *McGregor on Damages* (London, Sweet & Maxwell, 2009), p 657.

[26] Note by J Gun Cuninghame, *Calculating Claims of Interest*, www.goughsq.co.uk/documents/calculating_claims_of_interest.pdf

[27] Thomas & H McGregor, *McGregor on Damages*, above n 25, p 660.

[28] Gun Cuninghame, *Calculating Claims of Interest*, above n 26, p 11 referring to *Man Nutzfahrzeuge AG v Freightliner Ltd* [2005] EWHC 2347 (Comm). However, again this concerns a case in the commercial jurisdiction. The following paragraphs and case citations are based on his text.

[29] B.P. Exploration Co (Libya) Ltd v Hunt (No 2) [1979] 1 WLR 783, Robert Goff J.

In the UK, CPR rules 16.4(1)(b) and (2) require the claimant to state that s/he is seeking interest, and on what basis it is required, for what periods and at which rate. In the *Harmon* litigation, in *Aquatron*, 4 % were awarded. It is more common in the surveyed legal systems to apply the legal rate, for example in France, the legal rate of 0,93 %.

The Relationship Between Taxation and Damage

In the UK, an additional factor taken into account is the matter of taxation. In this respect, it has been held that while for damages themselves taxation may be irrelevant, for interest calculation the matter of taxation certainly matters in order to adjust the interest due. In the case below, Phillips J. awarded interest on only 75 % of the damages due to taxation matters, based on the following reasoning:

> Damages are awarded to compensate for the loss of money or its equivalent. Interest is awarded to compensate for the loss of use of money. In accounting terms damages compensate for the effect of wrongdoing on profit and loss, interest compensates for the effect of wrongdoing on cashflow. If in year one loss is caused which is shared between the plaintiff and Inland Revenue and in year five damages fall to be awarded which will be shared between the plaintiff and the Inland Revenue, it can be logical to disregard the effect of taxation when assessing the damages. But it does not follow that the plaintiff should receive an award of interest which compensates not only for his loss of use of money but in addition for the loss of use of the share which should have been received by the Inland Revenue.[30]

In France, by contrast, the Conseil d'Etat held the following:

> It follows that by holding that it was appropriate to evaluate the lost profits of Spie Est on the basis of its operating income, net of income tax, the Administrative Court of Nancy erred in law...[31]

---

[30] Deeny v Gooda Walker (No.3) [1996] L.R.L.R. 168 at 173 in D. A. THOMAS & H. MCGREGOR, *McGregor on Damages* (Sweet & Maxwell, 2009), p 674.

[31] CE, 19 January 2015, *Ste Spie Est* ECLI:FR:CESSR:2015:384653.20150119.

Another often neglected relationship is that of taxation in relation to damages awards. If the damages calculation reaches a sophisticated stage, courts have to assess whether to deduct interest claimable for the share of the award which would have been paid in taxation. While in the UK this seems to be the position, France has rejected such arguments in procurement; the calculation of lost profits is undertaken before taxation (see box above).

10.2.3.1   Interest as a Head of Damage? Interest as a Procedural or Substantive Matter?

From the EU law perspective, the conceptualization of interest is relevant for example if it is accepted that EU law should define the claimable heads of damages for a breach of law. Historically, interest has been conceived of on one hand *as* damage, namely damage to compensate for the late payment and the plaintiff's inability to use that money. On the other hand, interest could hold a special position within a specific item of damages. In England, both points of view were historically enshrined in the law.[32] In the context of arbitration, awarding interest is regarded as a procedural issue, thus allowing an appeal, while in other jurisdictions (e.g. Japan and Russia) it is a substantive matter, and is only challengeable under the arguably higher threshold of being contrary to public policy.[33] In line with the observation in previous parts, although interest is often treated as a head of damage, it is factually subsumed under the procedural autonomy considerations by the CJEU. For example, in *Metallgesellschaft*[34] the Court held: *"While, in the absence of Community rules, it is for the domestic legal system of the Member State concerned to lay down the detailed procedural rules governing such actions, including ancillary questions such as the payment of interest, those rules must not render practically impossible or excessively difficult the exercise of rights conferred by Community law."*[35] In this particular case the procedural autonomy considerations did not lead the Court not to intervene. From the formulation of the case, however, we can deduce that the court is willing to treat the interest question in a differentiated way depending on the right at stake. Under EU law more generally, interest tends to be mentioned in the same breath as actual damage and loss of profit. The availability of interest is a requirement of EU law, and the context indicates that the CJEU regards interest as a head of damage.[36] In the same vein, interest has been enshrined as part of full compensation in the new Competition Damages Directive.[37] It follows that interest is a head of damage that must be recognized in the area of public procurement as well.

---

[32] I Yoshida, 'Comparison of Awarding Interest on Damages in Scotland, England, Japan and Russia' (2000) *Journal of International Arbitration* 41, pp 52–53 citing the Civil Procedure Act 1833 as an example for interest as damage, and the Law Reform (Miscellaneous Provisions) Act 1934 regarding the special position.

[33] ibid, p 71.

[34] With regards to interest discussed by R Caranta, 'Damages: Causation and Recoverable Losses', in D Fairgrieve & F Lichère (eds), *Public Procurement Law: Damages as an Effective Remedy* (Oxford, Hart Publishing, 2011), p 175; and Joined Cases C-397/98 and C-410/98 *Metallgesellschaft and others* [2001] ECR I-1727, para 94.

[35] *Metallgesellschaft*, ibid, para 95.

[36] *Manfredi*, above n 9.

[37] Article 3(2) of Directive 2014/104/EU of the European Parliament and of the Council of 26 November 2014 on certain rules governing actions for damages under national law for infringements of the competition law provisions, OJ L 349 [hereinafter 'Competition Damages Directive'].

10.3 Provisions Regulating the Quantification of Damages

There are several structural elements which constrain and shape the way quantification is undertaken within the legal process. The degree of formal and doctrinal separation between the categories of constitutive and quantification criteria varies significantly between jurisdictions. In addition, quantification can occur in the same legal procedure as the establishment of liability, or as in some jurisdictions, there can be a separate quantification legal procedure in which the amount of damages is established. These factors influence the discretion accorded to the judge, which can be quite significant with regards to the ultimate damage award.

10.3.1 The Separation Between Constitutive and Quantification Criteria

The degree of separation between constitutive and quantification criteria of damages claims depends on the design of the legal system in question. In France, there is hardly any, and after establishing liability, a court will usually proceed to make an award in the course of the same legal procedure. Formal separation is stronger in other regimes, for example the Netherlands. Establishing liability and the quantification thereof are formally separated into two steps, the quantification provision being identical for both tort and contract. Similarly, in Germany, the legal regime distinguishes rather strongly between 'Haftungsbegründung' and 'Haftungsausfüllung'. Due to the definition of disputes by party submissions, the UK system is less formally separated, and proceeds in steps (see Harmon and Harmon II), thereby leaving ample room for the parties to come to a settlement.

The separation of a finding of liability from the ultimate quantification of an award impacts on how intensely quantification aspects are pleaded, and also on whether settlements are sought. Where quantification is embedded in the 'material' part of the procedure on the constitutive terms, a claimant may be primarily concerned with proving the constitutive elements of a claim. Consequently, quantification pleading receives less attention. When constitution and quantification are separate, it is also likely that the judge will have less discretion in estimating the amount of awarded damages. If an entirely new procedure is started to deal with the issues of quantification, those issues tend to become 'legalized'. Also, where the moments of constitution and quantification of damages are separate from one another, the likelihood of settlement proceedings increases. Usually, the outcome of a finding on the constitutive legal question will facilitate an out-of-court settlement on the amount of compensation, as opposed to a unilateral legal one imposed by the courts. Empirical data on these effects is unfortunately not available in the form of systematic studies, but such observations will be affirmed by most practitioners. It is clear that once there is a positive finding of liability, process economies will strongly encourage the responsible party to seek a settlement. Settling a dispute out

of court, at least partially, moves the dispute away from the formalized trial structure and hence moves disputes, in terms of result, away from the trial and the reach
of EU law, and into the private sphere.

10.3.2 Discretion of the Judge

The quantification of damages in the legal systems can be better understood by
looking at whether a legal system openly addresses and creates a formal doctrine of
damage quantification methods. Indeterminacy relates to the method itself, the
choice of method, or an open delegation to the judge's individual (not to say personal) assessment. In most legal systems, the quantification of damages is a
neglected topic. Quantification thus becomes a technical if not arbitrary exercise,
rather than one that is diligently dealt with by legal doctrinal discussions.
Paradoxically, this vacuum of common understanding and guidance puts the judge
in a position whereby, in the absence of legal determination, s/he has to exercise
discretion.

10.3.2.1 Indeterminacy, General Regimes, and Legislative Provisions
on Quantification

In the Netherlands (see Chap. 5), the burden of proof is thus incumbent on the
claimant and judges quantify damage by means of 6:97 BW. The most suitable
method is chosen according to the nature of the loss. The judge therefore has discretion in determining the method chosen. On the 'material' side, as opposed to factual
evidentiation, the judge does have the possibility of reducing the amount of damages for limitation and mitigation. Where damages seem to be incalculable, the
judge makes an estimate *ex aequo et bono*, implying that the duty to plead and
substantiate are not applicable. In this respect, the Dutch system is again characterized by informal means which allow the judge a lot of discretion. Also in the
Netherlands, the duty to plead extends only to claiming damage; further specification of losses at the outset of a case is not necessary. As such, the legal system is
more lenient than some of the others surveyed.

   In the English *Harmon* case (see Chap. 6), the judge enjoyed wide discretion to
estimate the damages. For example, there was a reduction in the amount of damages
for risk and hazards inherent to a sector by 35 % which was based on any specific
data (although one does not know how this issue played out in the hearing).

   In France (see Chap. 8), judges enjoy a broad discretion in their assessment of
the extent of the damage. From the jurisdictions that were scrutinized, France,
through its acceptance of the lost chance, holds the closest intrinsic connection
between constitution and quantification of damage. This is different in the
Netherlands and Germany, legal systems which follow a two-tiered model that
strives for conceptual distinction between the two steps.

The German legal system (see Chap. 7) discards heads of damages -as well as losses- rather swiftly where they are found not to be sustained. The interaction of the material and the procedural conditions surrounding damages claims in the provisions on recoverable losses can only be understood in the context of §287 ZPO, which grants extensive discretion to the judge in the determination of damage. Excepted from this discretion, however, is the determination of the reason for liability (*Haftungsgrund* or constitutive causality), establishing a damages claim.

Overall one can remark that the estimation of damages often lacks a more sound quantification method, and can incorporate rationales of reduction which come very close to comprising a material criterion. This material connection in terms of result often delivers 'proportional' liability due to the damage reductions undertaken.

10.4 Valuation Methods for Damages

To arrive at a monetary amount depends on the valuation of the losses. The previous section pointed out that the valuation exercise can depend to a great extent on the discretion of judges, and sometimes allows for their simple estimation. Thus, the extent to which a judge follows a specific evaluation method can vary even within particular jurisdictions and certainly according to different fields of law. The problem with this remains the same: valuation is in the hand of judges who are not specifically trained in these methodologies. For example, the double counting mistake regarding the valuation of actual damage and lost profits can be encountered in several investment awards.[38]

In public procurement, there are only few patterns of how lost profits are measured, both across jurisdictions and in jurisdictions where lost profit claims are common, such as France. Even at national level, beyond the enumeration of coverable losses, methods of quantification remain obscure. The following practices have been observed in the jurisdictions. In the UK *Harmon* case, the court has held that lost profits must be calculated on the basis of the gross margin, taking into account actual events and the specific financial position of the aggrieved bidder. In the few other cases that proceeded to the actual quantification, the details of the reference contracts and respective losses were covered in great detail. In the Netherlands, courts have given guidance (presumably in order to encourage a settlement process) on what kinds of questions can be taken into account when addressing the question. It is established that the profits to be taken into account should be net profits, however, in other cases the judge makes an approximate estimate under *ex aequo et bono*. In Germany, the courts have held that damages have to be determined on the basis of the *Differenzhypothese*. 'The question whether and to which extent a recov-

---

[38] S Ripinsky & K Williams, *Damages in International Investment Law* (London, British Institute of International and Comparative Law, 2008).

erable damage came to being, must be examined on the basis of the hypothesis of difference, the claimant's patrimony after the wrongful act is compared with the patrimony which would have existed without the wrongful act.' In France, the *Conseil d'Etat* has recently rendered cases providing guidance on the quantification of damages in public procurement. The margin of maneuver for judges narrowed, based on a two step calculation of first, the estimation of turnover, and second, the applicable profit rate.

On a general level, two main findings emerge. France, the jurisdiction with the most procurement cases, is equally the jurisdiction with the most sophisticated generalizable approach to the computation of damages awards in public procurement. The *Conseil d'Etat* has intervened in several instances in order to provide guidance with respect to the quantification of damages, notably stabilizing the doctrine of the different chances and heads of damages, applicable profit margins, the rate of interest and interest and taxation. The number of disputes stands in a positive relation to courts using more systematic and streamlined approaches rather than purely case-by-case analysis to the question of damages valuation. Secondly, the German jurisdiction demonstrates quite clearly that the theoretical availability of heads of damages is not sufficient to guarantee that such damages are effectively claimable. Aggrieved bidders are frequently rejected on the 'procedural' rather than the 'constitutive' side of claiming damages. For example, to rely on a margin of profit claim was rejected as an insufficient basis in order for the judge to proceed to an estimation of damages. In the Netherlands, where damages are not sufficiently determined, the judge is proceeding to estimate that damage *ex aequo et bono*. In Germany, by contrast, the same type of indeterminacy leads to a total rejection of the claim. Exclusions to the types of losses that are recoverable, the burden of proof and evidence for losses during the quantification stage can limit damages claims just as severely as at the constitutive stage.

10.4.1 Valuation in EU Law

The European Commission recognized the problem of valuation for the field of Competition law. It commissioned a systematic study of valuation methods that came out in 2010,[39] followed by the new Competition Damages Directive and guiding documents.[40]

---

[39] Oxera Consulting Ltd., 'Quantifying Antitrust Damages-Towards Non-binding Guidance for Courts. Study prepared for the European Commission' (2010) [hereinafter the 'Oxera-study']. This study systematizes and brings in the methodologies of two previous documents on the quantification of damages in national competition law regimes. Study on the conditions of claims for damages in case of infringement of EC competition rules (August 2004) and in the study on making antitrust damages actions more effective in the EU (December 2007), both available at http://ec.europa.eu/competition/antitrust/actionsdamages/index.html

[40] Commission, Communication on 'quantifying harm in actions for damages based on breaches of Article 101 or 102 of the Treaty on the Functioning of the European Union, 2013/C 167/07, and a

The guiding principle is full compensation. The counterfactual situation is based on a 'but-for' scenario,[41] comparing the actual position of the injured party with the position it would have been in but for the infringement.[42] The Practical Guide on Quantification presents several methods and techniques of valuation, such as comparator based[43]; and simulation models, cost-based and finance-based analysis and other methods.[44] It is clear that the guide does not prescribe specific valuation methods but follows a pragmatic approach which recognizes that the methods have inherent weaknesses and strengths, that the choice of method must be tailored to the individual case at hand. The guide also clearly states that these methods lead to an estimation only of the hypothetical value. However, the aim clearly is to approximate and model the actual losses as closely as possible.

10.4.2   Valuation in Public Procurement

Why would a common approach to the quantification methods be needed? The Commission, from the point of EU Competition law, cites reasons of 'clarity and transparency, completeness, and replicability of results'.[45] For the same reasons, in the United States the Daubert doctrine on scientific evidence, including 'economic and financial evidence on antitrust damages'[46] is applied.

In public procurement, disputes suffer from their relative rarity, which impacts first of all on the routine with which judges come to terms with assessing damages and also foregoes the search for replicability, as every damages award remains 'unique'. Secondly, since damages awards by courts are unpredictable factors, the disputes tend to phase out into the private sphere, and the parties come to settlements as regards the final amount of damages to be claimed. Overall, the discretion of the judge is broad, and from the damages awards we have seen, the judgments themselves are mainly devoid of discussions of the methodology for valuation.

This is especially so if compared to the growing sophistication of competition law on the matter. Although, as pointed out, not all of the findings in Competition

---

practical guide on Quantifying harm in actions for damages based on breaches of article 101 or 102 TFEU', SWD(2013) 205 [hereinafter, the 'Practical Guide on Quantification']. The Practical Guide on Quantification largely recalls the findings of the Oxera-study.

[41] Oxera Study, above n 39, (ii).

[42] Practical Guide on Quantification, above n 40, pp 9–10.

[43] Looking at the same market at a time before/after the infringement, a similar product or geographic market, see title II of the Practical Guide on Quantification.

[44] That is, the simulation of market outcomes on the basis of economic models, in the case of cost and approaches the approach to estimate a likely non-infringement scenario on the basis of costs of production and a reasonable profit margin or finance-based approaches use the financial performance of the claimant or the defendant. See Practical Guide on Quantification, above n 40, Title III.

[45] Oxera Study, above n 39, p 9.

[46] ibid, p 10.

law are directly applicable to public procurement, basic differences in computation are often ignored. A case in point being for example the quantification of lost profit as denoting either of the two methods of calculation: (counterfactual revenues – actual revenues=lost revenues) or (lost revenues – avoided costs=lost profit).[47] Methodologically, there is clearly much room for refinement in the valuation of damages.

From the methods discussed in the Practical Guide on Quantification, in particularly the cost- and finance-based methods will be relevant to the determination of damages in public procurement. cost-based method, which uses production costs for the affected product and a mark-up for a 'reasonable' profit margin to estimate the hypothetical non-infringement scenario In some instance, for example the calculations in the *Harmon II* judgment (See Chap. 6), the individual position of the aggrieved bidder that went into liquidation had to be taken into account, and necessitated the judge to make finance-based calculations on the basis of the financial performance of Harmon.

The gross margins vary with the markets and of course on the basis of the actual bids submitted, 3–15 % being fairly common profit margins. The gross margin was assessed at 15 % in *Harmon,* which is fairly high but was justified by the judge with reference to the high risk of such kind of project. In *Aquatron*, by contrast, the Court took old contract values as relevant indicators in order to calculate the contract value, and relied on an itemized cost assessment multiplied by units predictable on the basis of the old contracts in order to estimate the lost profits. Overall, the UK seems to rely on loss itemization. France has accorded various margins of profit rates, ranging up to 34 % in isolated cases, realistic margins being 5–15 % depending on the markets. France has the most sophisticated quantification methods. In Germany, 5 % profit margin were claimed; although here in another case the Court found that the bid was so low that it would not have included any profit margin at all.

There is no one valuation method suitable for all cases. However, a certain flexibility in allowing claimants to establish lost profits must be granted or else damages claims that have material merit fail for procedural reasons. Losses cannot always be substantiated sufficiently, but it should be possible to estimate the damage at least on the basis of generalized (conservative) profit margins. Rather than rejecting insufficiently substantiated claims altogether, a conservative estimate of the amount to be awarded should be accepted.

10.5 Conclusion

Due to the low number of cases and rare explicit treatment of quantification, the country studies' conclusions are hardly generalizable. The findings are therefore situated at conceptual level. Especially in public procurement, there is much room

---

[47] ibid, p 145.

and need for theoretical and methodological refinement regarding the quantification of damages overall. Particularly problematic is the mix of terminology for heads of damages. The European Commission and the CJEU consistently refer to loss suffered (*damnum emergens*), and loss of profit (*lucrum cessans*). As has been demonstrated, these terms are conceptually too ambiguous to be well received in Member States' legal systems.

The degree of formal and doctrinal separation between the categories of constitutional and quantification criteria varies significantly between jurisdictions. Quantification can occur in the same or in separate legal procedures as the finding of liability. These factors shape the discretion accorded to the judge, who often enjoys explicit powers of estimating damages – resulting in a rather rough appreciation of the value of an award. Available heads of damages and quantification methods can significantly determine the outcome of legal procedure in monetary terms and are therefore not negligible when it comes to assessing the effectiveness of damages.

Bibliography

Arrowsmith, S (2005) The Law of Public and Utilities Procurement, 2nd edition (London, Sweet & Maxwell).

Caranta, R (2011) 'Damages: Causation and Recoverable Losses', in D Fairgrieve & F Lichère (eds), *Public Procurement Law: Damages as an Effective Remedy* (Oxford, Hart Publishing).

Fairgrieve, D & Lichère, F (eds) (2011) *Public Procurement Law: Damages as an Effective Remedy* (London, Hart Publishing).

Gordon, D & Golden, M (2011) 'Money Damages in the Context of Bid Protests in the United States', in D Fairgrieve & F Lichère (eds), *Public Procurement Law: Damages as an Effective Remedy* (London, Hart Publishing).

Gotanda, J (2005) 'Recovering Lost Profits in International Disputes' 2 *Transnational Dispute Management*.

Gun Cuninghame, J *Calculating Claims of Interest.*

Honoré, T (1999) Responsibility and Fault (Oxford, Hart Publishing).

Jansen, CEC (2001) 'Aanbesteding en offertekostenvergoeding', in Bert van Roermund et al (eds), *Aanbesteding en aansprakelijkheid. Preventie, vergoeding en afwikkeling van schade bij aanbestedingsgeschillen* (Schoordijk Instituut Centrum voor Aansprakelijkheidsrecht).

Möller, H (1937) *Summen- und Einzelschaden. Beiträge zur Erneuerung der Schadenslehr vom Wirtschaftsrecht aus* (Berlin, de Gruyter).

Mommsen, F (1855) *Zur Lehre vom dem Interesse* (Braunschweig, Schwetschke).

Oskierski, JT (2010) *Schadensersatz im Europäischen Recht: Eine vergleichende Untersuchung des Acquis Communautaire und der EMRK* (Baden-Baden, Nomos).

Oxera Consulting Ltd. (2010) 'Quantifying Antitrust Damages-Towards Non-binding Guidance for Courts. Study prepared for the European Commission'.

Ripinsky, S & Williams, K (2008) *Damages in International Investment Law* (London, British Institute of International and Comparative Law).

Sousse, M (1994) *La Notion de Réparation de Dommages en Droit Administratif Français* (Libraire Générale de Droit et de Jurisprudence Librairie).

Spier, J, Hartlief, T, Van Maanen, GE & Vriesendorp, RD (2006) *Verbintenissen uit de wet en Schadevergoeding* (Deventer, Kluwer).

Thomas, DA & McGregor, H (2009) *McGregor on Damages* (London, Sweet & Maxwell).

Trybus, M (2011) 'An Overview of the United Kingdom Public Proucrement Review and Remedies System with an Emphasis on England and Wales', in S Treumer & F Lichère (eds), *Enforcement of the EU Public Procurement Rules* (København, DJØF Publishing).

van Rijn van Alkmade JMJ (2001) 'Overheidsaansprakelijkheid voor onrechtmatige verdeling van schaarse publieke rechten' *Overheid en Aansprakelijkheid* 69.

Wissink, MH & Van Boom, WH (1996) 'The Netherlands. Damages under Dutch Law', in U Magnus (ed), *Unification of Tort Law: Damages* (The Hague, Kluwer).

Yoshida, I (2000) 'Comparison of Awarding Interest on Damages in Scotland, England, Japan and Russia' *Journal of International Arbitration* 41.

Chapter 11
The Iridescence of the Lost Chance Doctrine in Damages Claims

Abstract The availability of procurement damages is best in jurisdictions that make use of the lost chance doctrine. The lost chance could provide a solution from a functional point of view to the problem of the hypothetical nature of aggrieved bidders' losses. This chapter surveys different understandings of the lost chance theory, namely as an autonomous loss, an alleviation of the burden of proof and as a proportional liability. It examines the general stance of the selected legal systems on the lost chance and in the area of public procurement particularly. The conclusions investigate the potential for a fruitful application of the lost chance doctrine in the EU public procurement context.

11.1 The Different Understandings of the Lost Chance Theory

In the country studies, the following pervasive obstacles for public procurement damages claims were identified: the problem of causality, and the question of whether an aggrieved tenderer can prove his or her chance of obtaining an award. The second serious limitation to successful damages claims lies in the availability of the heads of damages that may be claimed, i.e. the negative or positive interest, bid costs, and lost profits. Of course the determination of heads of damages is intrinsically linked to causality. In the abstract, the availability of a specific head of damage tells us nothing at all. Only through the factual constellations which are able to fulfill -or not- the constitutive requirements does the statement begin to acquire legal meaning.

In all selected jurisdictions, the hypothetical nature of a tender's potential chances of having obtained a contract, be it phrased as a question of the burden of proof, causality or the claimable head of damage, is *the* central difficulty standing in the way of a successful damages award. While a breach can often be readily proven, it is difficult to ascertain how the breach affected the position of an aggrieved bidder. The hypothetical nature of the future position of the aggrieved tender is thus almost subject to speculation. The main issue on which the success of a claim in procurement law hinges is the evaluation of the 'chance' of a tenderer receiving a tender. This, in its details, is judge-made law.

© Springer International Publishing Switzerland 2016
H. Schebesta, *Damages in EU Public Procurement Law*, Studies in European
Economic Law and Regulation 6, DOI 10.1007/978-3-319-23612-4_11

In the face of these notorious difficulties, the doctrine of the 'lost chance' is increasingly discussed as a potential solution. Without a doubt, this has partially been triggered by the fact that the terminology of 'lost chance' is used in the Utilities Remedies Directive and some General Court case law on Institutional liability regarding public procurement. As the country studies show, the acceptance and practice of a lost chance theory is positively linked to the availability of damages. We can conclude that damages claims in public procurement are most successful where there is an acceptance of the lost chance doctrine, independent of the type of lost chance doctrine followed.

The lost chance's potential lies in the fact that it is a compromise between the continuity of law and the liability allocation based views. In practical terms, it is an instrument that mediates between the interests of the aggrieved bidders in the protection of their rights, and the public interest in not having to pay too many damages suits. The lost chance is a compromise precisely because in a way it moves away from the full compensation principle which is enshrined in many legal orders.[1]

11.1.1   Different Understandings of the Lost Chance

The lost chance is sometimes seen as *the* lost chance, while, in reality, it is an iridescent legal doctrine. Conceptually, the lost chance is a chameleon that appears sometimes as a head of damage, sometimes as an alleviation of the burden of proof and sometimes as a proportional liability.

The country studies demonstrated that there are diverging concepts of the lost chance and it is apparent that differences exist in the way the lost chance is applied. At theoretical level, the concept of 'lost chance' takes one of three diverging forms:

1. The lost chance as a relaxation of *the burden of proof* for establishing full compensation;
2. *Proportional or relational liability*, in which the probability of the chance determines the lost chance as a proportion of the "final" or potential loss sustained; and
3. The lost chance as an *autonomous type of loss*.

Regarding (1), if the lost chance acts as a standard of proof, it is sufficient to demonstrate that there was the chance (sometimes serious chance) of the advantageous event arising had the breach of law not occurred. The lost chance fixes (lowers) the degree of probability required to demonstrate causation requirement. The compensation value, however, will correspond to full compensation. A chance of receiving €1000, which was not merely a remote possibility but a serious possibility, would necessitate the compensation of €1000.

---

[1] JT Oskierski, *Schadensersatz im Europäischen Recht : Eine vergleichende Untersuchung des Acquis Communautaire und der EMRK* (Baden-Baden, Nomos, 2010).

Regarding (2), the lost chance as proportional or relational liability, on the other hand, uses the probability of the advantageous event arising to determine which portion of the potential total loss will be compensated. The value of the hypothetical situation without the breach of law is multiplied by the likelihood of that event arising. For a chance of winning €1000, the probability of which is assessed at 10 %, compensation amounts to €100.

Regarding (3), a strong version of the lost chance theory requires a particular redefinition of the loss of a chance itself as a compensable damage. Based on a 'subjective-relational theory of value',[2] patrimony is a positive relationship between an individual and something of value in the individual's life/world. Damage to one's patrimony does negative harm to this relationship. A positive relationship can include mere potentialities. For example, the fact that I bought a lottery ticket gives rise to a positive relationship between me and the lottery prize. The damage to a positive relationship, even where the materialization of the value has not occurred, is damage to a 'becoming patrimony'.[3] On these theoretical grounds, the lost opportunity, the damage done to the 'becoming patrimony', is an autonomous type of loss.[4]

The lost chance of a lottery prize can be calculated conveniently on the basis of proportional liability. If 1000 lottery tickets were issued for a €1000 prize, the proportional liability would be €1. Such convenient and equal probability is often not a given in real life situations. The pure lost chance as an independent loss is therefore mostly applied to situations in which the uncertainty is uncertain, although it leaves the question open of how the value of the opportunity should be established.

The lost chance gives rise to doubt under accepted general principles of liability in that they challenge accepted notions of full causality (1); full compensation (2); or recognized types of losses (3). Below, the legal systems and the type of loss of chance arguments that are accepted are broadly described.

11.2   Country Overview in General

Before looking at the specific field of public procurement, the general stance on the lost chance theory in the legal systems covered is summarized and classified. These findings indicate under the EU comparative law approach whether there is a general tradition of Member States with regards to the lost chance doctrine.

---

[2] See, eg W Müller-Stoy, *Schadensersatz für verlorene Chancen - Eine rechtsvergleichende Untersuchung* (Albert-Ludwigs-Universität zu Freiburg, 1973), p 124, relying on Möller, below n 3.

[3] H Möller, *Summen- und Einzelschaden. Beiträge zur Erneuerung der Schadenslehr vom Wirtschaftsrecht aus* (Berlin, de Gruyter, 1937), p 124.

[4] Möller distinguishes these 'becoming patrimonies' as '*Anwartschaftsbeziehungen*' and sharply differentiates them from mere chances. This distinction is based on degree, as '*Anwartschaften*' are likely, and chances are merely possible. In Müller-Stoy, *Schadensersatz für verlorene Chancen – Eine rechtsvergleichende Untersuchung*, above n 2, p 124.

11.2.1 France

In France, the loss of chance theory (*la perte d'une chance*) has a long standing tradition, the *Cour de cassation* having permitted damages both for the loss of a chance and for future harm in 1932. The first traces of the prerequisite lines of argumentation appeared as early as 1896,[5] and manifested in an 1889 judgment on chances to win a process.[6] In specific fields of law, the doctrine is widely recognized – most pronounced in medical law since the 1960s. While it has been accepted since the end of the nineteenth century, France is a good example of how the understanding and the meaning accorded to the lost chance doctrine can oscillate. All variants of chance can be encountered.[7]

Clustering occurs, most commonly in separate fields of law and related typologies of case law. In addition, there is a difference between the case law of civil and administrative branches.[8] These jurisdictions deployed different concepts of the lost chance. In the 1960s, the *Conseil d'Etat*, the administrative jurisdiction, embraced the doctrine. Administrative courts were for a long time regarded as handling the notion of lost chance based on an alleviation of causality. Only since a judgment of the *Conseil d'Etat* of 5 January 2000 has the lost chance also come to be seen as an autonomous head of damage in the administrative branch of the judiciary.[9] The loss of a chance is not identical to the final loss, the *préjudice final*, as the French *Cour de Cassation* has also stressed on several occasions.[10]

The theory of lost chances in France is also subject to different conceptualizations – as one author noted in 1973: 'the problem of the chance in France is apparently situated on this fluid borderline, as the loss of a chance is on one hand certain (*"actuel et certain"*), but its realization on the other hand is doubtful (*"éventuel et hypothétique"*). Because of this, the lost chance is consistently treated under the section certainty of losses'.[11] In judging chances, the French general principles are:

---

[5] I Vacarie, 'La perte d'une chance', (1987) *Revue de la Recerche Juridique* 903, p 905 and fn 6.

[6] P Jourdain, J Ghestin & M Billau, *Traité de droit civil / T.II Les obligations 4e Partie Les conditions de la responsabilité* (Librairie Générale de Droit et de Jurisprudence, 1998), p 74, citing case of 17 July 1889 Cour de cassation.

[7] As observed, eg, by V Tacchini-Laforest, 'Reflexions à propos de la perte de chances', (1999) *Petites Affiches* 7, p 7, B.2.b: ('La position de la jurisprudence et d'une partie de la doctrine à légard de la perte d'une chance n'est pas exempte de paradoxe').

[8] The area of medical law is particularly interesting for the comparison of civil and administrative jurisdictions. Similar cases reached different jurisdictions depending on whether injuries were sustained in public or private hospitals.

[9] For greater detail on this distinction between administrative and civil jurisdictions, see J Boucher & B Bourgeouis-Machureau, 'Indemnisation de la perte de chances: le Conseil d'Etat poursuit sa conversion au probabilisme', (2008) *Acutalité Juridique Droit Administratif* 135.

[10] Tacchini-Laforest, 'Reflexions à propos de la perte de chances', above n 7, A.1., citing, eg Cass Civ 1re, 8 juillet 1997, J.C.P. 1997, II, 22921.

[11] '*Das Chancenproblem ist in Frankreich offenbar auf dieser fließenden Grenze anzusiedeln, weil die Zerstörung einer Chance zwar sicher ("actuel et certain"), ihre Realisierung aber zweifelhaft ("éventuel et hypothétique") ist. Demgemäß wird "la perte d'une chance" durchweg im Abschnitt*

the chance must be direct and certain in character and it must be real and serious, not merely hypothetical or eventual. Regarding the discretion of the judge, the *Cour de Cassation* held that the judge must lay down why a lost chance was certain, and held direct relation to the tortious act. The lost chance does not form part of the loss sustained, it is instead the value of the lost chance that is being compensated.

Characterized in this way, the lost chance forms part of a doctrine of possible losses and the evaluation of damages; but over time '*elle s'est métamorphosée en se dédoublant*'[12] – doubled because of it weakening the causality requirement. In the assessment of this loss, the judge must estimate the probability of a favorable chance materializing. The *Cour de Cassation* has repeatedly quashed judgments in which the lower courts granted compensation for the full damage without the required certainty that without the fault, the positive event would have materialized. The lost chance is necessarily a fraction of the losses incurred.[13]

11.2.2   The Netherlands

The Dutch Supreme Court applies different approaches to the loss of chance in specific circumstances.[14] In addition, specific fields of law have received better receptions in lower instances, especially in medical malpractice law.[15] The loss of chance is often quantified by means of judge's estimation (*ex acqua et bono*), for example by simply fixing a percentage of the amount claimed.[16] The lost chance is based on proportional liability. It has been applied by the Dutch Supreme Court in the *Nefalit/Karamus* case,[17] in the framework of 7:658 BW, a special provision on employers' liability for asbestos. In this case, the chance that the cancer was a result of exposure to asbestos was estimated at 55 %, from which the court reached the conclusion that 55 % of the claim was granted.

In the Dutch system, the default rule applied by the courts in determining damage is the all-or-nothing approach.[18] Recognition of loss of chance as a head of

---

über die "Certitude du dommage" behandelt' [translation by the author, footnote with doctrinal references omitted]. See also W Müller-Stoy, *Schadensersatz für verlorene Chancen - Eine rechtsvergleichende Untersuchung*, above n 2, p 7.

[12] JURISCLASSEUR, *Civil Code 14 juin 1999, 'Art. 1382 à 1386 > Fasc. 202-1-3: RÉGIME DE LA RÉPARATION'* (LexisNexis 28 October 2010).

[13] '*une fraction de la perte subie*' [translation by the author]. Ibid, listing relevant case law.

[14] Hoge Raad, 24 October 1997, NJ 1998, 257 (*Baijings/Mr. H.*).

[15] J Spier, T Hartlief, GE van Maanen & RD Vriesendorp, *Verbintenissen uit de wet en Schadevergoeding* (Deventer, Kluwer, 2006), p 217, with references to case law.

[16] ibid, p 218. One of the most famous examples is the Baby Ruth case, in which a late diagnosis negatively impaired chances of healing. Hof Amsterdam 4 January 1996, NJ 1997, 213.

[17] ibid, p 219; and HR 31 March 2006, RvdW 2006, 328.

[18] AJ Akkermans, *Proportionele aansprakelijkheid bij onzeker causaal verband. Een rechtsvergelijkend onderzoek naar wenselijkheid, grondslagen en afgrenzing van aansprakelijkheid naar rato van veroorzakingswaarschijnlijkheid* (Dissertation, Katholieke Universiteit Brabant, 1997), p 116.

damage in the Dutch system would amount to recognizing a new category of patrimonial loss covered under 6:95 BW.[19] The chance is thus quite controversial, not
least as it is difficult to fit within a rigid conception of the tort system in the
Netherlands. With the first applications by the courts, and several voices in the literature calling for the lost chance to be considered in Dutch law, one may assume
that the lost chance theory is on the rise. One has to note, however, that as in the
other legal systems, the relevance of the lost chance is strongly connected with the
specific typology of cases at issue and the kind of uncertainty (scientific, or hypothetical) that one is dealing with.[20]

11.2.3   Germany

In the German legal system, the recognition of lost chances is frustrated by the very
doctrinal and narrow reading of the principles of liability under German doctrine.
This is true in the field of medical liability as well as that of legal process, these
usually being the typical areas of the lost chance.[21]

Damages claims can be separately based on delictual or on contractual claims –
under the delictual scheme, following §823 I BGB, one distinguishes between violation, legally protected interest (*Rechtsgut*), and recoverable losses. Only those
legal interests which are protected by §823 I BGB may give rise to a damages claim;
as a purely pecuniary loss, the loss of a chance – according to the large majority of
doctrine – is not covered, so that the application of §823 I BGB for most factual
situations is precluded. For example, regarding the chance of healing, only a minority argues that such a chance would be covered by 'other legal goods' or the legal
goods of 'life' and 'health'. On German doctrinal grounds, this narrow interpretation
makes good sense. The provision in the BGB is seen as an explicit legislative choice
against a very wide general provision. Effectively, this reading limits liability claims
by imposing an enumeration of compensable harm arising out of delict akin to a
numerus clausus.

For contractual claims, on the other hand, the loss of a chance would have to be
fitted within the provision of the lost profit under §252s2 BGB.[22] The straitjacket of
the lost profit as defined by §252 BGB lies in the fact that it forces the lost profit as

---

[19] ibid, p 219.

[20] SD Lindenbergh, *Schadevergoeding* (Deventer, Kluwer, 2008), pp 52–53. Lindenbergh sees an
assured 'place' for the lost chance theory in Dutch law, the main question remaining as to in what
cases and how exactly one would handle it – in his opinion, with a 'definite degree of restraint'.

[21] See K Péguret, *Schadensersatzansprüche übergangener Bieter im Vergaberecht* (Dissertation,
Jenaer Wissenschaftliche Verlagsgesellschaft, 2010), pp 110–123 for a good summary on the
German doctrine, comparing the different factual situations of other areas of law with those of
public procurement procedures.

[22] §252 BGB – Lost profits: 'The damage to be compensated for also comprises the lost profits.
Those profits are considered lost that in the normal course of events or in the special circumstances,
particularly due to the measures and precautions taken, could probably be expected.'

a realization of the profits; as discussed above in the theoretical part, in order to conceptually accept the loss of a chance, however, a shift in perspective has to occur in order for the loss of the chance to become valued independently of the eventuality of the realization of the profits. While the lost chance is discussed, it is far from accepted in Germany.

11.2.4   England

The main authority for the lost chance in England dates to *Chaplin v Hicks* from 1911,[23] in which the court accepted the recovery of damages for loss of a chance based on a 25 % chance that the plaintiff would have won a beauty contest. *Hotson*[24] was a subsequent medical case denying recovery of a 25 % chance of causing damage to the plaintiff's hip. As many commentators have treated it as identical to *Chaplin v Hicks*, the case has called the authority of the latter into question. The major tension can be resolved based on a distinction that relies on the context, i.e. one being legal (*Chaplin v Hicks*), and the other medical (*Hotson*). Other explanations rely on characterizing *Chaplin* as a contractual and *Hotson* as a tort based claim, on past versus hypothetical facts, or probability theory.[25]

Without taking sides on the explanations advanced in this debate, it may suffice at this point to note that first of all the chance was, at least potentially, accepted in all its different theoretical manifestations, including proportional liability. At the same time, as the quite numerous commentaries suggest, the importance of the doctrine of the lost chance is not one that is close to being settled for English courts.

11.2.5   Evaluation

On a theoretical level, albeit to varying degrees, the lost chance theory is debated in all jurisdictions. The survey also demonstrated that different understandings of the lost chance theory persist next to each other, with countries exhibiting an internal equivocity regarding the theory.[26] Resistance to the lost chance stems from fundamental doctrinal considerations governing the legal systems. Generally, fundamentals bend more easily to particulars – this holds also true for the area of procurement law, which in many jurisdictions has found particular applications of the lost chance doctrine.

---

[23] *Chaplin v Hicks* [1911] 2K.B. 786.

[24] *Hotson v East Berkshire Area Health Authority* [1987] 2 All ER 909.

[25] H Reece, 'Losses of Chances in the Law', (1996) 59 *The Modern Law Review* 188.

[26] In a wider survey, Binon states that there is 'no unanimity' between the Member States with regard to the acceptance of the lost chance theory. See JM Binon, 'La Réparation de la Perte d'une Chance Dans la Jurisprudence Européenne : Une Question de Chance ?', in *Liber Amicorum Jean-Luc Fagnart* (Bruxelles, Anthemis, 2008), p 380.

11.3   The Lost Chance in Public Procurement Damages Claims

In relation to the lost chance, a strong tendency towards differentiation according to areas of law can be observed, the prime example being medical law. In adjudication, arguments on the lost chance theory in the abstract are heavily mitigated by the particular applications in specific fields of law. The reason is that specific fields of law come with repeated typologies and factual situations. They also exhibit particular patterns of uncertainty based on which the lost chance doctrine has different implications. This is also true for public procurement. As is evidenced by the country studies, all legal systems have developed rather 'idiosyncratic' interpretations of the lost chance in public procurement scenarios which to some extent deviate from the general doctrine. Therefore, discussions on the role of the lost chance in public procurement take on a largely national flavour, constrained by the available and existing national mould for providing damages in procurement contexts in the specific legal orders.

11.3.1   France

The lost chance is often understood in its form of a proportional liability, under which the lost chance – the lost opportunity – qualifies as an autonomous type of damage. Both civil and administrative jurisdictions apply the lost chance doctrine,[27] for both delictual and contractual claims.[28] It has been observed that the administrative courts have started to use the lost chance not in its version of proportional liability, but moving in the direction of a relaxation of the burden of proof. At least formally, this practice has been contradicted by the rulings of the higher courts, which insist on the proportional liability version of the loss of a chance.[29] The rendering of these judgments must so be seen as an admonition of the administrative courts for re-uniting their jurisprudence with the civil court developed doctrine. At the same time, one may question to what degree this 'general' understanding of the lost chance necessarily also finds its reflection in the case law pertaining to public procurement cases.

Proportional liability seems to remain confined to medical law, rather than also finding an application in public procurement law.[30] Globally speaking, there is strong evidence that the administrative courts are 'using the doctrine [of lost chance]

---

[27] Jourdain et al, *Traité de droit civil*, p 78.

[28] ibid, p 79.

[29] The following case are reverses the case law on the notion of chance: CE, 5 January 2000, *Telle*.

[30] F Lichère, 'Damages for violation of the EC public procurement rules in France' (2006) *Public Procurement Law Review* 171, p 176.

as a sort of presumption of causation'.[31] In this vein, Lichère remarked that it was unclear which version of the chance theory is deployed by the administrative judge in public procurement cases.[32] In the cases covered (see Chap. 7), the French system is seen to have oscillated over time, but now seems to have reached a point of stability in which the probability of the chance materializing for an aggrieved tenderer are fixed in categories. These categories are (i) having been *entirely deprived of a chance* of being awarded the contract, resulting in a preclusion of damages. Where the tender is assessed as meeting the highest requirement, namely (ii) a *very serious chance*, the lost profit is awarded. The classification in between of possible chances – those that are "merely" serious, but not very serious and the extent of damage these entail – is questionable.

The recent French cases link different qualities of chances (none/serious/very serious) to fixed categories of claimable losses (none/bid costs/lost profit). Looking only at the link between the chance and the claimable losses, the (serious) lost chance is therefore consistently used as an alleviation of proof, enabling the claimant to receive full compensation.

11.3.2   The Netherlands

In the Netherlands, the fields of law most touched by the lost chance doctrine are procedural errors and medical malpractice, as well as the asbestos line of cases. In public procurement, the doctrine did not gain ground for some time. The lost chance is discussed mainly in relation to the recoverable damage, and hence, as a head of damage. Although legal scholars discussed the advantages of the lost chance, for a long time there were only two court judgments in public procurement in which it had been applied.[33] However, as the overview of jurisprudence (Chap. 5) demonstrates, there are now several authorities in which the lost chance doctrine was applied in public procurement contexts.

The courts have used the lost chance doctrine in cases in which the wrongful behaviour of a contracting authority was clearly established and the aggrieved bidders were in privileged positions, ie they were one of a limited and identifiable number of competitors. The potential lost profits were then divided by the number of competitors, ie if there were 3 competitors 1/3 of the lost profits were awarded, if there was only one competitor, half. Although not numerous, these judgments consistently deploy a proportional approach to the lost chance theory.

---

[31] ibid, p 177.

[32] ibid.

[33] Utrecht DC, 4 July 2001, BR 2002/91; and Den Haag 29 March 2000, rolnr. 94/3490, as cited and discussed in EH Pijnacker Hordijk, GW Van der Bend & JF Van Nouhuys, *Aanbestedingsrecht. Handboek van het Europese en het Nederlandse Aanbestedingsrecht* (Den Haag, Sdu Uitgevers, 2009), p 661.

11.3.3   Germany

Principally, the German legal system is largely foreclosed for the lost chance doctrine. This is different in the field of public procurement as the legislator introduced the lost chance wording into the GWB, thus forcing doctrine to come to terms with 'the chance' as a concept. The wording relating to loss of chance was, in fact, changed during the legislative procedure, and has been the subject of some discussion within the preparatory documents for the implementing legislation. Therefore, the German courts' interpretation of chances is confined to the procurement damages article, namely §126 GWB, and is regarded as an exception to the general legal system.

11.3.3.1   The 'Real Chance' in §126 GWB – A Causality Requirement?

During the legislative process, the wording of §126 GWB was changed, as a result of which the nature of the norm – as being either an evidentiary or causality norm or a specific basis for claiming public procurement damages – became disputed. The initial proposal included the terminology of '*engere Wahl*' [34] – that is 'narrower selection' – which, in the course of the legislative procedure, was changed to the "real chance". The wording 'real chance' derives from Article 2(7) of Directive 92/13/EC. The national legislative proposal at the time interpreted the teleological purpose of the article to be that of lowering the burden of proof for the aggrieved tenderer. The wording '*engere Wahl*' was regarded as substantively equivalent to that of the real chance.[35] It has, however, been accepted by the courts that the norm does not just constitute a shift in the burden of proof, but that it constitutes an independent and specific action for claiming damages.[36]

In the interpretation of the 'real chance' criterion, different views prevail. One view defends a proper lost chance theory, in the sense that the lost chance itself becomes protected.[37] This view has generally been rejected under German law, particularly in other contexts. The loss of a chance under the second and prominent view is regarded as a modification of the causality element of the constitutive criteria granting an action for claims of damages under §126 GWB. However, one can also find commentators that interpret the 'real chance' approach as following the causal test of the *conditio sine qua non*.[38]

---

[34] Legislative proposal *Vergaberechtsänderungsgesetz* (VgRÄG) §135, BT-Drucksache 13/9340, p 9.

[35] ibid, p 22. The legislator additionally noted that the terminology had already been introduced by §25 3 (3) VOB/A.

[36] R Weyand, *Kommentar Vergaberecht. Praxiskommentar zu GWB, VgV, SektVO, VOB/A, VOLA/A, VOF* (München, Beck-online 2012), 42.5.

[37] Most convincingly C Alexander, 'GWB § 126 Anspruch auf Ersatz des Vertrauensschadens', in H Pünder & M Schellenberg (eds), *Vergaberecht,* 2nd edition (Baden-Baden, Nomos, 2011), rn 32–33.

[38] M Burgi, 'A Report about the German Remedies System', in S Treumer & F Lichère (eds), *Enforcement of the EU Public Procurement Rules* (København, Djof Publishing, 2011), p 25.

11.3.4   England

The main authority for public procurement damages cases in England is the *Harmon*[39] case. When addressing causality, *Harmon* used the lost chance theory instead of the general standard of the balance of probabilities. The lost chance in England is therefore applied as proportional liability. The court proceeded by applying *Allied Maples Group v Simmons & Simmons*.[40] In a remarkably explicit application of the lost chance doctrine, regarding the heads of damages of both lost profits and bid costs in *Harmon*, the court held:

> In summary therefore Harmon is entitled to recover its tender costs, taken by themselves, on the grounds that it ought to have been awarded the contract and would then have recovered its costs. If, notwithstanding, H of C had decided to place the contract elsewhere then Harmon would have been deprived of the chance of recovering its costs. I assess that chance as virtually certain – say 90 % – for I do not consider H of C would have been so perverse as not to accept Harmon's tender. It is not therefore truly an expression of a chance for the purposes of "loss of a chance" but more of probability. If H of C had decided to go for some other course such as to award the contract on the basis of a version of Option B2, but after giving the other tenderers the opportunity to tender on the basis of that option or to award it on the basis of a performance specification complying with certain design criteria but with the detailed design being provided by the tenderer, I consider Harmon would have stood as good a chance as any and better than most of being awarded the contract. Unlike the primary scenario (lowest price) there can be no certainty but there is surely a real and substantive chance that Harmon would have been awarded the contract. I therefore assess its chance of doing as 70 %. (I develop my reasons later.) I consider it quite improbable that H of C would run the risks inherent in starting all over again, but would have accepted Harmon's tender which was the lowest. Harmon's capabilities were denigrated solely to advance Seele/Alvis and Option B2. Issues 11(A) will be answered Yes and sub-issues (2) and (3): Not necessarily, it is sufficient if it ought to have been awarded the contract.

In this particular case, English jurisprudence strongly supports the idea of the 'true' proportional lost chance theory. However, in strands of law other than public procurement, this approach is highly contentious. While the procurement authority is clearly stated, it remains a fact that *Harmon* does not – even several years later – have the sufficient number of follow-up cases to conclude that the lost chance doctrine is steadily applied. In addition to the fundamental question of the validity of the lost chance doctrine, the question of how probabilities ought to be assessed remains open.

11.3.5   Evaluation

While on one hand the factual situations giving rise to damages claims are identical in all jurisdictions, doctrinally the jurisdictions differ from each other even more than one would suspect by simply looking at the differences of the causes of action.

---

[39] *Harmon CFEM Facades (UK) Ltd v The Corporate Officer of the House of Commons* [1999] EWHC Technology 199 [hereinafter 'Harmon'] and *Harmon CFEM Facades (UK) Ltd v The Corporate Officer of the House of Commons* [2000] EWHC Technology 84 [hereinafter 'Harmon II'].

[40] *Allied Maples Group v Simmons & Simmons* [1995] 3 All ER 907.

Of the selected jurisdictions, both France and the Netherlands have implemented the damages provision by means of a general tort law provision. However, the strength of the 'lost chance' doctrine generally in France has allowed for its application in public procurement disputes as well, while in the Netherlands it remains confined to isolated cases. Damages in England enjoy a strong authority for the proportional liability version of the lost chance. In Germany, by contrast, the lost chance is implemented through a legislative provision. One may conclude that the specific public procurement factual constellations have forced all jurisdictions to accept the lost chance theory in the field of public procurement in order to make damages available.

The counterargument is that at no point in the procurement procedure is the contracting authority actually required to award a contract. While a judge is under a duty to make a judgment, and the content of that judgment must be predicted, or the holder of a competition or lottery must hand out a prize, a contracting authority is free to contract. Thus, it has the theoretical possibility of reducing the bidder's chance to nil at any moment in the procedure is retained. This absolute uncertainty, which is grounded of course in party autonomy and the freedom to contract, is actually not chanceous, but on the contrary is a recognition of the right on the part of a public authority not to contract. The only way to remedy this doubt is to prove that the chance, that is the contract, indeed would have – or in fact has – materialized. Practically speaking, two real life situations giving rise to such a conviction would be the scenario in which the contract has wrongfully been awarded to another tenderer in the same procedure, or where -albeit in a different procedure- an identical contract is tendered out again.

As discussed above, this theoretical reasoning is accepted in Germany and the Netherlands, and applied by the courts in their determination of the heads of damages – under pre-contractual liability, lost profits are only claimable where the contract has actually come into existence in some way. In the research conducted for France or England, we have not come across this argument. Lost profits are granted for example to an aggrieved bidder that had a serious chance of being awarded a contract, regardless of whether or not the contracting authority ultimately tendered or not – hypothetically it is possible that the public authority would decide not to award a contract *tout court*.

11.4   Using the Loss of Chance Doctrine Fruitfully in Public Procurement?

Normative frameworks on the doctrine of loss of chance can depart from two differing logics: the first departs from doctrinal principles of compensation and an understanding of how the constitutive criteria of liability relate to each other. From this, one may dogmatically consider the chance as to how it fits within this doctrinal understanding of liability. The second approach stems from a bottom-up or fact-based approach, and looks at the nuanced versions of chances that typically present themselves in categories of situations. By approaching the law through the facts it is increasingly possible to have recourse to arguments of justice. This allows the point of view of recurring 'losers' to be taken into consideration in a dogmatic application of the law, which in particular sets of circumstances may be systematically sealed off from successful damages claims.

11.4.1 Causation in the Face of Uncertainty

In relation to damages, the most widely recognized of general principles of causality within the EU is the all-or-nothing approach[41] – granting full compensation where the causation can be established, but none where causation cannot be or has not been established. In these cases, either 'complete' certainty is required or, in the face of uncertainty regarding the link between an activity and a damage, a likelihood or specific threshold such as a percentage or a 'more probable than not' conclusion must be reached – all resulting in entire, full compensation. The result is a binary award of damages, which can differ massively with only marginal shifts in the degrees of certainty, a result that is often perceived as unfair. One way of alleviating the crudeness of the all-or-nothing approach lies in introducing elements of proportionality, through which degrees of probability of causation are matched by proportional compensation. The lost chance, or more appositely the lost opportunity, is situated here and from a functional point of view must be understood as an attempt to come to terms with uncertainty – however, the way this is done across legal systems is divergent, and can be categorized under the concepts of causality or head of damage.

The reason for recourse to the loss of a chance doctrine lies in the probably intuitive 'feeling' that unjust results are achieved through a strict application of the all or nothing approach. It is an acknowledgement of the fact that some liability claims are practically always precluded due to the problem of causality and the proof thereof. This is why as a variation on the material conditions, a shift in the burden of proof is often proposed. Apart from the obvious resistance to departing from established principles and doctrine, the dangers in terms of effect are seen to lie in the potentially unlimited proliferation of damages claims and overcompensation.

The merits of the loss of chance doctrine are comparable to those of a compromise. Bénabent summarized the lingering sentiment one faces in the presence of chances: "*In fairness, the process is perhaps less condemnable than purely logically considered: it leads to these kinds of compromises and rough-and-ready settlements which never satisfy anyone but which calm the spirits. One commits two small injustices instead of risking a big one. Perhaps the social order benefits from this.*"[42]

---

[41] Oskierski, *Schadensersatz im Europäischen Recht*, above n 1.

[42] '*En équité, le procédé est peut-etre moins condemnable qu'en logique pure: il aboutit à ces sortes de compromise et de cotes mal taillées qui ne satisfont personne mais appaisent les esprits. On fait deux petites injustices au lieu de risqué d'en faire une grosse. Peut-etre l'ordre social y gagne-t-il*' [translation by the author]. See A Bénabent, *La Chance et le Droit* (Librairie Générale de Droit et de Jurisprudence, 1973), p 191, fn 4, as cited in Müller-Stoy, *Schadensersatz für verlorene Chancen – Eine rechtsvergleichende Untersuchung*, above n 2, fn 96.

11.4.1.1   Coming to Terms with Criticism of the Lost Chance Theory

The lost chance theory is subject to fierce criticism, which target different aspects of liability, namely: (i) the maceration of causality. The lost chance doctrine does away with one of the fundamental constituent variables of responsibility – the causal connection.[43] (ii) Violation of the principle of full compensation. The compensation provided is partial only had it been justified, or, if in fact unjustified, constitutes overcompensation (iii) The use of probability in the statistical sense in order to establish the likelihood of a given effect materializing, therefore creating causality by means of a calculation is rejected. The attribution of liability is a case by case assessment of the particular and individual circumstances of the case under consideration, rather than an application of a generalized, average likelihood to be drawn from mathematical computation.[44]

11.4.2   How to Establish Criteria in an 'a priori' Account

Typically, comparative treatments of the lost chance doctrine have clustered different groups of cases together, the most typical of these being situations of competition: litigation chances, in the context of lawyers' liability for malpractice; professional careers of victims; and in the area of medical malpractice, the loss of a chance to heal. This is an indication of the fact that the need, acceptability, and practicability of the loss of chance doctrine are strongly determined by the factual situations and areas of law it is applied to.

In trying to create a typology of different factual situations, the following parameters influencing a legal system's stance on the lost chance have been identified[45]: whether the chance arises in contractual or delictual damages claims; regarding material versus procedural conditions; and the role of the judge in the evaluation of the damage, and his discretion. Criteria defining what constitutes a chance are mainly negative, defining those events which cannot be thus classified anymore for reasons of being too hypothetical, speculative, or contingent.[46] More specifically, chances should not be minimal chances – even though it is difficult to set a threshold in the abstract, the victim has to have invested some amount of time or money for the purpose of realizing the chance, hence mere 'chances of luck' are excluded.

---

[43] R Savatier, 'Une faute peut-elle engendrer la responsabilité d'un dommage sans l'avoir causé?' (1970) *Dalloz* 123.

[44] The process is not about '*d'établir une statistique générale, mais d'apprécier concrètement un cas particulier*'. See R Savatier, 'Note Cass. civ. 1re, 2 mai 1978, Mandryka c. Franck et autres' (1978) *Juris-Classeur Périodique* 18966, citing, eg the condemnation of instituting proportional liability practice by the Cour de Cassation belge 29 september 1974 (1976) *Juris-Classeur Périodique* II 18216.

[45] Müller-Stoy, *Schadensersatz für verlorene Chancen - Eine rechtsvergleichende Untersuchung*, above n 2.

[46] ibid, p 96.

Additionally, the lost chance if often accorded a subsidiary role, as only grantable where no other way of claiming damages is possible.[47]

One of the fiercest critics of the lost chance, Savatier,[48] based his criticism of the use of the notion of chance on an understanding of chance as probability – which is acceptable under certain circumstance only, but not in the case of a medical accident where statistical probability is inappropriate to predict the probable unfolding of events. He therefore only criticizes the doctrine of chance in certain circumstances or, phrased more positively, only accepts the doctrine under certain circumstances. This shows that the strengths of specific critiques of the lost chance vary with the underlying factual patterns of different domains. For example, Savatier – at least principally – accepted that in situations of participation in a competition, or even process chances, there are sufficient elements to give rise to the judge's estimation of the likelihood of the chance materializing in a concrete case – being, for example, the previous classification or preparatory classification of the participant in a competition, or on the likely outcome of foregone court proceedings. A similar distinction is drawn by Reece,[49] who argues that in deterministic cases the balance of probabilities ought to be used, while in indeterministic cases recourse to the lost chance is opportune. This author also bases the distinction on the underlying factual situations and the question what type of uncertainty is at stake, whether it is one which is inherently unknowable, or one wherein some forms of evaluation are possible.

Public procurement situations are characterized by similar features as competitions. In a procurement procedure indicators are established that may guide a judge on the probable hypothetical development of an award procedure; more strongly so because of the highly formalized procedures that are to be followed, and which define the future options – for example, a limited amount of competitors or previously established selection and award criteria, all of which would make the outcomes of award procedures much more predictable than an entirely open competition. In other words, there are indicators which make the lost chance to some extent measurable. *A priori*, such features provide a fruitful ground for the application of the lost chance theory.

11.5 Conclusions from an EU Perspective

There are three understandings of the 'loss of chance' doctrine: lost chance as autonomous damage, as causality alleviation and as proportional liability. This conceptual aspect is particularly relevant where the lost chance is used at EU level. If it is not sufficiently framed by a context, the lost chance terminology is burdened

---

[47] Williston, quoted in Müller-Stoy, *Schadensersatz für verlorene Chancen - Eine rechtsvergleichende Untersuchung*, p 94.

[48] Savatier, 'Une faute peut-elle engendrer la responsabilité d'un dommage sans l'avoir causé?', above n 43.

[49] Reece, 'Losses of Chances in the Law', above n 25.

by a significant inherent degree of indeterminacy. The legal term 'lost chance' with regards to the public procurement directives has not been assigned conceptual content at EU level,[50] and at the national level its content diverges. This is a classic situation for a conceptual and terminological misalignment in the implementation of EU law.[51]

Even internally, the legal systems expose a highly divided view on the loss of a chance and as to which version is best deployed. The internally inconsistent views are amplified when comparing across countries. There is, on a general level, a tendency towards exploring the lost chance theory and its relevance for particular legal systems. The equivocal state of the doctrine prevents a conclusion to the effect that a Member State tradition of the lost chance in general liability exists. The picture could vary with respect to highly specific areas of law, such as medical malpractice, legal process chances or as we explore public procurement claims. This assessment is, however, shy of constituting the existence of a common tradition regarding a *doctrine* of lost chance in public procurement.

Looking at damages claims in public procurement the picture is varied, as the lost chance has gained general acceptance in some jurisdictions (France), while in others it is specifically interpreted based on a legislative instrument (Germany), or still mostly ignored (the Netherlands).

11.5.1   Procurement Damages

Regarding the desirability of damages in public procurement, Reich summarizes the main arguments advanced in favor of making procurement damages more widely available: firstly, to *compensate* the bidder for losses unjustly suffered, under a "moral justification for compensation"; secondly, *to restore confidence in procurement processes*; and thirdly, to *create a deterrent effect*.[52]

Reich suggests following a truly proportional approach, which is the lost chance as interpreted in the English *Harmon* case, and proposed to couple it with a reversal of the burden of proof.[53] Provided that there was a material breach, a court would assess a bidder's chances of obtaining a contract and accord the corresponding percentage of the overall losses. Since it can be an onerous task to establish one's chances of being awarded a contract, and the contracting authority is generally in the better position in terms of information and evidence available, Reich makes the radical proposal to additionally shift the presumption of proof. Thus, the aggrieved

---

[50] I deliberately exclude the lost chance as applied by the General Court in its case law here.

[51] G Ajani, L Lesmo, G Boella, A Mazzei & P Rossi, 'Terminological and Ontological Analysis of European Directives: Multilingualism in Law', (2007) *International Conference on Artificial Intelligence and Law Journal* 43.

[52] A Reich & O Shabat, *The Remedy of Damages in Public Procurement in Israel and the EU: A Proposal for Reform*, SSRN eLibrary (2013) *at* http://ssrn.com/abstract=2244909, pp 28–29.

[53] ibid, 38.

bidder would be regarded by default as having had a 100 % chance of obtaining a contract, a presumption which can then be altered through evidence introduced by the contracting authority.

Since this approach advocates the lost chance in its proportional version, it is burdened with the relevant criticism (violation of the full compensation and causality principles, as discussed above). The proposal has the beauty of simplicity and efficiency. The incentives it creates, however, are probably strong enough to encourage plenty of 'cowboy litigation'.[54]

11.5.1.1 Own Appreciation

The particularities of the French lost chance version were previously described. It is a unique combination of categorization of lost chances which connects categories of chances to specific heads of damages. This categorization seems in effect to be a combination of different lost chance theories which comes to an effective, doctrinally acceptable, solution for public procurement fact typologies.

Where a tender was not devoid of any chance, bid costs are claimable; where s/he can prove a serious chance, the chance is assessed and lost profits are awarded. Under this approach, bid costs are awarded as something akin to the lost chance as a head of damage – one could say, bid costs are a pecuniary way of assessing this lost chance. In the category which enables lost profits ('a serious chance'), the lost chance approach works more in the function of alleviating the burden of proof. Here, the lost chance almost becomes a type of 'balance of probability' slanted in favour of the aggrieved tenderer. The approach is not strictly proportional, but the categories do fix the causality to the claimable damage in a rougher relation. This introduces an element of proportionality, which, however, sits easier with the principles of full compensation and causation.

The differentiation of the lost chance theories along different fields gives strong indications that a useful approach to the lost chance has to depart from the factual typologies it is designed to address. Reece (and Savatier) distinguish between different types of uncertainties or hypothetical situations in which the doctrine can come into play.[55] One type of indeterminacy is absolute and it is impossible to know anything about the possibilities of the chance's materialization. The other is merely uncertain, yet there are possible indicators to assess the chance.

Breaches of public procurement law result in different uncertainties with regard to the future position of tenderers. This can depend greatly with the type of procedure chosen, and also with the point in time at which a breach occurs.[56] Although

---

[54] LW Gormley, *Gordian Knots in European Public Procurement Law: Government Procurement Agreement: Standards, Utilities, Remedies* (Koln, Bundesanzeiger, 1997), p 5.

[55] See Sect. 11.4.2.

[56] In fact, case typologies are fairly common when discussing the lost chance in public procurement. By way of example see R Caranta, 'Damages: Causation and Recoverable Losses', in D Fairgrieve & F Lichère (eds), *Public procurement law : damages as an effective remedy* (Oxford,

the French solution is not put on this theoretical foundation, it seems to be able to accommodate these different kinds of uncertainties. Uncertainties with regards to chances lost are sometimes in some way measurable, while in other instances the position of an aggrieved tenderer is confined to the recognition of the fact that the deterioration of a potential future option has taken place – i.e. that he has suffered the loss of a business opportunity. The likelihood of that opportunity having occurred or value of that loss can often not be further specified. Where one simply cannot assess the uncertainty, merely proof that a tenderer was not devoid of a chance is required. For example, in an open procedure the unlimited number of competitors with valid bids might be so large as to preclude the tender from substantiating its specific advantageous position. It is an indeterminacy which is simply not specifiable. On the other hand, where a tenderer was shortlisted, and the award criteria were previously laid down by the contracting authority, indicators for the hypothetical assessments do exist. In this case, the position of the tenderer can be substantiated and the French system works simply as an alleviation of proof of a tenderers chances. Note that through the connection between the fixed categories of chance (no chance, not devoid of a chance, real chance) and the extent of damage claimable (bid cost, lost profit), a mitigated element of proportionality is introduced.

Comparative law can act as a feedback and interface to the national legal orders. In this respect, the suggested solution –while rendering damages claims more effective- also sits easier with the legal systems than strictly proportional liability. Other legal systems, next to France, seem capable of accommodating the proposal doctrinally. Although through different paths, the solution is similar in Germany; the statutory provision for bid costs and lost profits under the pre-contractual liability can arguably be interpreted along these lines.[57] The Netherlands has no general lost chance doctrine, but it was applied in a few cases in the area of public procurement. *Harmon* proposed the proportional version of the lost chance, making the UK arguably the system with the most divergent approach (and therefore potentially strongest opposition). Yet, since the proposed solution incorporates a gradual element of proportionality, the system could also be acceptable there – all the more so since *Harmon* does not have the necessary backbone of follow-up actions. Importantly, the suggested proposal would also be a defensible interpretation of the Utilities Remedies Directives damages article in relation to bid costs.[58]

Hart Publishing, 2011) and AJ Akkermans & EH Pijnacker Hordijk, 'Schadevergoeding en schade-berekening', in WH van Boom, et al. (eds), *Aanbesteding en aansprakelijkheid* (Schoordijk Instituut Centrum voor aansprakelijkheid, 2001).

[57] The biggest difference in Germany relates to the fact that an aggrieved bidder has to prove that the contract has or would have been awarded. In keeping in line with the 'private autonomy' rationale underlying this reasoning, I would defend a reversal of the burden of proof burdening the contracting authority with a rebuttable presumption that indeed it would have awarded a contract.

[58] Article 2(7) of Directive 92/13 requires that 'Where a claim is made for damages representing the costs of preparing a bid or of participating in an award procedure, the person making the claim shall be required only to prove an infringement of Community law in the field of procurement or national rules implementing that law and that he would have had a real chance of winning the contract and that, as a consequence of that infringement, that chance was adversely affected.'

Bibliography

Ajani, G, Lesmo, L, Boella, G, Mazzei, A & Rossi, P (2007) 'Terminological and Ontological Analysis of European Directives: Multilingualism in Law' *International Conference on Artificial Intelligence and Law Journal* 43.

Akkermans, AJ (1997) *Proportionele aansprakelijkheid bij onzeker causaal verband. Een rechtsvergelijkend onderzoek naar wenselijkheid, grondslagen en afgrenzing van aansprakelijkheid naar rato van veroorzakingswaarschijnlijkheid* (Dissertation, Katholieke Universiteit Brabant)

Akkermans, AJ & Pijnacker Hordjik, EH (2001) 'Schadevergoeding en schadeberekening', in WH van Boom et al, *Aanbesteding en aansprakelijkheid* (Schoordijk Instituut Centrum voor aansprakelijkheid).

Alexander, C (2011) 'GWB § 126 Anspruch auf Ersatz des Vertrauensschadens', in H Pünder & M Schellenberg (eds), *Vergaberecht*, 2nd edition (Baden-Baden, Nomos).

Bénabent, A (1973) *La Chance et le Droit* (Libraire Générale de Droit et de Jurisprudence)

Binon, JM (2008) 'La Réparation de la Perte d'une Chance Dans la Jurisprudence Européenne : Une Question de Chance ?', in *Liber Amicorum Jean-Luc Fagnart* (Bruxelles, Anthemis).

Boucher, J & Bourgeouis-Machureau, B (2008) 'Indemnisation de la perte de chances: le Conseil d'Etat poursuit sa conversion au probabilisme' *Acutalité Juridique Droit Administratif* 135.

Burgi, M (2011) 'A Report about the German Remedies System', in S Treumer & F Lichère (eds), *Enforcement of the EU Public Procurement Rules* (København, DJØF Publishing).

Caranta, R (2011) 'Damages: Causation and Recoverable Losses', in D Fairgrieve & F Lichère (eds), *Public procurement law: damages as an effective remedy* (Oxford, Hart Publishing).

Gormley, LW (1997) *Gordian Knots in European Public Procurement Law: Government Procurement Agreement: Standards, Utilities, Remedies* (Koln, Bundesanzeiger, 1997).

Jourdain, P, Ghestin, J & Billau, M (1998) *Traité de droit civil / T.II Les obligations 4e Partie Les conditions de la responsabilité* (Libraire Générale de Droit et de Jurisprudence).

Lichère, F (2006) 'Damages for violation of the EC public procurement rules in France' *Public Procurement Law Review* 171, 176.

Lindenbergh, SD (2008) *Schadevergoeding* (Deventer, Kluwer).

Möller, H (1937) *Summen- und Einzelschaden. Beiträge zur Erneuerung der Schadenslehr vom Wirtschaftsrecht aus* (Berlin, de Gruyter).

Müller-Stoy, W (1973) *Schadensersatz für verlorene Chancen - Eine rechtsvergleichende Untersuchung* (Albert-Ludwigs-Universität zu Freiburg).

Oskierski, JT (2010) *Schadensersatz im Europäischen Recht: Eine vergleichende Untersuchung des Acquis Communautaire und der EMRK* (Baden-Baden, Nomos).

Péguret, K (2010) *Schadensersatzansprüche übergangener Bieter im Vergaberecht* (Dissertation, Jenaer Wissenschaftliche Verlagsgesellschaft).

Pijnacker Hordijk, EH, van der Bend, GW & Van Nouhuys, JF (2009) Aanbestedingsrecht. Handboek van het Europese en het Nederlandse Aanbestedingsrecht (Den Haag, Sdu Uitgevers).

Reich, A & Shabat, O (2013) 'The Remedy of Damages in Public Procurement in Israel and the EU: A Proposal for Reform', 28–29.

Savatier, R (1970) 'Une faute peut-elle engendrer la responsabilité d'un dommage sans l'avoir causé?' *Dalloz* 123.

Savatier, R (1978), 'Note Cass. civ. 1re, 2 mai 1978, Mandryka c. Franck et autres' *Juris-Classeur Périodique* 18966.

Spier, J, Hartlief, T, van Maanen, GE & Vriesendorp, RD (2006) *Verbintenissen uit de wet en Schadevergoeding* (Deventer, Kluwer).

Tacchini-Laforest, V (1999) 'Reflexions à propos de la perte de chances' *Petites Affiches* 7, 7.

Vacarie, I (1987) 'La perte d'une chance' *Revue de la Recherche Juridique* 903, 905.

Weyand, R (2012) *Kommentar Vergaberecht. Praxiskommentar zu GWB, VgV, SektVO, VOB/A, VOL/A, VOF* (München, Beck-online).

Part IV
Conclusions and the Way Forward

Chapter 12
Conclusions

Abstract The concluding chapter provides a brief outline of the book and presents its main findings. It concludes with a section on the way forward and recommendations for a legislative proposal on public procurement damages.

12.1 Summary

While the law is often highly harmonized at EU level, the ways in which it is realized in the various national courts are not. This book looks at enforcement through damages claims for violations of EU public procurement rules. Despite important recent amendments to the procurement remedies regime, the damages provision remains indeterminate. The legislative inertia pressures the CJEU to give interpretations and raises the question as to how the Court should deal with damages.

The requirements on damages claims are clarified under both general and public procurement EU law. The action for damages is conceived as a legal process which incorporates the national realm. Therefore, a comparative law part (covering England, France, Germany and the Netherlands) examines national damages litigation in public procurement law. A horizontal discussion of the legal issues which structurally frame damages claims is provided. The remedy of damages is analyzed as a bundle of rules and its constitutive and quantification criteria are studied, thereby refining the Member States' common conceptual base of damages claims. Functionally, the lost chance emerges as a compromise capable of mitigating the typically problematic nature of causation and uncertainty in public procurement constellations.

12.2 Main Findings

The legislative inertia with regards to damages in procurement forces the CJEU to come to terms with the open question of damages. (Chap. 2)

1. Directive 2007/66 greatly strengthened the overall private enforcement of procurement law by amending the existing remedies regime. Except where the ineffectiveness of contracts is now required under the Directive, the potential role of damages actions remains important as the only available post-contractual remedy.

H. Schebesta, *Damages in EU Public Procurement Law*, Studies in European Economic Law and Regulation 6, DOI 10.1007/978-3-319-23612-4_12

2. The damages provision was left unchanged and is still but a vague obligation. Despite the known difficulties of damages claims in procurement, the Commission so far has not taken legislative action. This legislative inertia results in the CJEU coming under increasing institutional pressure.

The general EU law on damages is indeterminate. (Chap. 3)

3. The two main doctrines formulating general EU law requirements on damages are the doctrines of 'effectiveness' of EU law and Member State liability, both of which are characterized by significant legal uncertainty.

4. The doctrine of procedural autonomy has developed over time and is currently unstable. While initially it served only to describe effectiveness and equivalence, it has become increasingly normative, with the potential to shield national law from EU influence.

5. Three uses of 'effectiveness' can be distinguished: effectiveness as a standard, a balancing exercise, and judicial protection as a fundamental right. The latter is increasingly autonomous from general 'effectiveness'.

6. Member State liability, equally, has emerged as an indeterminate doctrine: there is *internal uncertainty* concerning the scope and constitution of its liability. In addition, there is *external or structural uncertainty* resulting from the fact that the relation to *parallel* remedies granted by EU law is ambiguous, as is its relation to other domestic remedies at the national level.

The damages obligation in EU procurement law is also indeterminate. (Chap. 4)

7. There are several gateways for further interpretation of the damages provision. Overall, remedies in procurement became more closely regulated through Directive 2007/66. As an integral part of that remedial system, the significance of damages must be interpreted as relative to the remedial context at EU level. A systemic interpretation must consider the divergent wording of the damages provisions in the general and the Utilities Remedies Directives.

8. The legislator should consider giving some clarification of the meaning of the lost chance in the Utilities Remedies Directive and aligning the general and Utilities Directives by including the lost chance provision for both regimes. A systemic interpretation by the CJEU may reach the same results.

9. The CJEU has consistently subjected cases on enforcement rules in procurement to the effectiveness test; however, even in a confined area of law, the use of the doctrine of procedural autonomy is extremely divergent. In *Simvoulio*, the CJEU went so far as to speak (for the first time) of the procedural independence of the Member States, while in *Strabag*, procedural autonomy did not preclude the Court from striking down a fault requirement. In *Combinatie Spijker*, the Court took a deferent attitude to procurement damages under the effectiveness and equivalence test (without calling it procedural autonomy), only to hold that the damages provision is an expression of Member State liability. The doctrine does not constrain the Court in predictable ways and the effect of applying procedural autonomy in the legal reasoning of the Court, even in one specific area of law, is highly uncertain.

10. Damages are subject to a conflationary trend of interpretation. The *Combinatie Spijker Infrabouw* ruling assimilated Member State liability into the field of procurement with the damages article of the Remedies Directive. This transcending interpretation is aggravated by the extension of the institutional liability of the EU.
11. By analyzing the EU legal system through the lens of legal processes, Member State liability and effectiveness can be endowed with diverse damages and liability rationales. Member State liability damages are a constitutional remedy securing the systemic and structural functioning of the EU legal order, while 'effectiveness' ensures the performative function of EU law.
12. Member State liability is vested with a normative framework based on considerations of supranational justice, within which it provides 'tertiary protection' of EU integration through the protection of EU rights. Thus conceived, damages awarded under the doctrine of Member state liability are distinct from other types of damages awarded under EU law ('separation thesis').

The action for damages is a legal process that incorporates the national realm. (Part II)

13. In order to understand damages actions for the purposes of EU law, one must also examine national damages litigation. The thesis presented four jurisdictions in a comparative law part: the Netherlands, the United Kingdom, Germany, and France.
14. In the Netherlands (Chap. 5), the available actions for damages are the general tort law and pre-contractual liability. Bid costs are generally not awarded alone as full compensation involves all (including lost profit) or nothing. Under pre-contractual liability, bid costs can be recoverable alone. Damages claims are not rare, but legal certainty regarding the outcome is low.
15. In the UK (Chap. 6), the theoretical availability of damages in the UK is vast. The main authority *Harmon* established as main different causes of action breach of statutory duty, implied contract and public misfeasance. The claim for bid costs is subsidiary to lost profits, and the lost chance is available as a head of damages. There are only a few examples of successful damages claims.
16. The German landscape of damages claims (Chap. 7) for breaches of public procurement rules is characterized by a number of parallel actions. The multitude of available causes of action combines a statutory public procurement action, possible claims developed under *culpa in contrahendo* duties, and those based in one way or the other on the liability of the State.
17. In France (Chap. 8), an aggrieved tenderer that was not devoid of the chance to obtain a contract will be granted bid costs. A serious chance usually leads to the award of lost profits. The special solution of France mediating between the lost chance can be described as one of 'categorized proportional liability'.
18. As the cases discussed in the country studies demonstrate, in none of the jurisdictions is it entirely predictable whether and in how far an aggrieved bidder can claim damages. Legal uncertainty persists.

The frayed nature of national damages actions calls the viability of treating damages actions at the national level as unitary into question. (Chap. 9)

19. Member States' enforcement attitudes depend to some extent on how high up procurement policy is on the national public agenda. In addition, the implementation of EU law by Member States is contingent on the strength of the specific obligation at EU level. The structural implementation mechanisms of the damages article vary between specific legislative implementation, case law developed procurement liability actions and the applicability of general tort law clauses. In a field that is highly regulated, such as that of EU public procurement remedies, vagueness at EU level leads to equally vague implementation at Member State level.

20. At the institutional level, damages claims are brought in different types of procedures. The generally uneasy relationship between EU law and alternative dispute settlement mechanisms is a shared concern in the procurement sector. However, requirements on the organization of tribunals are defined in the procurement directives, so that as a *lex specialis,* the requirements set in the Remedies Directives prevail.

21. The Rome II Regulation is pertinent to the determination of the applicable law for damages claims under international private law.

22. The causes of actions exhibit the broadest divergence between Member States. Statutory liability, tort and contract coexist, and have diverging implications at the level of quantification. Member State liability, within the national legal system, may be an identical action to damages (NL), a parallel action to damages claims (UK), interpreted by national State liability and hardly of significance (D), or simply not discussed at all for procurement damages (FR). Conceptually, the unitary damages action from an EU point of view actually emerges as a plurality of possible actions, which exhibit different liability rationales and raise questions as to their accumulability.

23. Under the influence of EU law, procurement law moved from an administrative towards a competition rationale and strengthened bidders' rights considerably. The personal scope of EU law instruments is defined at EU level. In public procurement, a specific interpretation prevails as the Remedies Directives extend to 'any person with an interest'.

24. Time limits in Member States cover a broad range – from 30 days to 6 years. The CJEU has set a standard on the starting point of a time limit in *Uniplex.*

25. According to *Strabag,* fault criteria are not permissible. Germany has one action without fault, but the remaining ones do refer to fault criteria.

26. The frayed nature of national damages actions, coupled with the close interplay between different constitutive rules, call the viability of treating damages actions at the national level as unitary into question. Damages actions conceptually emerge as a bundle of rules.

The quantification stage of procurement damages particularly needs conceptual and methodological refinement. (Chap. 10)

27. Positive and negative contractual interest are not congruent with lost profits and bid costs sustained. The causes of action influence the available compensation as some jurisdictions conceive of procurement damages in tort, while others resort to (pre)contractual considerations. Where bid costs and lost profits or *damnum emergens* and *lucrum cessans* are claimed in parallel, an appropriate method of evaluation must be used in order to avoid double counting. Bid costs do not necessarily correspond to *damnum emergens*; the concept of bid costs can be split between the cost of preparation and the cost of participation, or also costs relating to the performance of a contract. The jurisdictions all hold divergent views as to what exactly bid costs are, as well as to whether they are claimable and in parallel to lost profit. The mixed terminology used in relation to heads of damages is highly problematic in light of the CJEU's standard use of the terms *damnum emergens* and *lucrum cessans*, which translate badly into the national legal orders.
28. The availability of interest is a requirement of EU law; the context indicates that the CJEU regards interest as a head of damage.
29. The degree of formal and doctrinal separation between the categories of constitutional and quantification criteria varies significantly between jurisdictions. Quantification can occur in the same or a separate legal procedure as the finding of liability. These factors shape the discretion accorded to the judge, which impacts significantly on the ultimate damage award.
30. The amount of damages received varies with the kind of computation chosen. In pursuing the aim of approximating the actual losses as closely as possible, the pragmatic approach of choosing the valuation methodology according to the available data is well accepted.
31. Due to the low number of cases and the rarity of explicit treatment of quantification, it is hardly possible to generalize based on the country studies' conclusions. There is considerable room and need for theoretical and methodological refinement regarding the quantification of damages overall, and especially in public procurement.
32. The available heads of damages and quantification methods are significant in determining the outcomes of legal procedures in monetary terms and are therefore not negligible when it comes to assessing the effectiveness of damages.

The lost chance emerges as a compromise capable of mitigating the typically problematic nature of causation and uncertainty in public procurement constellations. (Chap. 11)

33. In all of the selected jurisdictions, causality emerged as one of the prime doctrinal issues for successful damages claims. Damages actions in public procurement are most successful where there is acceptance of the lost chance doctrine, independent of the type of lost chance doctrine followed.
34. The concept of the 'lost chance' takes on three theoretically different forms: the proportional lost chance, lost chance as an autonomous head of damage, and as an alleviation of the burden of proof.

35. The lost chance theory is debated in all jurisdictions, but different understandings of the lost chance theory persist alongside one another. Not all countries accept the lost chance at the general level, for example it meets with doctrinal resistance in Germany.

36. The surveyed countries diverge largely in terms of their recognition of the lost chance, but all of them provide an idiosyncratic solution particular to the field of public procurement. These are, with the partial exception of the German statute on the lost chance, judge made solutions. In procurement cases, Germany accepts the lost chance in terms of the narrow statutory provision, the Netherlands has applied it in only two judgments, the UK in *Harmon* followed a proportional liability approach, and France exhibits special forms of categorized lost chances.

37. The consensus across jurisdictions falls shy of constituting a 'common tradition of the Member States' regarding a doctrine of lost chance in general or in public procurement specifically.

38. The lost chance is more easily accepted in special areas of law. Procurement is characterized by factual patterns with typical hypothetical causal relations. To these, the lost chance is a particularly appealing solution that mitigates the interest of aggrieved bidders and contracting authorities at the level of outcome.

39. At a functional level, this book suggests the adoption of the lost chance approach as it is followed in the French legal system. It has a unique system of categorization of lost chances, which connects categories of chances with specific heads of damages. The categories align the causality to the claimable damage, thereby introducing a moderate element of proportionality. This makes a better compromise between adherence to the full compensation principle and the *conditio sine qua non* on the one hand, while at the same time providing an effective solution to accommodate the inherent uncertainty of typical factual procurement situations.

12.3 Proposal for a Revision of the Damages Article in the Procurement Remedies Directive

At EU level, with respect to damages, Competition law is a clear forerunner. While damages had been a contentious issue already in the 60s, it was the CJEU which (much later) gave the damages debate some impetus. In 2001, the Court rendered the landmark *Courage* judgment, which postulated the full effectiveness and the practical effect of how Article 101 TFEU would be put at risk if individuals could not claim damages for loss caused.[1] The judgment was confirmed in 2006 in *Manfredi*,[2] which held that individuals seeking compensation would be entitled to

---

[1] Case C-453/99 *Courage v Crehan* [2001] ECR I-6297.
[2] Joined Cases C-295/04 to C-298/04 *Manfredi and Others* [2006] ECR I-6619.

claim actual loss and loss of profit, plus interest. The European Commission had initially responded with a Green Paper on damages in 2005, but in legislative terms nothing happened. After a long silence, on 11 June 2013 the Commission tabled a long awaited antitrust damages actions legislative package, including a proposal for a directive on rules governing actions for damages under national law for infringements of the competition law provisions. The Competition Damages Directive was adopted on 26 November 2014.

The package is of significance also for the procurement sector. From a political point of view, it seems clear that the Competition legislation package is a pilot test case with regard to the political acceptance of enhanced legislative action regarding damages enforcement in the Member States. The Competition damages initiative and the fact that the Member States agreed on (some) damages harmonization, have an important signalling effect. It is a sign to the EU legislator that other sectors could equally be harmonized by means of legislative measures. Public procurement would seem as the most obvious and suitable candidate for being the next in line. The successful legislative action in the field of Competition law damages could further act as an inhibitor for the CJEU to develop damages further. This shifts the institutional responsibility onto the legislative process. In the light of these developments, it seems that the EU legislator could reconsider its reluctant stance to intervene in damages in public procurement. Public procurement is a cornerstone of the internal market, and at the heart of several policy initiatives. In addition, it is a field already disposing of detailed remedial secondary legislation, in which the damages provision stand out through their indeterminate nature.

The present research has demonstrated the difficulty of the Court to position itself in the judicial policy making space that has opened up, in particular with respect to the notions of procedural autonomy and effective judicial protection (Chap. 4). While the Court may have to come to terms with the precise limitations inherent in the developing concept of procedural autonomy, it is important to understand it as an adjudicative principle. The legislative is not restrained by it as the competence to harmonize enforcement rules follows from the substantive competence. At the same time, the principle of effective judicial protection, as a general principle of EU law, enshrined in the European Charter of Fundamental Rights as well as the European Convention on Human Rights, provides legitimacy to elaborate a law of damages at EU level for both, the Court and the legislative.

From the country studies, it appears that the opaque nature of the EU obligation to provide damages results in a lack of incentives for Member States to regulate damages and clarify the regime because formal compliance is achieved without transposition measures being necessary (Chap. 9). Since public procurement remedies are highly regulated at EU level, it is unlikely that Member States are going to pass further reaching damages legislation in the area on their own initiative.

The number of references to the CJEU related to damages claims in the field of procurement confirms the need for clarification of the provision. Legislative action would be an opportunity to remedy the vagueness of the damages article.

A proposal should include a *codification* of the case law rendered by the CJEU in the field (see Chap. 4); in particular that the damages may not be made contingent upon fault (*Strabag*, Portuguese case line), but also with respect to standing rules.

Further, it could be an opportunity for *clarification*. The time limits for an action in damages in the area of procurement law in the UK are only 30 days, while other countries provide several years (see discussion in Chap. 9). The new Competition Damages Directive provides for a minimum period of 5 years, and detailed condition on when it starts to run. The Court, in *Uniplex* has stressed the need for rapidity and legal certainty in the specific context of public contracts, arguments that ought to be considered. 30 days, on the other hand, might be too short as to provide a real opportunity for aggrieved bidders to mount an effective damages action. The legislative process is in a much better position than the Court to proceed to evidence-based rule making and ascertain the needs of bidders in the specific field through empirical studies.

However, the most important modification of the procurement damages provision would be the specification of the extent to which damages must be claimable.

An obligation of result stipulating which heads of damages must be made available seems the most suitable recommendation given the frayed nature of different causes of action in the legal systems. Member States could accommodate the stipulated heads of damages through their respective causes of action. Where a Member State feels that a solution sits uneasy with the general system, a specific statutory exception can respect the coherency of the overall system, while reaching the desired results.

Regarding the available heads of damages, Competition law follows the full compensation doctrine. The Competition Damages Directive provides in Article 3(2): 'Full compensation shall place a person who has suffered harm in the position in which that person would have been had the infringement of competition law not been committed. It shall therefore cover the right to compensation for actual loss and for loss of profit, plus the payment of interest.' However, the uncertainty that is regularly involved in public procurement constellations means that a strict all-or-nothing approach is not always suitable. A damages provision in public procurement, therefore, must be careful not to simply replicate solutions devised for Competition law situations.

The heads of damages which are regularly discussed in procurement are bid costs, the lost chance, and lost profits (plus interest). Regarding bid costs, the Public Sector and the Utilities Remedies Directive should be aligned. Utilities Remedies Directive 92/13/EEC contains a more specific damages provision in Article 2(7):

> Where a claim is made for damages representing the costs of preparing a bid or of participating in an award procedure, the person making the claim shall be required only to prove an infringement of Community law in the field of procurement or national rules implementing that law and that he would have had a real chance of winning the contract and that, as a consequence of that infringement that chance was adversely affected.

Under the Utilities Remedies Directive, bid costs are currently available on the basis of proving a real chance only. A condition of having to prove that a contract would have been awarded to the aggrieved bidder is not permissible. At a very minimum, this solution ought to be extended to the Public Sector Directive. This head of damages addresses the losses of aggrieved bidders in legal systems which still do not habitually award bid costs. In systems following a pre-contractual approach, it addresses situations that fall outside of protected contractual relationships.

Regarding further reaching heads of damages, a pure application of the principles of full compensation leads to unjust results in public procurement. All surveyed jurisdictions have modified their approach in recognition of the lost chance, either as a head of damage (the UK and the Netherlands) or as an alleviation of the burden of proof (Germany and France with respect to bid costs, France also with respect to lost profits). It is a less straight forward issue whether EU law should require the lost chance, either as a head of damage or as an alleviation of proof. The solution presented as the 'categorized proportional' liability (proposed in Chap. 11) opts for a version in which a (very) serious chance results in the availability of lost profits. An alternative is to stipulate the lost chance as a head of damage, proportional in some way to the quality of the chance that an aggrieved bidder is able to establish. The choice for one of these solutions would essentially depend on what ultimately proves more acceptable in the political process. However, it ought to be clear that a mere stipulation that 'lost profits must be available' will be insufficient in order to provide a better secondary protection of aggrieved bidders' rights.

A too rigid conception of proving harm has been shown to prevent successful damages claims, in particular in Germany, but also the Netherlands (see Chaps. 7 and 5 respectively). The Competition Damages Directive in Article 17 provides that 'Member States shall ensure that the national courts are empowered, in accordance with national procedures, to estimate the amount of harm if it is established that a claimant suffered harm but it is practically impossible or excessively difficult precisely to quantify the harm suffered on the basis of the evidence available.' It makes sense to include a similar provision in a procurement legislative regime.

In public procurement, the valuation methods used by judges in the area of procurement were far less sophisticated than quantification in Competition law currently is. A first step would be to establish a quantification culture that recognizes different methodological approaches of calculating bid costs and lost profits. Legislative action on this point is probably not suitable, and a change in practice could be effected through framing measures such as conferences or trainings perhaps followed by a Commission communication.

Overall, there is a compelling case for legislative action. In the ruling in *Combinatie Spijker Infrabouw*, the Court has indicated deference to the legislative with respect to public procurement damages. One may also read this as an invitation; action on damages in the field will not come from the Court, it must be legitimized in the political process.

Printed in Great Britain
by Amazon

45023366R00143